Prevention's

DIABETES
BREAKTHROUGHS
2007

NEWS YOU CAN USE TO
MANAGE DIABETES EFFECTIVELY

Prevention's

DIABETES

BREAKTHROUGHS

2007

NEWS YOU CAN USE TO
MANAGE DIABETES EFFECTIVELY

from the editors of **Prevention** magazine

RODALE

© 2007 by Rodale Inc.
Insert photographs © 2007 by Rodale Inc.

Prevention is a registered trademark of Rodale Inc.

Printed in the United States of America
Rodale Inc. makes every effort to use acid-free ⊗, recycled paper ♻.

Photo credits: © Hilmar (pages 110–115, 153–158, 172–176, 183–189, 193–198);
Mitch Mandel/Rodale Images (pages 311, 313, 314, 316, 318, 351–357);
Alan Neider (page 56); and Kurt Wilson/Rodale Images (pages 312, 315, 317, 358)

ISBN-13 978–59486–647–0   hardcover
ISBN-10 1–59486–647–3   hardcover

4   6   8   10   9   7   5   hardcover

RODALE
LIVE YOUR WHOLE LIFE™

We inspire and enable people to improve their lives and the world around them
For more of our products visit **rodalestore.com** or call 800-848-4735

Contents

Part I
Take Control

Part II
Eat Right

Part III

Lose Weight

Part IV

Move It

Part V
Stress Less

Part VI
Avoid Complications

Part VII
Diabetes Cookbook

You Are Not Alone

In 1998, the World Health Organization predicted that 22 million Americans would have diabetes by the year 2025. As usual, we're a nation of overachievers, so we're way ahead of schedule. We reached 21 million in 2005. The number of Americans with diabetes increased 14 percent from 2003 to 2005. Currently, 7 percent of the US population has diabetes.

And we're careening ahead on our dangerous path—41 million Americans ages 40 to 74 now have prediabetes. If present trends continue, by 2030, up to 70 million Americans will have prediabetes.

So you're certainly not alone in your fight against diabetes.

And we're right there beside you. We hope that this book will help you to battle this complicated illness and regain control—of your disease and of your life. In Part I, you'll learn how to "Take Control." It offers the basic information you need to know about diabetes, presents a two-part strategy to help you lower your risk of complications, includes critical info on insulin and noninsulin drug treatments, and assists you in assembling your diabetes medical team.

Part II will help you to "Eat Right." Slim down and control blood sugar with our breakthrough eating plan, learn how to keep carbs in check throughout the day, and discover insider grocery-shopping secrets. In Part III, you'll find our very best advice on how to "Lose Weight." The diabetes–weight loss connection is so strong that an increase of only 1 centimeter in waist size (that's less than $^1/_2$ inch) could raise the risk of developing type 2 diabetes by 28 percent for women and 34 percent for men. If you struggle with your weight, this part of the book can help. Here, you'll take a quiz to determine if you're really ready to commit to a diet. "Your Diet Datebook" will arm you with hints for surviving the biggest dieting tests in the year ahead, and "The Diabetes Weight-Loss Exercise Circuit" will help you to lose your belly, drop pounds, and control your diabetes all in one fell swoop.

We hope that Part IV will inspire you to "Move It." Our exercise section includes a walking plan that's as easy as ABC. Foot health is critical to people with diabetes, so you'll find our solutions to the 10 most common walking injuries. Don't have to time exercise? Learn "The Multitasker's Workout" and "The TV-Lover's Workout."

It's been said that stress is the biggest threat to women's health. Learn how to "Stress Less" in Part V. This part includes advice straight from the folks who really know—stress experts and six extremely stressed-out women.

Complications are a terrible—and all too common—by-product of diabetes. Learn how to "Avoid Complications" in Part VI. Here you'll find the latest breakthroughs on heart disease, kidney disease, and vision loss—and on Alzheimer's disease and cancer, which, sadly, experts now believe are also linked to diabetes.

Finally, in Part VII, the "Diabetes Cookbook," we offer our secrets for effortless meal planning and 100 delicious, nutritious, diabetes-fighting meals and snacks. We hope that you enjoy them all.

Here's to your best year ever!

Jennifer Bright Reich
Editor

PART I

TAKE CONTROL

CHAPTER 1

DIAGNOSIS DIABETES

From what it is to what to do,
here are the basics you need to know

Once you've been diagnosed with diabetes, you need to understand the basics of your condition before you can go about taking control of it and regaining your good health. That's why we posed some of the most common diabetes-related questions to James Rosenzweig, MD, associate chief of adult diabetes and director of the Office of Disease Management of the Joslin Diabetes Center—an internationally recognized research, education, and treatment center for people with diabetes. In this chapter, Rosenzweig explains what you need to know about diabetes, using easy-to-understand language.

Even if you've had diabetes for a while, it'll take only a few minutes to read through the following basic information. Think of it as a refresher course that will help you make better use of the chapters that follow. You may also want to share this chapter with family members and close friends, so they can have a better understanding of your condition and how it's treated and managed.

1. WHAT IS DIABETES?

When you have diabetes, something is wrong with your production of insulin—a vital hormone made by your pancreas. Insulin helps your cells take in fuel in the form of blood sugar. (This blood sugar, also called glucose, is produced when your body digests food.) If glucose doesn't get into the cells, those cells begin to weaken. Then the sugar from your food builds up in the bloodstream, damaging everything from your blood vessels to your organs. Here's a quick explanation of the different types of diabetes.

Type 1 Diabetes

In type 1 diabetes, sometimes referred to as juvenile or insulin-dependent diabetes, the pancreas no longer produces insulin or doesn't produce enough of it. Type 1 diabetes often occurs in people younger than age 30 who are not overweight. The cause is not yet known—in 90 percent of cases, the children who have it do not have a family history of diabetes—so it is not yet preventable. Insulin shots are required to regulate blood sugar levels in people with type 1 diabetes. Children can also develop type 2 diabetes.

Type 2 Diabetes

In type 2 diabetes, formerly known as adult-onset diabetes, your pancreas makes insulin, but your body isn't able to use it properly. Type 2 diabetes typically develops in people over 30 who have one or more risk factors for the disease.

Type 1.5 Diabetes

About 2 million Americans—10 to 15 percent of all adults now diagnosed with type 2 diabetes—may actually have a hybrid form of diabetes known as type 1.5 diabetes, also called LADA (latent autoimmune diabetes in adults). Type 1.5 is caused by a problem in the immune system. People with type 1.5 have immune systems that slowly kill off the body's vital insulin-producing beta cells. Without insulin, blood sugar levels soar. This condition often goes undiagnosed in people who aren't at risk for diabetes. If it is misdiagnosed as type 2 diabetes, it may be difficult to control because insulin injections are required, and type 2 diabetes is usually treated with oral medications that don't work on type 1.5.

If you have been diagnosed as type 2 but aren't responding well to oral meds, talk with your doctor about whether you need to take insulin. You can try asking for a blood test for type 1.5, called GAD_{65}, but it's not widely used in doctors' offices, and insurance may not cover it. If you have no risk factors for diabetes but have some of the symptoms—such as thirst, fatigue that won't quit, frequent need to urinate, or unexplained weight loss—ask for a fasting blood sugar test, which can detect diabetes.

Gestational Diabetes

Gestational diabetes appears only in pregnant women who haven't previously had either type 1 or type 2 diabetes, and it occurs in about 2 to 5 percent of pregnancies. After the pregnancy ends, so does the diabetes. The risk factors are the same for gestational diabetes as for type 2 diabetes (see list at right). But even women with none of these risk factors can develop gestational diabetes, which is why pregnant women who are at risk (those over the age of 25 or those under age 25 who are obese) are screened with an oral glucose tolerance test between the 24th and 28th weeks of pregnancy.

Gestational diabetes slightly raises the risk of birth defects, can lead to low blood sugar in the fetus, and often results in the baby being large, which can make it difficult to deliver. This is one reason that doctors may choose to induce early labor or recommend a Caesarean section in mothers who develop gestational diabetes.

If you develop gestational diabetes, you'll need to be tested about 6 weeks after you deliver, to make sure you don't develop type 2 diabetes later. If the results are normal, it's recommended that you be tested for diabetes every 3 years, since gestational diabetes is a risk factor for type 2 diabetes. You should also be on the alert for gestational diabetes in future pregnancies.

2. WHO IS AT RISK?

You may be at risk for type 2 diabetes if any of the following are true.

- You have a family history of diabetes.
- You are 20 percent over a healthy weight or obese. (Your doctor can tell you whether or not you're in this category.)
- You lead a sedentary lifestyle.
- You are African-American, Latino, Pacific Islander, Asian, or Native American.
- You had diabetes during pregnancy or had a baby who was 9 pounds or more at birth.
- You are age 45 or older. (While it's wise

to be tested as early as age 25 if you're at risk, the older you are, the greater your risk becomes.)

- You have low HDL (good) cholesterol or high overall cholesterol levels.
- You have very high blood pressure or very high triglycerides.

3. IS DIABETES CURABLE?

Neither form of diabetes is curable. But with the right treatment, you can get your blood sugar levels back down to normal. As long as you keep your glucose levels at an acceptable point, you should be able to live a normal, healthy life.

4. WHAT CAN HAPPEN IF I DON'T CONTROL MY BLOOD SUGAR?

Many people feel fine while they have elevated blood sugar, but long term, they will be at a greater risk for the major complications of diabetes, including eye, kidney, and nerve damage and all sorts of problems related to blood vessel damage. All these complications occur with increased frequency if you let your diabetes stay out of control for long periods of time. You can also develop a life-threatening condition called ketoacidosis (see Q & A: "What Is Ketoacidosis?" on page 8) if your blood

sugar is uncontrolled for a long time. In addition, there are some more immediate problems that can occur when your blood sugar spikes too high or drops too low.

High blood sugar (also known as hyperglycemia): Your blood sugar may go too high if you don't take care of your condition or when you are sick or under a lot of stress. Symptoms of high blood sugar include headaches; blurred vision; thirst; frequent urination; and itchy, dry skin. Drink lots of water when you are sick or have high blood sugar, and work with medication and lifestyle changes to get it back down.

Low blood sugar (also known as hypoglycemia): It is possible to have too little glucose in your system. This can be caused by taking too much diabetes medicine, eating too little or not at all, exercising too hard or too long, and drinking alcohol without eating. When your blood sugar drops, you feel shaky, tired, hungry, confused, and nervous.

5. WHAT SHOULD MY DOCTOR BE DOING?

Your doctor should be seeing you on a regular basis, sending you to the eye doctor at least once a year for a dilated eye exam if you've had type 1 diabetes for

5 years or more or type 2 diabetes. Your doctor should be looking at your feet and checking your blood pressure, blood sugar, and cholesterol very carefully. And it's important that the doctor communicates well with you. (See Chapter 2 for a complete rundown of the tests and exams you'll need each year and Chapter 5 for tips on making sure you get what you need from your doctor.)

6. WHAT SHOULD I BE DOING?

Once you are diagnosed, you and your doctor will discuss the lifestyle changes and possible medications that may be needed. But as we've said before, diabetes and your health are totally under your control. By doing the right things (which you'll find all throughout this book), you'll live a long, happy, healthy life!

Test your blood sugar daily. Even though you get your blood sugar tested at doctor's visits, it varies over the course of the day. A random sample that a doctor might get will not give a complete picture of your overall blood sugar control. By testing periodically throughout the day, you see how your blood sugar goes up in response to factors such as exercise and diet. You should be testing on a regular basis and

---

Protect Your Family

Unlike many other diseases, diabetes isn't obvious. Often you feel just fine. And its complications can mask themselves as other health problems first. It hides behind cardiovascular disease, kidney disease, nerve damage, and eye disease. Most of the diagnoses are delayed by an average of 7 years. So by the time people know they have it, it's typically both firmly established and difficult to treat, and long-term complications have already gained a foothold. Of the nearly 21 million people with diabetes, only 15 million realize they have it.

Diabetes tends to run in families (although you *can* develop diabetes even if no one else in your family has it). If you have diabetes, encourage your children, siblings, and parents to have their blood sugar tested too, so that they can begin treatment early if, in fact, they do develop diabetes.

then bringing the records to your doctor for review. Based on your own situation, your doctor will tell you how often to test daily. (For tips on testing blood sugar, see Chapter 2.)

Give your diet a makeover. Different people adapt better to different kinds of approaches. Some people like to use the exchange system. Others prefer to count carbohydrates. Ideally, you should meet with a nutritionist who knows how to care for diabetes, because a nutritionist will be able to get an idea of your individual preferences and capabilities and adapt a meal plan accordingly. (For a meal plan that could help you control your diabetes, turn to Chapter 29.)

Follow your doctor's orders. Take all medications as directed. Get the tests your doctor recommends. Make sure you understand all of the instructions you're given so you can follow them correctly. By properly following a healthy diet and treatment plan, most people can successfully control their blood sugar.

Live a healthy lifestyle. To optimize your health—whether or not you've got diabetes—it's important to eat right, exercise regularly, get enough sleep (about 8 hours a night), avoid stress, and get regular checkups, as recommended by your doctor. You'll feel better, look better, and be better able to deal with whatever life dishes out—including your diabetes.

Q&A

What is ketoacidosis?

If your body has very high levels of blood glucose for a long time, it becomes overwhelmed by the sugar and begins to metabolize fat (instead of sugar) to provide energy. The breakdown of fat produces large quantities of ketones and acidosis, which make the blood more acidic than the tissues of the body. When that happens, you get quite ill. If the accumulation of acids and high blood glucose is very severe and the condition is not treated, you can go into a coma. Most people with ketoacidosis are very dehydrated, urinate a lot, and often get sick to their stomach so they can't eat. The key to preventing all this is just to monitor your blood sugar and keep it under control.

CHAPTER 2

TESTING, TESTING

Follow this two-part strategy to lower your risk for complications

Don Werkstell's motto is "check, check, and recheck." An aviation security inspector for the Department of Homeland Security, Werkstell is responsible for ensuring that cargo flying in and out of Dallas–Fort Worth Airport poses no threat. Diagnosed with type 2 diabetes in 2004, he now applies the same "check and check again" philosophy to his blood sugar.

"I have to know what my numbers are. It's the only way to keep my blood sugar low and avoid all complications of diabetes," says Werkstell, 58. "I check my blood sugar all the time and guide my exercise and food choices by it. And every 3 months, I get a long-term test called an A1c. Diabetes runs in my family, and I've seen what can happen if you don't take care of yourself."

Most of the 14 million Americans with type 2 diabetes aren't as "in control" as Werkstell. In May 2005, a shocking new survey by the American Academy of Clinical Endocrinologists of 157,000 women and men with diabetes revealed that while 85 percent think they're keeping the lid on high blood sugar, two out of three actually have dangerously high levels that can lead to kidney failure, blindness, amputation, heart attack, and stroke.

What's gone wrong? Study participants said they know that daily sugar checks are vital, but they simply didn't understand the importance of a relatively new, high-tech-sounding check called the A1c (short for "glycated hemoglobin A1c") test. This extremely important test measures long-term blood sugar levels and can turn up problems that daily blood checks can miss.

"High blood sugar doesn't hurt. It's invisible. You only know you have it by testing," says diabetes specialist Jaime A. Davidson, MD, of the Dallas-based Endocrine & Diabetes Associates of Texas. "But you can't test round-the-clock. Even careful daily blood sugar checks may not catch specific times of day when your sugar might be high, such as first thing in the morning, after Sunday brunch, or when you're under stress. That's where the A1c test comes in. It shows you how well your blood sugar has been controlled for the past 2 to 3 months. If it's high, your diabetes management plan needs some changes. If it's on target, your plan is working."

A LIFESAVING ONE-TWO PUNCH

You need two tests—daily at-home glucose tests and periodic laboratory A1c tests—to learn how to keep blood sugar within a healthy range, experts say. "Daily glucose checks and A1c tests look at blood sugar in two very different ways," says Francine Kaufman, MD, former president of the American Diabetes Association (ADA), head of the Center for Diabetes and Endocrinology at Children's

Ouchless Testing

Checking blood sugar may soon be as simple as slicing an onion. A new study from India reveals that tears may be just as effective as blood samples at tracking blood sugar levels. The discovery will allow researchers to develop a new kind of test strip that could measure blood sugar levels simply by being placed near the corner of the eye.

Hospital Los Angeles, and author of *Diabesity: The Obesity-Diabetes Epidemic That Threatens America—And What We Must Do to Stop It*. "A daily finger-stick glucose test is a snapshot. Taken with a blood sugar meter, it tells you what your level is at one moment. It's very useful for finding out how high or low your blood sugar is at key times of day—first thing in the morning before you eat, before a meal, after exercise—or to see how well your body handles the natural rise in blood sugar after you eat."

In contrast, Dr. Kaufman says, the A1c is like a full-length movie. It tells you what's happened, on average, to your blood sugar over the past 2 to 3 months. It works by measuring the amount of sugar attached to hemoglobin in your bloodstream. Found inside red blood cells, hemoglobin carries oxygen from your lungs to cells throughout your body. But it also links up with sugars such as blood glucose along the way. Like Christmas cookies rolled in sweet sprinkles, hemoglobin picks up more and more sugar if there's an excess in your blood.

"With results of both tests, you can see if there's a disconnect between your diabetes management plan and your real blood sugar levels," Dr. Kaufman explains. "What if your daily checks look good, but your A1c is high? You may discover that the meter you use for daily checks isn't working right or that there's a time of day when your sugar's much higher than you ever realized. You may need to alter your medication dosage, the size of your meals, or your food choices; work on lowering stress; or resolve to exercise more. If you weren't getting A1c checks periodically every few months, you'd never know there was a problem."

Knowing your A1c results is vital to your health: Research confirms that every 1-point rise in your A1c level significantly raises your risk for heart attack; stroke; and damage to eyes, kidneys, and nerves. For every 1-point drop in your A1c, you lower your risk anywhere from 14 to 41 percent. (See "High Stakes" on page 14 for more details.)

But having the A1c done doesn't lessen your need for daily checks. Both are necessary for complete diabetes management. "The A1c cannot give you the quick results you need to see if a new sugar-control strategy is working," Dr. Kaufman says. "You need to know right away if your medication is effective, or whether a new food raises your levels too high, or how physical activity impacts your blood sugar. Everyone's body is different. Daily tests let you see just how your body is reacting, so that you can fine-tune your plan."

Our quick and simple blood sugar test guide that follows will help you use this powerful two-test strategy to keep your blood sugar—and your complication risk—low.

DAILY BLOOD SUGAR CHECK

Think of it as: Instant feedback about your blood sugar level.

Good for: Discovering your unique blood sugar patterns and reactions and getting up-to-the-minute info on how your meal choices and portions, physical activity, stress levels, and medications affect your blood sugar. Regular checks are vital if you take insulin or other diabetes medications, have low blood sugar episodes without warning signs (a risk when you take diabetes medications), or have a difficult time controlling your diabetes.

Not good for: Knowing with certainty whether your blood sugar has been in control all day and all night—simply because you can't test 24/7 and therefore can't catch every rise and fall.

Best test equipment: A glucose monitor that's less than 3 years old or an older meter that has been checked against laboratory blood sugar tests by your doctor, says Karmeen Kulkarni, MS, RD, president of health care and education for the ADA. "After a while, meters start to wear out," she says. "New meters have some great features. You can store your previous readings, then plug them into a program in your home computer to see patterns in your sugar levels.

"Some also let you record your food intake, exercise levels, medication, and dose so you have a record of what was going on when you took a reading. But if all of that's too confusing, you can just use the meter to get your blood sugar number."

Another reason to consider upgrading to a new monitor: "You get results in a matter of seconds, instead of waiting 2 minutes, as you did just a few years ago," says certified diabetes educator P. J. Pugh, RN, director of the diabetes center at Baylor Regional Medical Center in Grapevine, Texas. "And new meters use much less blood. Older meters needed a pretty healthy-size drop, equivalent to about 10 microliters of blood. New meters today need just one-thirtieth as much, about $3/10$ of a microliter. That means drawing blood is easier these days."

Cost: Meters may cost as little as $10 for a very basic model to more than $300 for a sleek glucose meter that doubles as a personal digital assistant (PDA). Supplies, such as lancets and test strips, cost extra.

Money-saving tip: Check with your insurance company first to see which meters they cover or how much they'll kick in. Some insurers also cover the cost of test strips.

When to check: "That's up to you," Pugh says. "If you've just been diagnosed or are starting a new medication, your doctor may ask you to test more often. Once you've settled into a plan, the frequency may change because the more often you test, the more information you get. But be realistic and try to mix up the times of day that you test. If you're going to test twice a day, don't always do it before breakfast and dinner. One day, test first thing in the morning, so you can see how much glucose your liver produces overnight, while you're fasting. Check before a meal to see what's going on. Check

2 hours after breakfast one day, after lunch the next. That way, you'll have a more complete idea of how your sugar levels rise and fall."

Shoot for these numbers: On a fasting test or before a meal: 90–130 mg/dl (110 mg/dl is ideal); 2 hours after a meal: less than 180 mg/dl (although less than 140 mg/dl is preferable).

Smart Testing Tips

Write it down. If you don't use a meter that records your readings, be sure to use a logbook. And take your readings to every diabetes checkup so your doctor can review them with you.

Sidestep the pain. Sticking your finger to obtain a blood sample can hurt. To reduce the pain, Kulkarni suggests adjusting your meter so that the lancet penetrates as little skin as possible. "You want to get a usable blood sample with the least penetration," she says. "You may have to experiment." Always use a fresh lancet for each test. Reused lancets grow dull and hurt, she says. Another way to ease the pain: Try taking your blood sample from your palm or from the side of your finger. Some meters can also test on your thigh or upper arm.

High Stakes

A growing stack of research confirms that keeping your A1c in a healthy range (a reading of 6.5 to 7 percent for people with diabetes; lower, if possible) is a powerful, effective strategy for sidestepping a host of serious complications. Here's how a high A1c threatens your health.

Heart trouble: In a recent British study of 10,232 women and men with type 2 diabetes, University of Cambridge researchers found that every 1-point increase in A1c levels raised heart disease risk 28 percent for women and 24 percent for men. Other research shows that it doubles heart failure risk.

Brain attacks: The same study found that stroke risk rose 30 percent when A1c levels rose above 7, and it tripled at levels above 10.

Nerve damage: Tulane University scientists found in a recent study of 4,526 women and men that an A1c over 7 triples the risk for peripheral vascular disease.

Blindness: In a study of 11,247 women and men, researchers from the International Diabetes Institute in Australia found that the odds for retinopathy—damage to the tiny blood vessels inside the retina—rose 25 percent when A1c levels were over 7.5 percent for up to 4 years and rose 50 percent when A1c remained high for more than 8 years.

Kidney damage and failure: The higher your A1c, the greater the odds for kidney failure, say Israeli researchers.

Scary? Yes, but there is a bright side: You're in control. University of Oxford scientists say that reducing your A1c (by tightening your blood sugar control) cuts all of these risks dramatically. A 1-point drop in your A1c level will reduce heart attack risk 14 percent, lower heart failure risk 16 percent, cut stroke risk 21 percent, cut risk for amputation due to peripheral vascular disease by 41 percent, and reduce risk for blindness or kidney failure by 37 percent.

A1C TEST

Think of it as: Your blood sugar "batting average"—a sign of your overall level for the past 2 to 3 months.

Good for: Seeing if your long-term diabetes management plan is working.

Not good for: Judging how your blood sugar responds to specific meals, foods, exercise sessions, or a single dose of medication.

Best test equipment: At your doctor's office or a commercial lab. "Home A1c tests are available, but I still recommend having one performed by your doctor," Pugh says. "People with diabetes need to see their doctor on a regular basis anyway to have their blood pressure, cholesterol, and foot health checked. And your doctor should discuss your A1c results with you."

Cost: $40 at a private lab (though insurance may cover most or all of the cost).

When to check: "If your A1c is high, have it rechecked every 2 to 3 months," says Dr. Davidson. "If your blood sugar is in good control, three times a year is enough."

Shoot for these numbers: An A1c reading of 6.5 to 7 percent. "Normal A1c levels for people without diabetes are 6 percent or lower," Dr. Davidson says. "The closer to normal, the better. But be reasonable. If your A1c is high and you bring it down, you've reduced your risk for complications."

Smart Testing Tip

Ask for more. Many doctors test A1c just once a year. Request more frequent checks, Dr. Davidson suggests, especially if you've started a new medicine or have difficulty keeping your daily blood sugar under control.

CHAPTER 3

THE DIABETES MEDICINE CABINET

Here's a rundown of insulin and noninsulin methods, plus promising new drugs and treatments on the horizon

If you think that having diabetes means you need to take insulin shots, think again. While many people with diabetes do need to take insulin daily, others are able to manage their blood sugar with oral medications and lifestyle modifications (namely, a healthy diet and regular exercise).

When taken properly, diabetes medications can lower your blood sugar level, reduce your symptoms, and lessen your risk of diabetic complications, such as nerve damage and vision loss. Remember, though, that no matter what diabetes drugs you take, it's still crucial to eat well and get regular physical activity. Here's an overview of the options available to you right now.

ORAL MEDICATIONS FOR DIABETES

If you have type 2 diabetes, your doctor will likely prescribe oral medication. Currently, those available stimulate the pancreas to produce or release insulin, enhance the effectiveness of insulin, reduce the liver's production of glucose, and delay the digestion of sugars and starches in the intestines.

Diabetes pills belong to five classes of drugs, all of which lower blood glucose levels in different ways. You may need to try more than one type of medication, a combination of pills, or oral medication plus insulin. Also, if you plan to become pregnant, you'll need to control your diabetes with lifestyle changes or with insulin, rather than oral diabetes medications.

Sulfonylureas

These drugs—which include glipizide (Glucotrol and Glucotrol XL), glyburide

---

Avoid Prescription Drug Errors

Taking a number of drugs at the same time can lead to dangerous interactions or unpleasant side effects, or it can render one or more of the drugs ineffective. Here are some simple ways to help your doctor and pharmacist avoid future (and current) mix-ups.

Carry a list of your meds. Always keep a complete record of your prescription medications in your wallet. Include each medication's name, the dosage you're taking, the prescribing physician, and the prescribing pharmacy. Also include any environmental and drug allergies you have as well as any vitamin supplements, herbal remedies, and over-the-counter medications you're taking. Make sure the list is readable and up-to-date at all times. This can come in especially handy when you go to a new doctor or if you are hospitalized unexpectedly.

Share it with your health care team. Every time you see members of your team, even if it's not to receive a new medication, show these professionals the list you've compiled so they can be alert for symptoms of side effects or drug interactions.

Read the package inserts. When you get a new medication, whether it's prescription or over the counter, read the information that comes with it. If you don't understand it or can't read all that fine print, ask your doctor or pharmacist for an explanation.

(Micronase, Glynase, and Diabeta), and glimepiride (Amaryl)—cause the pancreas to release more insulin. For these medications to work, your pancreas has to already be able to make some insulin.

What you should know: To avoid low blood sugar reactions while on these medications, pay close attention to eating on schedule.

Meglitinides

Like sulfonylureas, these drugs, which include repaglinide (Prandin) and nateglinide (Starlix), increase the pancreas's production of insulin, but they are shorter acting. They're taken before each of three meals.

What you should know: Because meglitinides stimulate insulin release, it is possible to experience hypoglycemia (low blood glucose levels) while taking this medication. You must eat if you have taken meglitinides.

Biguanides

Metformin (Glucophage) reduces the amount of glucose produced by the liver and makes muscle tissue more sensitive to insulin. Metformin may help you lose a few pounds when you start to take it, which can help you control your blood sugar and also improve blood fat and cholesterol levels, which are often high if you have type 2 diabetes. It's usually taken two times a day.

What you should know: If you have a kidney problem, metformin may build up in your body. Make sure your doctor knows how well your kidneys work before you begin taking this medication.

Thiazolidinediones

These drugs—which include rosiglitazone (Avandia) and pioglitazone (Actos)—help insulin work better and reduce glucose production in the liver. They're taken once or twice a day with food.

What you should know: Medications in this group don't cause blood sugar to drop too low. But if you take other diabetes medications along with pioglitazone or rosiglitazone, your blood sugar might drop too low.

Alpha-glucosidase inhibitors

These drugs—which include acarbose (Precose) and miglitol (Glyset)—delay the digestion of starches and sugars from the intestines, leading to lower blood sugar after meals.

What you should know: Because they work in the gastrointestinal tract instead of the bloodstream, these medications can cause side effects such as bloating and gas.

INSULIN

Although it is common for doctors to try pills before insulin, your doctor may start you on insulin based on several factors, including your overall health, how long you've had diabetes, your blood sugar level, and other medications you may be taking.

If your doctor says you need to take insulin, you should know that different types of insulin vary in how fast they work and how long they stay in your system. Your doctor can best guide you toward the type that's right for you. Once that is decided, you have several options for getting the insulin into your body. Here are the basics on each.

Insulin Needles

Most people give themselves injections of insulin with a bottle and a syringe. You can purchase more than one bottle of insulin at a time, but extras must be kept refrigerated.

Insulin Pens

Instead of drawing insulin out from a bottle, you dial the amount of insulin into a device that looks like a pen and has a needle at the end. You keep using the insulin until the cartridge is finished, and then you replace either the cartridge or the whole pen. These pens are used widely in Europe, but the United States has been slower to adopt this method.

Insulin Pumps

Instead of taking a series of injections during the day, this device delivers the insulin as an infusion from a small plastic catheter under the skin. The pump is a little smaller than a cigarette pack, and it has a computerized system that delivers insulin gradually throughout the day. The advantage of the pump is that it offers you a lot more flexibility in how to deliver your insulin. The disadvantage is that you are attached to this little device. There are certain people who really like using the pump because it helps them achieve control, and there are some people who don't do as well. It's important that you realize that if you're using an insulin pump, you must be prepared to do a lot of blood sugar testing and keep a careful watch on it.

Your doctor should offer you these options. Sometimes the insurance companies will decide for you, but in most cases, it's up to you.

ON THE HORIZON: NEEDLE-FREE INSULIN

Researchers and pharmaceutical companies are studying a variety of needle-free alternatives to administering insulin. Among them are these options.

• An oral insulin spray (absorbed into the bloodstream from the mouth)

• Inhaled insulin (administered in a device similar to an asthma inhaler)
• Insulin pills (specially made to protect the insulin from breaking down in the stomach)
• Skin patches (resembling those now used for some forms of heart medication and birth control)

Every day, the medical community is discovering new drugs, treatments, and ways of administering medications that can help improve your ability to take control of your diabetes. At each doctor visit, ask your physician if any new methods or therapies may help you gain better control over your blood sugar.

CHAPTER 4

DRUG DANGER

Are you getting the latest meds you desperately need?

You can't judge your diabetes by the number of pills you take. You should gauge it by your blood sugar.

When Harvard Medical School researchers recently checked up on diabetes care at 30 of the nation's top university medical centers, they uncovered a shocking trend: Half the time, people with diabetes were sent home without the medicines they needed to lower dangerously rising blood sugar—leaving them at unnecessary risk of potentially fatal complications.

For the 1,765 people in this study, rising blood sugar levels signaled that their diabetes was progressing—a normal event that happens when the body makes less and less insulin yet needs more and more in order to coax resistant cells to absorb blood sugar.

Yet 60 percent of those with slightly high sugar levels and 40 percent of those with alarmingly elevated levels didn't receive prescriptions for new drugs or higher doses of their current medicine—a pattern experts say is being repeated by family doctors and specialists treating millions of people with diabetes across North America.

"Most people with type 2 diabetes will need more medications as time goes by, and it's not their fault," says Kenneth J. Snow, MD, acting chief of the Adult Diabetes Division at Boston's Joslin Diabetes Center. "It's not a personal failure. It's just the natural progression of diabetes. But doctors don't always explain this. And people are very surprised and troubled when it happens."

In interviews with top diabetes experts, we learned that doctors—and people with type 2 diabetes—often bungle, misunderstand, or simply ignore the crucial moment when blood sugar tests reveal that diabetes is progressing. Research shows that while physicians know when it's time to take action, they may delay doing so for years. People with diabetes often bargain for more time on a single drug or promise to clobber blood sugar with radical lifestyle changes. Others become discouraged and feel they've failed or avoid the issue out of fear that upping the meds is a sign of disaster.

"You can't judge your diabetes by the number of pills you take," Dr. Snow says.

"You should gauge it by your blood sugar—and by how well your treatment-plan mix of diet, exercise, and medication is working to keep it low. If adding another drug brings it back down, that's a success. But lots of people with diabetes don't understand this."

That's why you need to take the initiative and work with your doctor to make sure you're getting the most effective drug treatments.

IT'S NOT YOUR FAULT

Chances are, even if you are religious about diet and exercise, your condition will progress. British scientists tried to get a handle on the odds of progressing diabetes recently by tracking 4,075 women and men with newly diagnosed type 2 diabetes. All started out controlling their diabetes with diet alone or by using a single drug (either metformin, which fights insulin resistance, or a sulfonylurea, which stimulates insulin production). After just 3 years, 50 percent of the drug group saw blood sugar rise to dangerous levels. After 9 years, 75 percent needed several drugs. Just 9 percent of the lifestyle-only group saw blood sugars stay within a safe range for the whole 9 years. Even more eye-opening: The researchers concluded that in less than 10 years, most people with type 2 will need insulin shots to keep blood sugar low.

"It's a huge shock for people to hear this," Dr. Snow says. "They see the need for more help as a personal failure or as a sign that their diabetes is really bad—that complications have already started. Neither is usually true."

And yet, don't assume that your doctor will initiate giving you new medications. Consider this: In a 12-year study of 570 people with diabetes, researchers at Kaiser Permanente Northwest found that doctors "followed" their patients' high blood sugar levels for months or even years before upgrading their drug treatments. They often waited until results of A1c tests—a measure of long-term blood sugar control—topped 9 percent, even though the American Diabetes Association recommends changes at 7 percent and other experts advocate starting even sooner.

In Canada, a study of 2,502 people with type 2 diabetes found that just 37 percent of those with high blood sugar got a drug upgrade from their family physician. People who saw endocrinologists— diabetes specialists—did only slightly better; 45 percent got the treatment they needed for progressing diabetes.

What's going on? "We call such behavior clinical inertia—recognition of the problem but failure to act," says diabetes expert Lawrence S. Phillips, MD, an endocrinologist at Emory University School of Medicine. Dr. Phillips says doctors often overestimate how well their treatments are working and hesitate to recommend additional drugs or even insulin injections to reluctant patients, even though treatment goals aren't being met. Sometimes, too, doctors don't feel an urgent need to treat a problem that causes no immediate symptoms. After all, high blood sugar doesn't hurt—at least not in the short term.

WHY YOU SHOULDN'T WAIT

Delaying or ignoring this diabetes turning point raises your risk for other health problems. Complications such as heart attack, stroke, blindness, kidney failure, and amputation are more likely if your diabetes treatment isn't optimal. "The worst thing is when patients and physicians let fear or denial or false hope get in the way and wait until blood sugar is really high before adding the next pill," says Anne Peters, MD, director of the University of Southern California's clinical diabetes program in Los Angeles and author of *Conquering Diabetes: A Cutting-Edge, Comprehensive Program for Prevention and Treatment.* "Each new pill or shot tends to lower long-term blood sugar only so much. If you wait too long, it could become very difficult to get blood sugar back into a healthy range."

How it matters: High blood sugar (an A1c level above 7 percent) raises heart attack risk 25 percent, ups stroke risk 30 percent, and triples your odds for nerve damage in legs and feet.

TAKE CONTROL BY TAKING CHARGE

Based on this information, you may have to be the catalyst in your diabetes drug therapy. Take these four steps to overcome misinformation, fear, self-blame, and even a reluctant doctor to get the proper medications you need to control your blood sugar.

Step 1: Update Your Attitude

Don't blame yourself if your diabetes progresses. "The truth is, you could have a perfect regimen, doing everything right, and your blood sugar can still start to slip," says endocrinologist Steven Edelman, MD, a professor of medicine at the University of California, San Diego. "It's easy to blame yourself—or for your doctor to even blame you when it's really just the diabetes progressing. But you shouldn't—and neither should your doctor."

Step 2: Track Your Blood Sugar

Regular blood sugar checks at home, plus the doctor-administered A1c test two to four times a year, will keep you up on important changes as they happen.

A clue that it's time for a change: an A1c over 7—or higher than your personal A1c target. "I don't wait," Dr. Peters says. "The A1c shows long-term blood sugar levels. It is high blood sugar over time that damages the body, not just a high reading after a meal. If your average blood sugar level over 3 months goes up, it's a sign that something serious is going on and a change in treatment is needed."

Another sign: If your daily blood sugar checks are consistently higher than the targets you and your doctor have set, then it may be time for a new drug regimen. (For example, many suggest daily levels between 90 and 130 mg/dl before meals or in the morning and under 140 to 160 mg/dl 2 hours after a meal.)

Step 3: Ask This Question

See your doctor every 3 months for checkups, and at each visit ask: Am I still at my target? If not, is it time for something new? "Every time you see your doctor about your diabetes, you should discuss how well your treatment plan is working and whether it needs to be changed," Dr. Snow says. Cutting-edge diabetes treatment calls for aggressive care.

If your doctor seems behind the curve, ask why you don't need a new plan (or find a new physician). This is especially important if you're in your thirties, forties, fifties, or even sixties. "If your diabetes is diagnosed when you're younger, or if you plan on living a long life, there's less room for error," Dr. Peters says. "High blood sugar is more dangerous when it goes on for years and years."

Step 4: Strike a Balance

"Start with the fundamentals," says endocrinologist Richard Hellman, MD, a clinical professor of medicine at the University of Missouri/Kansas City School of Medicine and medical director of the Heart of America Diabetes Research Foundation. "The foundation of good diabetes care is always a healthy diet and regular exercise. Often, if you see your blood sugar levels slipping on daily checks, it's because of that. Even

Quick Tip

If you aren't getting the A1c test two to four times a year, ask your doctor to order it. Most people with diabetes don't get this crucial test as often as they should—so their doctors don't have the info they need to see if it's time to change their treatment plan.

if you need more medication, your diet still helps because it can help prevent weight gain, it supplies important nutrients, and it will still have an impact on your blood sugar. Exercise helps muscle cells become more insulin sensitive."

What about drugs? Your doctor has lots of choices today. Until the mid-1990s, doctors had two drug choices for type 2: sulfonylureas (such as Diabeta, Diabinese, Glucotrol, Micronase, and Orinase), which prompt your pancreas to make more insulin, and insulin itself.

Why Blood Sugar Rises

Type 2 diabetes is a progressive disease—even with treatment, blood sugar rises over time because of changes inside your body. Here's what's happening and why you need to constantly monitor and perhaps change your diabetes medications.

Less insulin: Your pancreas normally produces this important hormone, which tells cells in your muscles and organs to absorb blood sugar. For reasons scientists are still probing, insulin production drops lower and over the years in type 2 diabetes. "High blood sugar is sort of toxic to insulin-producing beta cells in the pancreas," says researcher Richard Pratley, MD, director of the Diabetes and Metabolism Translational Medicine Unit at the University of Vermont College of Medicine in Burlington. "But there are other factors. People with diabetes have lower levels of a protein called GLP that acts as a growth factor for beta cells. This loss of beta cells is a big problem, causing the need to go onto multiple drugs and even move to injected insulin."

More insulin resistance: Due to inactivity, overweight, and aging, cells throughout your body tend to ignore insulin's signals more and more over time, says Anne Peters, MD, director of the University of Southern California's clinical diabetes program. Blood sugar rises as a result. You can control insulin resistance with exercise, weight loss, and medication.

"Now there are 15 different oral medications in five different categories," Dr. Snow says. "And there are several combination drugs that can make it easier and more affordable if you have to take more than one medication."

As discussed earlier, your doctor may suggest you take metformin—which improves insulin sensitivity and seems to turn down the liver's production of blood sugar—plus a sulfonylurea. Another type of insulin sensitizer called a glitazone (brand names include Actos and Avandia) may be added. If your blood sugar soars after meals, the doctor may suggest a starch blocker (such as Precose or Glyset) or a meglitinide (such as Prandin or Starlix), which triggers a short burst of insulin.

If your doctor prescribes insulin, don't balk. "Insulin is still the most powerful agent we have for lowering blood sugar," says Dr. Hellman. "Doctors want to make patients happy and give them lots of choices, but some of the new diabetes pills won't work well if your body isn't producing some insulin on its own. Don't overlook insulin if it's what you need to get the job done. It's not a setback. It's preserving your health and your life."

CHAPTER 5

TIP-TOP DIABETES CARE

Assemble an A team and get the high-quality care you deserve

When you have diabetes, it's important that you get the best quality care you can. The good news is that the quality of your care begins with you. The more informed you are about what constitutes good diabetes care, the more effective you can be in taking control of your diabetes and avoiding complications—and the more you help your doctors help you.

Whether you've lived with diabetes for a while or have just been diagnosed, this chapter offers an easy three-step way to the best care: making your health a team effort, getting the most from your team, and keeping on top of the tests you need. The benefit: a happier, healthier life and the satisfaction of knowing that you control your diabetes, rather than the other way around.

STEP 1: PUT TOGETHER YOUR TEAM PLAYERS

Seeing your primary doctor regularly to keep tabs on your diabetes care is crucial. But to achieve optimum health and stop potentially dangerous diabetes side effects well before they start, you should enlist the assistance of several more health care providers. A group of physicians, nutritionists, counselors, and other health professionals—a sort of diabetes A team—can work in tandem to ensure that you achieve the best diabetes control.

The benefits of a team approach are considerable. In a study of a dozen health clinics in New Mexico, when 1,465 people with diabetes received team care, the number of those who got important eye exams and kept their LDL (bad) cholesterol within safe limits doubled. In addition, the number of people who set goals for controlling their condition (and the heart risks that go with it) quadrupled.

Here are the people you should include on your A team. (To determine if they will provide good diabetes care, see "'Interview' Your Doctor" on page 31.)

Primary physician: This can be your current primary care doctor, an internist who specializes in diabetes, or an endocrinologist. However, for most people, it is sufficient to see an endocrinologist only occasionally or even just once, soon after being diagnosed. Regardless of which you choose, your primary physician should be knowledgeable about dia-

betes so that you can be appropriately evaluated and treated.

Nutritionist/dietitian: A nutritionist can help you develop an eating plan that's right for you and identify and resolve any problems you have sticking with a healthy diet. Your primary physician can recommend a nutritionist. Don't let concerns about cost deter you from seeing one; Medicare and private insurance cover some visits.

Certified diabetes educator (CDE): The CDE plays a pivotal role on a diabetes care team, says Carole Mensing, a CDE and president of health care and education at the American Diabetes Association (ADA). "CDEs help you sort out strategies and resources and provide a little more comprehensive view," she says. Your CDE will show you how to do glucose testing, record your results, and map out a self-care plan based on your results. If your doctor doesn't have a CDE, ask for a referral or contact the ADA for CDEs in your area.

Mental health counselor: Research has shown that having diabetes doubles your odds of depression. That's no surprise. Dealing with the daily demands of diabetes can be stressful, even for the strongest people. To care for your emotional well-being as well as your physical health, ask your doctor or CDE to recommend a good mental health counselor.

Exercise physiologist: If you're generally in good health and stay moderately active, you may not need an exercise physiologist. But if you have a heart condition or participate in a high-intensity sport such as marathon running, you may want to add one to your team. Your doctor or CDE can give you a recommendation.

One more thing: If you're already getting good care from your doctor, stick with him as your primary physician. The same holds true if you already have a nutritionist, CDE, mental health counselor, or exercise physiologist you're happy with.

Managing Your Team

After you have all the people in place and have had your initial consultations with them, here's how to get ongoing benefits from your team.

Set goals and monitor your progress. Goal setting is a matter of hitting important targets for things such as blood sugar and blood pressure, getting eye exams, and controlling weight to prevent complications. You might want to keep track of these results on your own and share them with a member of your team.

Stay on top of your appointments. "We recommend that people should be seen every 3 to 4 months by their primary doctor for their diabetes care, and then annually with a CDE or attend an ADA–sponsored program for an update," says Mensing. Make sure all lab tests, examinations, and routine follow-ups such as foot checks and eye exams are in place. Ask your doctor to provide you with a checkup checklist. And see your nutritionist, counselor, and exercise physiologist as often as each recommends or when you have a problem that needs to be addressed.

Get to know the support staff at your doctor's office. They can be extremely helpful in getting you more time with your doctor or helping you smooth over any rough patches in your care, such as insurance issues, questions you have about your treatment, or when you need a quick answer to a concern.

STEP 2: MAXIMIZE EVERY APPOINTMENT

Studies have shown that, currently, an average doctor visit lasts 22 minutes or less. When you have diabetes, that's not a lot of time to address all of your symptoms, test results, concerns, and

"Interview" Your Doctor

Would you hire an employee without interviewing him? Then don't "hire" the members of your diabetes team without asking them these important questions. Their answers can help you decide if they will provide good diabetes care.

1. How often do you treat people with diabetes? You want someone who has a lot of experience with patients with diabetes.

2. How do you stay current on diabetes management? Good team candidates will say they go to conferences, stay on top of the latest diabetes studies, confer with colleagues about new treatments, or regularly read journals related to their discipline (diabetes, nutrition, exercise, etc.).

3. What other professionals do you refer patients to? You want to determine that your health care providers have multiple resources in place and that they encourage patients to see those individuals—for example, nutritionists, podiatrists, eye doctors, nurse practitioners, etc.

4. How much time do you allot for annual physicals and regular doctor visits? One doctor might allow 5 or 10 minutes; another might allow 30. The more time a doctor usually allows, the more time you'll have to broach your questions and concerns.

questions. Here are some simple ways to make the most of the minutes you do get with your doctor or member of your diabetes team.

Make a list. Once you're in the exam room, it's easy to forget the topics, symptoms, and concerns you wanted to discuss with your doctor. So bring a small notepad on which you've listed what you want to bring up. As you cover each item, note your doctor's recommendations and comments, then cross it off your list. Even if you get sidetracked (or your doctor does), don't let your doctor go until you've covered everything on your list.

Talk about tests. If you have had any lab tests done since your last visit, discuss the results with your doctor. It's also a good idea to go over your observations regarding your daily blood tests. Then ask your doctor if you're due for any important screening tests in the near future, so you can schedule them before your next visit.

Explain symptoms clearly. If you are experiencing any symptoms or side effects, your doctor will want to know how your symptoms feel, how long you've had them, what you are doing when the symptoms begin, whether you're having other symptoms at the same time, and if anything you do makes the symptoms go away. The more information you provide, the easier it will be for your doctor to make an accurate diagnosis.

Discuss medications. Before you leave home, make a list of the medications you're taking, including both prescription and over-the-counter drugs. Remember to write down nutri-

---

Get the Most from Your Insurance

Maria Gargano, a registered nurse who reviews medical records and claims for a large health insurance plan in North Carolina, offers her advice on getting the most out of your health insurance.

- Read your benefits book. Most people have no idea what their coverage is and expect all claims they submit to be covered.
- Don't assume that because a doctor wrote you a prescription, the service or item will be covered. Coverage is usually based on necessity, not convenience.
- If your insurance company has a case management department, use it. Case managers can help patients get services they need and negotiate with nursing homes and equipment companies.
- Use your insurance company's Web site to find information on doctors in the plan, medical policies, and covered conditions.
- When troubles arise, call your insurance company and find someone there willing to be your advocate.

tional supplements (such as multivitamins and calcium) and herbal treatments as well. Update your doctor on any changes, and discuss how the treatments he or she has prescribed are working and if they seem to be causing any unpleasant side effects. Also inform your doctor if you intend to modify your diet or start exercising, since these lifestyle changes can reduce your need for certain medications.

STEP 3: KEEP ON TOP OF THOSE TESTS

Along with daily blood sugar checks, the following tests can help keep you from developing painful and even possibly life-threatening complications from diabetes. If you haven't had any of these tests recently, call your doctor and ask to schedule them. After you have them, write on your calendar when you should have them repeated, so you won't forget them.

Every 3 to 6 months: hemoglobin A1c (HbA1c) test. Beyond daily, at-home blood sugar testing, people with type 2 should also have their long-range blood sugar levels checked two to four times a year. That blood test—called the HbA1c test—-measures the amount of sugar attached to hemoglobin, revealing your average blood sugar level over the previous 2 to 3 months. This test also helps predict the risk of diabetes complications, including heart disease, stroke, kidney failure, vision problems, and circulation problems. It's possible to take this test at home (see "Ask about This Do-It-Yourself Test" on page 35).

At least once a year: foot check. Diabetes can cause poor circulation in the feet, which makes them more susceptible to infections. When examining each foot, your doctor should check the pulse, see whether the foot is getting good circulation by looking at capillary refill in the toes, and look for any severe calluses, cuts, bruises, or infections. Your doctor should also do a special sensory exam to test whether the sensation in the feet is adequate. Your leg reflexes can also be tested, which can indicate nerve loss or damage.

If, between visits, you notice bruises, injuries, or areas of infection on your feet, or if you have ingrown nails or excessive calluses, have a podiatrist take care of them right away.

At least once a year: eye screening. Diabetes can damage tiny blood vessels in the retina (the light-sensitive inner layer of the eyes), increasing the chances of vision problems and even blindness. A special eye check can detect this damage early on, allowing for prompt treatment to prevent vision loss.

People with type 2 should have this exam every year. Currently, people with type 1 diabetes are advised to get an eye check within 3 to 5 years of their diabetes diagnosis.

Once a year: lipid panel. People with diabetes have a high risk of heart disease and stroke because of the circulatory problems caused by the excess glucose in the bloodstream. A high cholesterol level makes matters worse, further boosting your risk of heart disease and

---

Ace Your Tests

Diagnostic tests are essential for your health, but they can cause you to worry. Here are a few ways to calm your nerves and get all the information you need before heading to the lab.

Learn the details. Tests are scariest when you don't know in advance what to expect. Ask your doctor to describe the test in detail. Will there be pain? How long will the discomfort last? How long does it take to get results? The more information you get, the less nervous you are likely to be.

Also, don't hesitate to ask other people, including those in the doctor's office, about their experiences with the tests and what they did to relax and reduce the discomfort.

Know what's normal. When your doctor gives you the results of a test, ask for the normal range. Your doctor should explain what the numbers mean and how they affect your long-term health.

Discuss a plan of action. If your test results are normal, your doctor might tell you to keep doing what you're doing. But if they're not normal, make sure you fully understand what you need to do in the months and years ahead.

Ask about This Do-It-Yourself Test

Until recently, the hemoglobin A1c (HbA1c) test was available only in a doctor's office or by prescription. Now it's possible to check HbA1c levels at home with the FDA-approved Metrika A1cNow monitor. About the size of a deck of cards, this monitor uses a drop of blood, which you get from pricking your finger, to measure glycated hemoglobin levels without a prescription. Results are available in 8 minutes. Each test kit can be used once. HbA1c levels better predict risk of diabetes complications, including heart disease, stroke, kidney failure, blindness, and circulation problems. For more information, log on to www.metrika.com. Some experts still recommend having this test done at your doctor's office.

stroke, which is why it's important to have this test annually.

Typically, the lipid panel measures total cholesterol, HDL (good) cholesterol, LDL (bad) cholesterol, and triglycerides. Your doctor will use all of these measurements to assess your cholesterol profile and determine if any action should be taken. He may recommend that you take a cholesterol-lowering statin drug and a daily low-dose aspirin.

At least once a year: kidney check. At least 40 million Americans have kidney disease or are at high risk for it—and many have diabetes, according to a recent analysis of government statistics conducted by the National Kidney Foundation. Experts recommend that people with diabetes get an annual blood pressure check, a blood test for creatine, and a urine check for proteins, all of which will be used to assess kidney function. Ask your doctor for an albumin-specific dipstick test or to have your urine sent to a lab to check for even lower levels of proteins.

MEDICAL BREAKTHROUGHS

Here's the latest and greatest diabetes research to help you take control.

PLAY YOUR ODDS

One in three Americans likely has a gene that mutes the body's response to insulin—raising the odds for insulin resistance and, eventually, type 2 diabetes, according to new research from Wake Forest University School of Medicine in Winston-Salem, North Carolina.

Blood tests of 1,895 volunteers revealed that 35 percent had a quirky variation in a key gene that altered the way their bodies processed sugar. "Someday, this test may be part of tests assessing diabetes risk before trouble starts," says researcher Donald W. Bowden, PhD, associate director of the university's gene research.

For now, your best screen is your family tree. The results suggest that you likely have the gene if a few of your relatives are diabetic, making it crucial that you exercise, stay trim, eat plenty of fiber, and get regular blood sugar tests.

NEW HOPE FOR TYPE 1

For the 1 million Americans with type 1 diabetes, cell transplants can seem miraculous. A recent National Institutes of Health report concluded that 60 percent of people who had islet cell transplants—the cells produce insulin—didn't need painful daily insulin shots a year later. Doctors hope the risk of type 1 complications (blindness, kidney failure, even amputation) will plummet.

But they're not for everyone—yet. "Islet transplants are still very experimental," says Camillo Ricordi, scientific director of the Diabetes Research Institute at the University of Miami. Here's what you need to know.

- Islet transplants are performed as research only. You have to meet certain criteria to be accepted.
- Transplant recipients need to take potent immune-suppressing drugs for life. These drugs boost the risk of infection, high blood pressure, cancer, and other problems.
- Donor cells come from organ donors, so there are only enough to perform a few thousand transplants each year.
- Transplants start losing function after 1 year. And researchers are still puzzling out the reasons.

KNOW YOUR HEART RISK

People with diabetes have a high risk of heart disease and stroke because of the circulatory problems caused by excess glucose in the bloodstream. One of the biggest heart disease risk factors is a complete mystery to 58 percent of people—and to 83 percent of their doctors, a World Heart Federation (Switzerland) survey found.

An expanding waistline raises your risk of heart disease as well as your risk of two other related problems with long-term implications for your health: high blood pressure and elevated cholesterol.

Next time you see your doctor, have your waist measured. Chances are, however, your physician doesn't know how to take an accurate reading, and measuring the wrong way can give you a false result. Follow these steps to get it right.

1. Take off or raise your shirt above your midriff and loosen your belt.
2. Place a measuring tape midway between the top of your hip bone and the bottom of your rib cage.
3. Relax your stomach and breathe out while you measure. Healthy waistline maximums are 35 inches for women and 40 inches for men, no matter what your height.

STOP BLAMING MOM

Bad diet and a sluggish lifestyle—not "the way you were raised"—give rise to midlife insulin resistance. A British study of 379 people reveals that the largest contributors are body fat and waist circumference—accounting for 22 percent of the risk in men who had insulin resistance and 34 percent in women. High birth weights from moms' excess weight gain and early diets had little effect.

INHALE THIS

According to a *British Medical Journal* study of 4,572 adults, people who regularly breathe in secondhand smoke—even if they've never taken a puff—are more likely to develop prediabetes than former smokers.

DOZE AWAY DIABETES

Sleep has a sweet bonus: Getting just the right amount of z's each night could protect against type 2 diabetes.

A Yale University study of 1,709 men found that those who regularly got less than 6 hours of shut-eye doubled their diabetes risk; those who slept more than 8 hours tripled their odds. Previous studies have turned up similar findings in women. "When you sleep too little—or too long because of sleep apnea—your nervous system stays on alert," says lead researcher Klar Yaggi, MD, an assistant professor of pulmonary medicine at Yale. This interferes with hormones that regulate blood sugar. A recent Columbia University study found that sleeping less than 5 hours also doubled the risk of high blood pressure.

For a good night's rest, avoid caffeine after noon, leave work at the office, and skip late-night TV. Oversleeping may be a sign of depression or a treatable sleep disorder, so talk with your doctor.

GO CHROME

The best mineral for diabetes? Chromium. The mineral that unlocks a cell's ability to absorb blood sugar might be the must-have diabetes supplement. But here are a few things you should know before you take it.

It may help control diabetic health risks. In a 10-month study of 27 people with diabetes, insulin sensitivity was twice as good in chromium takers as in those who got a fake supplement. And a new Slovenian study of 60 people with diabetes found that taking chromium supplements for 3 months shortened their QTc interval—a heart rhythm that may become fatal if the interval lengthens.

Safety questions haven't been answered. We need more studies to be sure chromium is safe, says Robert Rizza, MD, president of the American Diabetes Association. The studies here used 1,000 micrograms per day, but the current federal recommendation is only 50 to 200 micrograms per day. Doses higher than 1,000 micrograms may threaten the liver and kidneys.

The bottom line. Try to get chromium from foods such as whole grains and vegetables. If you want to try a supplement, check with your doctor first (and remember, don't take more than 200 micrograms a day).

GET MILK

Don't toss those calcium pills yet. Researchers are questioning the supplement's value in preventing bone fractures, but a landmark study suggests that calcium plus vitamin D offers powerful protection against diabetes.

In a 20-year study of 83,779 women by scientists at Tufts–New England Medical Center in Boston, those who got the highest levels of the combo—more than 1,200 milligrams of calcium and more than 800 IU of vitamin D—had a 33 percent lower risk of type 2 diabetes than women who got the lowest levels. The nutrients also worked alone, though not as well. About 75 percent of the women got less than the recommended levels of calcium, and 97 percent got too little D. Aim for one to two servings of low-fat dairy and a 500-milligram supplement of calcium daily. And add a D pill containing 400 IU.

TAME INFLAMMATION

Aspirin isn't the only salicylate that saves lives. A new Harvard study reveals that prescription salicylates—aspirin's chemical cousins—may help reverse insulin resistance in people with type 2 diabetes. Researchers found that weight gain leads to diabetes by triggering low-level inflammation in the liver, which makes the body's insulin receptors less responsive because the two systems cross paths in the body. Taking prescription salicylates can reduce inflammation (so can losing weight), says study author Steven Shoelson, MD.

POSSIBLE RELIEF FOR KIDS WITH TYPE 2

Pills for adults with type 2 diabetes work as well as insulin injections for kids.

Metformin and sulfonylureas—often the first-choice pills for grown-ups with type 2 diabetes—work as well as insulin injections for children, says new research from Ohio State University.

Although the study is small—it followed 42 kids, ages 9 $^1/_2$ to 16, for 5 years—the results could help close a troubling treatment gap. "The epidemic of childhood obesity and the growing epidemic of children with type 2 diabetes have outstripped what we know about diabetes drugs in children," says Milap Nahata, PharmD, MS, the study's principal investigator and a professor of pharmacy and pediatrics. "Most kids with type 2 get insulin because it has been well studied in children with type 1 diabetes—the only type of diabetes most children ever used to get. Doctors aren't sure how diabetes drugs in pill form will affect kids." (In type 1 diabetes, the body stops producing insulin; in type 2, over-weight and inactivity make the body ignore insulin's signals.)

The results: Pills and insulin all lowered kids' A1c levels—a sign of long-term sugar control—by a respectable 2.5 percentage points. "That can help reduce the risk for complications in the future," Dr. Nahata says. Pills can be very helpful for teens, who may not take insulin injections as often as they should. Pills seem safe and effective for kids over age 10.

DELAY INSULIN SHOTS

Experimental "gliptin" drugs—under development by researchers at five international drug companies—might one day help people with type 2 diabetes put off the need for insulin shots.

In a study of 552 people with type 2 diabetes, sitagliptin—a type of gliptin being developed by Merck—lowered levels of A1c, a measure of long-term blood sugar control, by as much as 1 percentage point. And when 107 people took vildagliptin—Novartis's gliptin drug—for up to 1 year, their A1c levels fell 1.1 percent. A 1-point drop in your A1c level will reduce heart attack risk by 14 percent and lower heart failure risk by 16 percent, stroke risk by 21 percent, amputation risk by 41 percent, and kidney failure by 37 percent.

Unlike many other diabetes drugs, gliptins don't seem to cause weight gain.

"Increased levels of GLP-1 reduce food intake," says vildagliptin researcher Daniel J. Drucker, MD, director of the Banting and Best Diabetes Centre at the University of Toronto.

Part II

EAT RIGHT

CHAPTER 6

THE BREAKTHROUGH DIABETES EATING PLAN

Slim down and control blood sugar in three easy steps

Diabetes researchers have developed a breakthrough eating plan that not only controls sugar levels but also satisfies your appetite, tames diabetes-related heart risks, and shrinks dangerous belly fat. Best of all, it's a food plan you can stick with—happily—for life.

"This is not a drastic, short-term weight loss diet but lifelong lifestyle changes," says Osama Hamdy, MD, PhD, director of the Clinical Obesity Program at the Harvard-affiliated Joslin Diabetes Center in Boston, where experts developed the new strategy. "Most people with diabetes or at risk for it are overweight. The foods in our guidelines help make weight loss easier—and lead to metabolic improvements that help lower blood sugar and reduce heart risks and heart attacks, too," he explains.

DANGEROUS FAT TARGETED

Smart yet practical, this plan is based on hundreds of studies looking at the interactions of food, weight, health, and fitness. It's beneficial whether you have type 2 diabetes or you're at risk (as are 40 percent of American adults) due to overweight, inactivity, a family history of diabetes, or a too-snug waistband. Diabetes risk rises if your waist measures more than 35 inches for women or 40 inches for men, even if your weight is normal.

"These guidelines really target visceral fat—the fat inside your abdomen that pumps out hormones and other inflammatory substances that lead to insulin resistance [when the body's cells can't obey insulin's signals to absorb blood sugar]," Dr. Hamdy says. "Americans typically carry at least 6 to 8 pounds of this dangerous visceral fat at their midline. Studies show that the waistlines of American women and men increased by more than an inch between 1994 and 2000 alone, due to overeating, lack of exercise, stress, and genetics. This visceral fat contributes to diabetes and heart disease.

"We suggest cutting calories by 250 to 500 per day and getting at least 2 1/2 to 3 hours of exercise per week, and ideally 60 to 90 minutes most days of the week," Dr. Hamdy continues. But don't go lower than about 1,000 to 1,200 calories for women and 1,200 to 1,600 for men. Here's your new blueprint for eating to control diabetes.

CARBS: LESS IS MORE

New goal: Get 40 percent of daily calories from carbs, and keep to a minimum of 130 grams per day. "This is a significant change from the standard 50 to 60 percent of calories from carbs," says Joslin dietitian Amy Campbell, RD. "Too much raises blood sugar and also raises heart disease risk, usually by increasing triglycerides [a type of blood fat]." The slightly lower carb intake may also help reduce abdominal fat.

On your plate: If you're following a 1,500-calories-a-day plan, get about 600 calories (150 grams) from carbs. This is about the amount in 5 servings of starch (whole grains, starchy vegetables such as potatoes and peas, and beans), 2 servings of fruit, 2 1/2 servings of low-fat dairy (including 1 serving of milk), and 3 servings of nonstarchy vegetables.

Quick Tip

Stock up on frozen fruits and veggies as well as the precut and packaged vegetables you'll find in the produce department. It will make preparing these healthy carbs a snap.

- Have whole fruit instead of juice. It's more filling, it provides comparable amounts of vitamin C and antioxidants for less carbs and calories, and the fiber slows the rise in blood sugar.
- Swap and downscale. If you love pasta and bread, switch to whole grain varieties and scale back the portion sizes. "Have 1 cup of noodles instead of 3 or one piece of toast instead of two," Campbell suggests.
- Fill half your plate with veggies and be creative with color, variety, and taste. Try chopped tomatoes with a splash of vinegar, oil, garlic, and basil, or make low-fat vegetable soup by adding frozen mixed veggies to a low-sodium canned variety.

FAT: REACH FOR THE GOOD GUYS

New goal: Get 30 to 35 percent of daily calories from good fats. "This is higher than we've recommended in the past," says James Rosenzweig, MD, director of Joslin's Disease Management Program. "We've found that having a little more fat, in place of some carbohydrates, helps people lose weight more easily. And good fats can help protect your arteries and heart."

On your plate: Aim for approximately 450 to 530 calories (50 to 60 grams) a day from good fats if you're following a 1,500-calorie eating plan—about the amount in 2 tablespoons of olive or canola oil or trans-free margarine and a handful of nuts, plus a serving of salmon. "The higher the percentage of calories that comes from fat, then the lower the percentage from carbohydrate," says Dr. Rosenzweig, "which makes diabetes easier to control." How to get there:

Snack on nuts. Nuts are packed with heart-healthy monounsaturated and poly-unsaturated fats; in addition, walnuts contain omega-3s. (Although nuts and oils are heart-healthy, they are high in calories, so limit your portions.)

Have oily fish twice a week. It's good for you. "Omega-3–rich fish include salmon, mackerel, lake trout, herring, and sardines," Campbell says. An easy fish dish: Mix canned salmon with low-fat mayo to make salmon salad for sandwiches.

Use olive or canola oil. Rich in mono and polyunsaturated fats, they're good for cooking and salads.

PROTEIN: SATISFACTION SECRET

New goal: Unless you have kidney problems, get 20 to 30 percent of daily calories from protein. "Research shows you can lose more weight if your diet has more protein, and your blood sugar, unhealthy LDL cholesterol, triglycerides, and blood pressure can also improve," Dr. Hamdy says.

On your plate: Have 300 to 450 calories (75 to 113 grams) worth of protein for a 1,500-calorie meal plan. This is about the amount in two scrambled egg whites and 1 cup of fat-free milk for breakfast, a sandwich with 2 ounces each of low-fat cheese and chicken plus $1/2$ cup of fat-free milk at lunch, and 6 ounces of codfish at dinner. The tricky part? Avoiding extra fat. These strategies can help.

• Choose skinless chicken and turkey. To keep poultry moist, cook it with the skin on, then remove it before serving. Make burgers and meat loaf with skinless ground poultry.
• Think vegetarian. Add canned black, red, or white beans (rinsed) to vegetable soup. One serving of beans is $1/2$ cup.
• Go for skinny dairy. Drink fat-free milk and snack on fat-free yogurt, for instance, and choose reduced-fat cheeses.

Quick Tip

Keep your cholesterol intake to under 300 milligrams per day, or under 200 milligrams daily if your LDL (bad) cholesterol is more than 100 mg/dl.

Fiber: More Is Better

Joslin Diabetes Center's new fiber recommendation of 50 grams per day is nearly double the 25 to 30 grams advocated by groups such as the American Heart Association—and three times more than the average American actually eats!

"Studies show that people who eat that much fiber have better blood sugar control," says Joslin dietitian Amy Campbell, RD. "You can get there if you eat high-fiber cereal for breakfast, whole grains, and lots of fruit and vegetables." Or sprinkle a super-high-fiber cereal over fat-free, no-sugar-added yogurt for a fiber-boosting snack. If you want to add a fiber supplement, try psyllium or beta-glucan. (Beta-glucan is found naturally in oatmeal, oat bran, and barley.)

CHAPTER 7

CARB CONTROL

These simple, delicious menu choices will help you keep carbs in check throughout your day

Great low-carb recipes sure make low-carb cooking easier, which is why Part VII of this book serves up 100 delicious, nutritious, low-carb offerings for breakfast, lunch, dinner, snacks, and desserts. But we also know that meals often get thrown together at the last minute—without a cookbook. That's why we put together the following helpful fast-fix meal guidelines, along with handy charts to help you figure out how many calories and grams of carbohydrates you need each day. Read them over now to help you get a feel for making smart low-carb choices at each meal throughout the day.

BRIGHTEN UP BREAKFAST

Many people skip breakfast or eat the same thing every morning. Neither approach is a good way to start the day. The key to a healthy diet is variety. And if you are going to eat carbs, breakfast may be the best time to eat them. One study shows that our bodies are more receptive to the insulin rush of carb-rich foods in the morning. Keep breakfast fresh with some of these ideas.

Switch to whole grains. If you're a big fan of cereal, try a whole grain or high-fiber version such as All-Bran, oat bran or oatmeal, whole rolled wheat or rye, kasha (buckwheat), or unsweetened puffed grains such as brown rice, corn, or whole wheat. Top it with a bit of cow's milk or soy milk and some fruit such as blueberries or strawberries. For a variation, try a few whole grain crackers, a whole wheat matzo, a whole wheat tortilla, or some whole wheat toast spread with cream cheese, almond butter, or macadamia nut butter.

Get creative with eggs. This excellent source of protein can be scrambled, hard-cooked, poached, fried, or mixed with other ingredients. Add leftover vegetables and meats and some reduced-fat cheese to eggs to make a quick omelet or frittata. Leftover quiche also makes an excellent breakfast dish (or microwaved lunch).

Give cottage cheese a makeover. For a great breakfast "sundae," mix cottage cheese with a teaspoon of all-fruit spread, cut-up whole fruit, and a sprinkle of cinnamon. Or try it with some chopped vegetables or a chopped hard-cooked egg and season with a little salt and pepper.

Eat nonbreakfast foods. In Japan, it's customary to start the day with a bowl of warming soup. In Mexico and Britain, beans are often served with breakfast. Beans are a terrific source of protein and make an excellent accompaniment to eggs. Try some seasoned lentils or kidney, pinto, navy, or Northern beans. No time to cook? Reheat the leftovers from yesterday's dinner.

ENJOY A GOOD LUNCH

For most Americans, lunch is a grab-and-go meal. Fortunately, plenty of satisfying low-carb lunches are up for grabs. You just need to know where to look.

Make a salad out of almost anything. There are so many varieties of greens and prepared salads readily available in supermarkets and fast-food restaurants that you can have a different kind every day. Toss chopped raw vegetables with sliced cooked ones. For instance, the contrast of raw, leafy vegetables with hot, cooked cauliflower or sugar snap peas tastes fantastic. For protein, add chunks or slices of fish, hard-cooked eggs, meat,

What's a Serving?

Here's a guide to smart low-carb serving sizes. Use these to help you control your portions. Also read "What to Eat Each Day" to find out how many daily servings to eat from each food group, based on your calorie intake and your goals.

FOOD GROUP	AMOUNT IN 1 SERVING
Protein	1 oz cooked lean beef, pork, lamb, skinless poultry, fish, or shellfish
	1 oz hard cheese (preferably reduced fat)
	1 egg
Fat, unsaturated	1 tsp ghee (clarified butter)
	1 tsp oil (such as olive, canola, walnut, or flaxseed)
	1 tsp regular mayonnaise
	1 Tbsp low-fat mayonnaise
	1 Tbsp oil-and-vinegar dressing
	5 large olives
	$1/8$ medium avocado
Fat, saturated	1 tsp butter
	1 slice bacon
	1 oz salt pork
	1 Tbsp heavy cream
	1 Tbsp cream cheese
	2 Tbsp sour cream
	2 Tbsp shredded unsweetened coconut

FOOD GROUP	AMOUNT IN 1 SERVING
Nuts	1 oz, without shell
	2 Tbsp peanut butter
Vegetables	$1/2$ c raw, chopped, or cooked
	$3/4$ c vegetable juice
	1 c raw, leafy greens
Starches	1 slice whole wheat bread
	$1/2$ whole wheat bagel or muffin
	$1/2$ c cooked whole grain cereal or pasta, brown rice, or other whole grain
	$1/2$ c cooked beans, corn, potatoes, rice, or sweet potatoes
Fruits	1 small to medium piece
	1 c whole strawberries or melon cubes
	$1/2$ c canned or cut fruit
	$3/4$ c fruit juice
	$1/4$ c dried fruit
Dairy	1 c fat-free milk
	1 c fat-free or low-fat unsweetened yogurt
	$1/2$ c low-fat ricotta cheese or cottage cheese
	$3/4$ c unsweetened soy milk

poultry, or shellfish or some chickpeas or other beans.

Create a wrap with lettuce. Soft lettuce leaves such as Boston make excellent

tortilla substitutes in "wrap" sandwiches. Simply top a large lettuce leaf with tuna, egg, chicken, turkey, shrimp, or crabmeat salad and roll it into a neat pack-

What to Eat Each Day

Most people who now consume a high-carbohydrate, low-fat diet (the standard American weight loss diet) will likely lose weight by cutting carbohydrates down to 125 grams (180 grams if that is too much too soon) and replacing them with protein and fats. To do that, follow the plan below. Simply eat the daily number of servings of food listed under that plan.

If you're trying to lose weight, don't choose a goal weight—just reduce your current calorie intake by 500 to 1,000 calories a day. (Note: Never go below 1,500 calories per day unless under the supervision of a doctor.) This will lead to safe, effective weight loss of 1 to 2 pounds per week. For instance, if you currently take in 2,300 to 2,500 calories a day, try reducing your daily intake to 1,800 to 2,000 calories. This will be your new daily calorie level. If you're not trying to lose weight, ask your doctor what your daily calorie intake should be.

Find your optimal calorie level below, then try to eat the amounts of each food group listed. This will automatically make you cut back on your carbs yet make sure you get enough of the right foods.

CALORIES	1,500–1,800			1,800–2,200		
Food Group	**Servings**	**Calories**	**Carbs (g)**	**Servings**	**Calories**	**Carbs (g)**
Protein	9	495	0	14	770	0
Fats	6	270	0	8	360	0
Nuts	1	200	4	1	200	4
Vegetables	5	125	25	5	125	25
Starches	4	320	60	4	320	60
Fruits	2	120	30	2	120	30
Dairy	1	45	6	1	45	6
Total		1,575	125		1,940	125

age. Fasten with toothpicks to make it easier to transport. You can also use spinach, which contains lots of essential nutrients including vitamin A, folate, and magnesium.

Have a low-carb sandwich. If you like sandwiches at lunchtime, just remember to use whole grain bread, light whole wheat bread, whole wheat pitas, or whole wheat tortillas for wraps. You could also make an open-face sandwich with just one slice of bread to reduce your carb intake; to make it easier to hold, top the contents with a lettuce leaf.

Use eggs for lunch. If you haven't had eggs for breakfast, have an omelet for lunch. Include some finely chopped vegetables and cheese, meat, poultry, or seafood.

MAKE DINNER MEMORABLE

Dinner is by far the easiest low-carb meal to plan because most dinner menus have some type of protein food at the center, a serving or two of vegetables, and relatively few carbohydrates. Part VII includes nearly two dozen main-dish recipes that serve as excellent examples. Here are a few things to keep in mind when planning dinner.

Be well-balanced. Start with at least one protein food, and try to include one or two vegetables (cooked or raw) and a starch if you have not already eaten much from these food groups during the day.

Vary your protein source. Eating the same food over and over may hinder or even halt your weight loss and your efforts at blood-sugar control. To avoid flavor fatigue, rotate different sources of protein in and out of your diet every few days. Try these protein options when you get stuck in a rut: beef, lamb, pork, chicken, Cornish hen, turkey, shrimp, crab, lobster, or any type of fish.

HAVE HEALTHY SNACKS

Here's some great news: Snacks are good for you! In fact, you should eat or drink something every 2 to 4 hours to avoid setting yourself up for a starvation-binge scenario. If you're used to having breakfast, lunch, and dinner every day, also make sure to add a snack midway between those mealtimes. Here are a few simple ideas for keeping carbs low when snacking.

Nibble on nuts. Nutritious, filling, and

Take Your Low-Carb Habits Out to Eat

Dining out the low-carb way is pretty simple—especially since typical entrées focus on protein rather than carbohydrates. Still, some dishes that seem low-carb may not be. Here are some tips to help you keep your carb count down when eating out.

Stay away from these. The following menu terms may indicate extra carbohydrates.

- À la mode
- Barbecued
- Breaded
- Creamed
- Crispy
- Crust
- Fruited
- Glazed
- Gravy
- Honey-baked
- Loaf
- Parmigiana
- Potpie
- Stuffed
- Stuffing
- Sweet and sour
- Tetrazzini

Ask questions. When ordering, don't be bashful. Many restaurants are willing to make something special or to substitute a serving of vegetables or small salad for a potato, rice, pasta, or other starchy dish. Also ask whether foods are prepared with flour, bread crumbs, or sugar. For example, meats, poultry, or fish may be dredged in flour, or a dish may include a gravy, sauce, or breading not mentioned on the menu.

Beware the bread basket. If you have bread with the meal, remember that an average-size dinner roll is the equivalent of 2 servings of starch. It's unlikely that you'll be able to get whole grain bread or pasta or even brown rice in many restaurants. But if you eat out only occasionally, it won't hinder your weight loss or adversely affect your health to enjoy the refined versions of these foods now and then.

The Smart Low-Carb Food Pyramid

1. Sweets: Eat sparingly
2. Dairy: 1 daily serving
3. Fruits: 2 daily servings
4. Nuts: 1 daily serving
5. Fats: 6–8 daily servings
6. Starches: 4 daily servings
7. Protein: 9–14 daily servings
8. Vegetables: 5 daily servings

Note: Based on daily intake of about 1,800 calories and 125 grams of carbohydrates

a source of protein and monounsaturated fats, nuts make a perfectly healthy snack. It takes a few minutes after eating nuts to feel satisfied, so eat them slowly. Allow yourself at least 10 minutes before reaching for something else.

Stuff some celery. Spread with a little peanut butter or seasoned cream cheese, celery sticks make an easy, satisfying, and portable snack.

Try a little fruit. A piece of fruit is a natural at snack time. Try to combine it with nuts to reduce its effect on your blood sugar. For instance, have a banana or apple with some peanut butter. Or munch on a mix of raisins and peanuts.

Go with crackers. Whole grain crackers with nut butter or reduced-fat cheese make a satisfying, low-carbohydrate nibble that you can enjoy anytime.

CHAPTER 8

LOW-CARB SUPERSTARS

Here are the tastiest low-carb foods in the supermarket and the five must-haves for your carb-watching kitchen

It's a safe bet that you've probably heard of low-carb eating as a successful means of losing unwanted pounds. You may even have heard that it's a good way to help control your blood sugar. But perhaps you've never considered trying low-carb eating because it seems so different from the way you eat now. Or perhaps you simply didn't know what to do or where to begin.

The great news is, going low-carb doesn't require a major overhaul of your eating habits. In fact, when you flip through the pages that follow, you'll be amazed at how easy eating low-carb can be. Read on for a few simple tricks for trading sugar and white flour for healthier alternatives as well as adding some good protein sources to your menu.

UPGRADE YOUR SWEETENERS

Sugar crops up in so many foods, it's nearly impossible to avoid. Fortunately, when you're the one choosing the food or adding the sweetener, you're in control.

You've likely already encountered saccharin (found in Sweet'N Low) and aspartame (Equal) and maybe even sorbitol, a sweetener found in some diabetic candies—all of which allow you to enjoy a sweet flavor without eating sugar. Following, you'll find some other all-natural sweeteners that have fewer calories than sugar, are absorbed more slowly, or have the benefit of additional nutrients that are lacking in table sugar.

Spreadable fruit: Unlike jelly, which is loaded with sugar and/or corn syrup, spreadable fruit is made with 100 percent fruit, which means, as a bonus, it provides some vitamins, too. Try spreadable fruit on bread and muffins or use it instead of sugar to sweeten desserts such as fruit pies, compotes, and even some snack cakes.

Brown sugar: When it comes to replacing sugar, nothing tastes or performs quite the same way in cooking. However, you can reduce your carbohydrate intake by using brown sugar instead of white sugar. Brown sugar is a mixture of white sugar and molasses, which gives it a slightly lower carbohydrate content than that of white sugar. If you swap brown for white, you'll save 15 grams of carbohydrate in every $1/4$ cup you use.

Stevia: This herb (available in liquid or powder form in health food stores or large supermarkets) has enormous sweetening power. For cooking, liquid stevia is the most convenient choice because it measures easily and stores in the fridge. But go easy. One-eighth of a teaspoon of liquid stevia is equivalent to $1/2$ cup of sugar.

Splenda: This product is the commercial form of sucralose, a sugar substitute processed from real sugar that has been modified so that it isn't absorbed by the body. And it's a real breakthrough for low-calorie, low-carbohydrate cooking. It measures cup for cup like sugar, it performs almost like sugar in recipes, and—when used in moderate amounts—it doesn't have the cloying aftertaste associated with artificial sweeteners. Splenda is especially useful in baking, but keep in mind that it doesn't caramelize like sugar. Some recipes may work better if you split the difference and use half sugar and half Splenda.

SWAP THE "WHITES" FOR "BROWNS"

We can't say it often enough: One of the best (and easiest!) switches you

The Scoop on Sugar

Sugar, per se, is not bad for you. You need to be able to regulate the amount of fast-acting carbohydrate—which sugar is—and adapt it to the insulin or the medications you're taking. Most diabetic meal plans currently don't prohibit sugar; in fact, sugar can be used in your diet in moderation. Many people who have diabetes end up using artificial sweeteners or sugar alternatives, but the idea of totally eliminating sugar from the diet has really gone by the wayside.

can make is from refined grains (such as white flour) to whole grains. When whole wheat flour is refined into all-purpose white flour, it loses 100 percent of its bran, 86 percent of both manganese and vitamin E, 85 percent of its magnesium, 72 percent of its B_6, 68 percent of its copper, and 40 percent of its chromium. Similar nutrients are lost when other grains such as rice are refined.

Whole grains can also help you lose weight, largely because they have a healthy amount of fiber (most of which is lost when grains are refined). Fiber helps you to feel full, so you're not tempted to overeat, and it can reduce your risk of heart disease. Here are some tips on using fiber- and vitamin-rich whole grains.

Swap white pasta for whole wheat pasta. You'll get more fiber and more flavor. Whole wheat noodles have a more complex, nutty taste than refined white pasta, and they can be used in your favorite pasta recipes. Most supermarkets carry a variety of whole wheat pastas, including spaghetti, linguine, and rotelle. Look for them right next to the refined white pastas.

Exchange white rice for brown rice. Brown rice is higher in fiber and vitamins than white rice, and it has a more chewy texture and nutty flavor. Both short- and long-grain varieties work well in casseroles and as simple side dishes. And when it comes to flavor, brown rice mixes beat the white rice mixes, hands down.

Reach for whole grain bread. Good choices include 100 percent whole wheat bread and 100 percent rye bread. Read the ingredients list on the label to make sure that the first flour used is a whole grain flour, such as whole rye, whole wheat, or whole oat flour. Light whole wheat bread is the best choice for reducing carbohydrates; it is cut thin and is slightly smaller than a traditional loaf. Slice for slice, light whole wheat bread has 5 fewer grams of carbohydrate than white bread.

Switch to whole wheat bread crumbs. For example, to bread fish or chicken, use whole wheat bread crumbs instead of regular bread crumbs. To make half a cup of fresh whole wheat bread crumbs, place two slices of whole wheat bread in a food processor and process until fine crumbs form. Use immediately or freeze to use another time.

Incorporate whole grain flour. If you bake, try mixing in some whole grain flour along with the all-purpose flour. You can even use whole grain flours for thickening sauces and dredging meats.

USE YOUR BEAN(S)

Beans are one kind of carb you can't get bored with: After all, there are more than 100 different varieties and plenty of recipes that call for them. Beans provide all the protein, carbohydrates, fats, vitamins, and minerals needed for plants to grow and mature. That's why they're so nutrient-rich and healthy for people to eat. It's true that beans are not superlow in carbohydrates, but they are one of the best sources of fiber. Bonus: Numerous studies have demonstrated the cardiovascular benefits of eating beans.

Try canned beans. They are already soaked and cooked, so they are ready to use, which makes them a great choice when you need a quick meal. Keep several varieties in your pantry at all times. Ideas: Add canned beans to salads and pasta dishes, or puree them and add spices to make a delicious dip.

To reduce the sodium content of canned beans, drain and rinse them before using. Rinsing until all the bubbles disappear removes up to 40 percent of the sodium as well as some of the gas-producing oligosaccharides.

Try dried beans. Some recipes, such as soup, taste remarkably better made with dried beans. That's because as the beans cook, they release their delicious flavors into the soup (some of the flavor of canned beans goes down the drain with the canning liquid). And dried beans aren't as difficult to use as you may think: They simply need to be soaked before cooking.

GIVE SOY A SHOT

Here's another bean that's bursting with benefits. For starters, soybeans are one of the most nutrient-dense beans available. What's more, numerous studies show that soy protein helps to lower blood cholesterol levels and may help reduce the risk of osteoporosis and some forms of cancer. Here's how to include soy in your cooking.

Enjoy soy milk. It's so creamy and delicious, it can stand in for cow's milk in cereal, shakes or smoothies, sauces, or baking. One big advantage of soy milk is that it's lower in carbohydrates than cow's milk because it does not contain a type of sugar called lactose. Its protein content is about the same as that of cow's milk. And most brands are fortified with calcium, vitamin D, and vitamin B_{12} so that soy milk is nutritionally similar to cow's milk.

When selecting soy milk, read labels carefully. Some brands are sweetened with malt, rice syrup, or other sweeteners. The carbohydrate content can range from 8 to 36 grams. For the fewest carbs, buy unsweetened soy milk.

Cook with soy flour. Lower in carbohydrates than wheat flour, soy flour is a smart addition to your shopping list. Soy flour is excellent for dredging and sautéing foods such as fish fillets or chicken because it browns beautifully and quickly. In baking, things get a little trickier. It's best to replace no more than one-quarter of the wheat flour (or other flour) called for in a baking recipe with soy flour.

Go for tofu. If you eat meat, there's no reason to replace meat with tofu. But you might want to use tofu in other ways for the health benefits associated with soy protein. Firm tofu can be cut into cubes, browned, and tossed into a stir-fry. Or it can be cut into thick slabs, marinated, and grilled, baked, or broiled. You can also buy premarinated, prebaked tofu that's ready to be eaten right out of the package or tossed into salads or stir-fries.

GET A LITTLE NUTTY

The ancient Romans often served nuts with dessert or afterward; hence, we have the phrase "from soup to nuts." Take a

A Low-Carb "Cheat Sheet"

Keeping carbs in check doesn't mean eliminating your favorite food groups. A simple switch to a similar food in the same "family" can satisfy your craving without

INSTEAD OF . . .	TRY . . .	CARBS SAVED (G)
BREADS, PASTA, AND FLOUR		
Bagel, plain (4")	Bread, whole wheat (1 slice)	25
Bread, white (1 slice)	Bread, light whole wheat (1 slice)	2
Flour, all-purpose (1/4 c)	Flour, soy (1/4 c)	14
Flour, whole wheat (1/4 c)	Flour, oat (1/4 c)	12
French toast (1 slice)	Omelet, ham and cheese (2 eggs)	12
Lasagna noodles (2 oz dry)	Eggplant or zucchini slices (1 c)	35
Pancakes, from mix (two 6")	Eggs, large (2)	56
Spaghetti, cooked (1 c)	Spaghetti squash, cooked (1 c)	30
Tortilla, flour (6")	Tortilla, corn (6")	6
DESSERTS, SWEETS, AND DAIRY FOODS		
Cake, yellow, with vanilla frosting (1 slice)	Cheesecake (1 slice)	18
Ice cream (1/2 c)	Gelatin, diet (1/2 c), with whipped cream (2 Tbsp)	14
Maple syrup, pure (2 Tbsp)	Maple syrup, low-calorie (2 Tbsp)	14
Milk, fat free (1 c)	Milk, soy, unsweetened (1 c)	9
Pie, apple (1 slice)	Pie, pumpkin (1 slice)	10
Sugar, granulated (1/2 c)	Splenda (1/4 c) or stevia (1/8 tsp)	48
Sugar, granulated (1/4 c)	Brown sugar (1/4 c)	15
Yogurt, frozen soft (1/2 c)	Fruit juice bar (2.5 oz)	2
Yogurt, with fruit (1 c)	Yogurt, plain, unsweetened (1 c)	30
FRUITS		
Apple (medium)	Celery (1 rib)	18

sending your carb count sky-high. Try these substitutions, whether you're dining at home or elsewhere.

INSTEAD OF . . .	TRY . . .	CARBS SAVED (G)
Banana (6")	Kiwifruit	10
Blueberries, fresh ($^1/_2$ c)	Strawberries, fresh ($^1/_2$ c)	5
Honeydew ($^1/_4$ medium)	Grapefruit ($^1/_2$ medium)	13
Juice, apple (1 c)	Cider, apple (1 c)	8
MAIN DISHES, SAUCES, AND SOUPS		
Beef potpie, frozen (1 serving)	Meat loaf (1 serving)	40
Linguine with white clam sauce (1 serving)	Manicotti with tomato sauce (1 serving)	31
Pasta salad, seafood ($1^1/_2$ c)	Tuna salad ($1^1/_2$ c)	3
Sandwich, chicken, fast food	Hamburger, fast food	8
Sandwich, roast beef, fast food	Soup, chicken rice (1 can)	29
Soup, tomato, canned (1 c)	Soup, gazpacho (1 c)	12
Thousand Island dressing (2 Tbsp)	Oil and vinegar (1 Tbsp each)	4
SNACKS AND BEVERAGES		
Cashews, dry-roasted ($^1/_3$ c)	Brazil nuts, dry-roasted ($^1/_3$ c)	9
Fig bars (2)	Gingersnaps (2)	20
Pretzels, hard twists (10)	Popcorn, air-popped (2 c)	35
VEGETABLES AND SIDE DISHES		
Carrot (medium)	Celery (1 rib)	5
Onion rings, fried (8)	Mozzarella sticks, fried (5)	9
Onions, chopped ($^1/_2$ c)	Scallions, chopped ($^1/_2$ c)	3
Potato, baked (1 medium)	Corn on the cob (1 medium)	34
Potatoes, mashed (1 c)	Turnips, mashed (1 c)	26

tip from the ancients, and reap a wealth of health benefits by including nuts in your daily diet. Nuts contain protein, iron, and other important vitamins and minerals. Here are some nutty ideas.

Choose the freshest nuts for the most flavor. Autumn and winter are generally considered nut season, but nuts are available year-round. If you buy fresh nuts in bulk, shop at a store with fast turnover. Shelled nuts can become rancid fairly quickly because of their high fat content. For the freshest nuts, buy them in the shell. Avoid any that feel light for their size or have holes or splits in the shell. These are most likely past their prime.

Keep nuts in a cool, dark place. They'll generally last about a month at room temperature. They will last longer and taste fresher when stored in a cool, dry place away from light (or in the refrigerator). If you have a large stockpile of nuts, keep them in airtight containers in the freezer, where they will last for up to a year.

Toast nuts to bring out the flavor. Simply place them in a dry skillet over medium heat and stir frequently until lightly colored and fragrant. This should take only 2 to 3 minutes. Or you can place the nuts on a baking sheet and toast them in the oven at 350°F for 3 to 5 minutes.

Add them to your favorite foods. Nuts are incredibly versatile. They can be eaten as is or added to almost any dish—both savory and sweet. Sprinkle nuts on cereal, yogurt, or pasta; into bread dough, cookie batter, or casseroles; or over salads or desserts.

Go unsweetened. If you like peanut butter, try the unsweetened variety, also called natural peanut butter. Unsweetened peanut butter is made without hydrogenated fats, sugar, or other flavoring agents. It has a more peanutty taste and is absorbed by your body more slowly than most commercial varieties, so it won't raise your blood sugar as rapidly.

CHAPTER 9

SUPERMARKET SLEUTHING

Insider grocery shopping secrets

Have you ever gone to the market for milk, bread, and bananas, and come home with milk, bread, bananas . . . and a family-size bag of cheesy corn chips?

You're not alone. Shopping for food is an eternal tug-of-war between intention (don't forget the asparagus!) and temptation (hey, look, Sludgy-Fudgy cookies are on sale!). Of course, temptation usually wins. And if you need evidence of its power, know that a recent *Prevention*/Food Marketing survey found that 58 percent of health-conscious people eat unhealthy foods on a regular basis.

But grocery stores aren't there just so you can indulge your dietary demons. They also have mountains of produce, cases of low-fat dairy products, and aisles of other good-for-you comestibles that can liven up your dinner table without sabotaging your waistline. How you use your supermarket is up to you. Because most of us do a lot of shopping (84 percent of consumers prepare home-cooked meals—presumably with store-bought ingredients—at least three times a week), it's important to learn to sleuth out the healthiest products while navigating the supermarket smorgasbord.

For guidance on how to be a smarter shopper, *Prevention* enlisted Lisa Sasson, RD, a clinical assistant professor at New York University, a mother of two, and a twice-a-week shopper who lives by this motto: "If you resist it at the grocery store, you only have to resist it once. If you take it home, you have to resist it every hour of every day." Still, it's easier said than done, as we learned when she took us on a tour of ShopRite in Hackensack, New Jersey, a typical US supermarket. Read on for hands-on lessons on how to track down the most nutritious foods, what temptations and distractions to avoid, how not to get caught in the impulse-buying trap, and, most important, how to complete your healthy shopping mission.

GO PREPARED

Savvy shopping starts before you leave the house, says Kelly Brownell, PhD, director of the Yale Center for Eating and Weight Disorders, and his pretrip advice is simple: "Make a list, and only stray from it if the item is a healthy one." He also recommends shopping after you've eaten and, if possible, when you're in a calm, stable mood. Hunger and stress make you more susceptible to—you guessed it—temptation.

And try to go without the kids. Sasson, who's shopped with and without them, advises that your health goals can be met more easily if you leave little ones at home (where they can't pester you for candy). If that's not practical, you can always exercise your parental prerogative and just say no to such purchases.

However, Dr. Brownell points out that shopping with kids, handled correctly, can be a positive experience. The key is to turn shopping into an educational activity. To that end, "charge the kids with finding the healthful choices," he says. "Take them to the fruit section and say, 'You can have anything you want; you get to pick.'" In other words, shopping with kids doesn't have to be a fight to the death over junk food. It can be a fun game in which everybody wins.

HIT THE WALLS

Even before we walk through ShopRite's sliding doors, Sasson starts strategizing. "The first thing we're going to do is shop the perimeter," she explains. "That's where the whole foods action is." In this case, that also means walking through a bakery piping out dangerously enticing, fresh-from-the-oven smells.

Pulling me into produce, Sasson explains that supermarket design is changing, and not necessarily in a healthy shopper's favor. Until recently, fruits and vegetables were the first thing you saw when you entered. Today, 88 percent of supermarkets have in-store bakeries, and some are near the entrance, meaning you have to run the gauntlet of cakes, muffins, and doughnuts just to grab a bag of spinach. "Smells, especially cinnamon, will get shoppers to buy baked goods," warns Kevin Kelley, founding partner of Shook Kelley, a marketing firm that consults with national grocery chains. So hold your nose if you have to.

BEWARE OF "INNOCENT" FOODS

The produce section definitely wins the market beauty contest. It has pyramids of gleaming fruits, big leafy greens, stacks of bright red berries, and—tucked beside the stack—cream cheese dip loaded with fat and calories. What's that doing there? "They're trying to tempt you by offering a healthful food with an unhealthful one, as if there's innocence by association," Sasson says. "There's also a caramel-apple kit next to the apples. I'm seeing this more often, and I tell my clients, 'Buy the fruits and vegetables, but skip the dip and candy coating. You don't need them.'"

Kelley agrees with Sasson that healthy-unhealthy adjacencies in supermarkets are a trend. Marketers call it vignetting. Like the boutique that wants to sell you a scarf with your sweater or a handbag with your shoes, the supermarket wants to sell you the processed cheese with your trans-free crackers or the Alfredo sauce with your whole wheat pasta. Stick to your list.

Before leaving the produce section, we ask Sasson for some buying tips. "It's easy," she says. Because most markets get more produce delivered on Fridays and Saturdays for the weekend rush, you'll find a greater selection of fresh fruits and vegetables if you shop on Friday afternoon or Saturday morning. We grab some Fuji apples, a couple of sweet potatoes, and a head of lettuce.

Then, just as I reach for some radishes, I get a damp reminder of another marketing tactic—the mister. Even though glistening produce looks fresher, Sasson frowns on the growing trend of spritzing fresh produce. Too much moisture can make vegetables go bad faster, she says. We skip the rained-on radishes and head to the fish counter.

KNOW THERE'S NO FREE LUNCH

Before we get there, we're waylaid by a smiling employee handing out samples of the rich, fatty-looking dips we just saw in the produce section. One taste couldn't hurt, could it? Well, maybe—if free samples add unwanted pounds.

"If you don't want a food in your house, don't sample it," Sasson says. Once you've tasted it, you're much more likely to buy it. (Dr. Kelley adds that most supermarkets "sample" poor selling products as a way to get them into your cart and out the door.) A similar principle applies to coupons. "Don't clip a coupon if it's not for a healthy food," says Sasson. In other words, if you can get a discount on the soy milk or granola you'd buy anyway, great. But the chance to get three bags of leftover Christmas candy for the price of one is no health bargain, no matter how much money you save.

RETHINK FRESH FOODS

"Is there any possible way to tell which of these is going to taste best?" we ask Sasson as we peruse the fish counter. "Time your fish buying according to your market's schedule," she replies. "Try not to shop for fish on Sundays— there aren't many deliveries over the weekend. Ask your local supermarket manager when fish comes in, and shop that day or the next. Then cook it the same day."

Fish labeled "fresh," notes Kelley, doesn't mean fresh off the boat; it just means that the fish hasn't been frozen. But freezing is usually your best bet for food-safety reasons.

The deli is a different story. Here, the word *fresh* does have meaning. "When you're buying deli meat, choose fresh over the processed versions, which are more likely to be high in salt, sugar, and preservatives. Your butcher will know the difference," Sasson says. She steers us away from the white deli salads made with lots of high-calorie, high-fat mayonnaise, such as macaroni and potato salads and coleslaw. Better nutritional options include carrot salad, hummus, and coleslaw made with vinegar.

BE A CHEESE WHIZ

Most markets, ours included, have two cheese sections: one with domestic cheeses such as American and sliced pepper jack; and a second, usually near the deli, with a wider variety of imported and fancy cheeses with equally fancy hard-to-pronounce names. This second section is where she urges us to shop. The reason: "You'll find a lot of more flavorful choices—blue, Parmesan, Camembert. A little of these varieties goes a long way, so you use much less, and that means fewer calories and fat for all the flavor."

Sasson learned this while doing supermarket comparisons in Europe, where many people eat cheese every day and don't get as fat as Americans do. Tiny portions of flavor-packed cheeses (which, by the way, are not diet food by any measure) may help explain that paradox.

CHOOSE SELECT MEATS

We now hit the meat section, where Sasson warns me not to buy based on the government grades of prime and choice; they indicate marbling—a polite way of saying "lots of fat." A better idea: Choose "select" cuts, which are the leanest, most healthful, and most affordable meats you can find.

Most meat is packaged in family-size cuts. But portion control is key to weight control, and supersize beef doesn't help. The fix: Ask the butcher to package the exact amount you need. Buying less doesn't guarantee you'll eat less, but it sure makes it easier.

Before we go, we toss a top round London broil into the cart because it's nice and lean and, even better, on sale. "Wait a minute," says Sasson. "Beware of perishables like dairy, produce, and meat on sale. They're often at the end of their life." Sure enough, when we check the expiration date, today is the last day to buy my steak. I skip it.

SHOP LIKE A MAN

While we're standing in front of the store's interior, staring at miles of candy, chips, and chocolate, Sasson makes an announcement: "Wherever there's temptation, like here, we're going to shop like a man." Turns out, there's a big gender gap in shopping styles. Men do surgical-strike shopping. They know what they want, and they go get it. Women browse, pause, read, and choose.

There are times when each strategy is more useful and yields healthier results. For example, if you're in relatively healthy territory, such as the store's periphery, it makes sense to browse and select with care. But when you're in the kind of danger zone we're in now, browsing yields to temptation. (By the way, Dr. Kelley studied the difference by taping real shoppers, and stores all over the country use this research.)

Sasson demonstrates how to man-shop the snacks. They're prime temptation territory—almost 60 percent are bought on impulse—so we enter the aisle with a macho purpose, bypassing chips and stopping at the unshelled nuts. "Nuts are a healthful snack, but they're high in calories. Buying them whole ensures that they don't have added sugar or salt, and shelling them slows you down so you may eat less," Sasson says.

But junk isn't totally off-limits. For indulging, Sasson likes the trend of "fun size" single-serving packs of sugary treats, which are often 100 calories each. Read labels, though, and make sure it really is a single serving. (We check a snack pack of chocolate cookies that looks like one serving but—surprise—is actually four servings, each with 140 calories.)

SKIP THE BEVERAGE AISLE

"There's nothing here you want," Sasson warns, advising me to nix the smoothies, juices, sodas, and sports drinks because of the sugar they all contain. "Kids grow up associating satisfying their thirst with a sweet drink, and that's one of the culprits in pediatric obesity." Which leads to adult obesity.

Sasson says that, with increasing frequency, high-calorie drinks aren't limited to the beverage aisle. More than 10 percent of the calories Americans consume come from a combination of soft drinks and juice, and food companies are making it easier to guzzle your calories. She's right. At this store, there are sugary yogurt drinks in with the plain yogurt; high-calorie smoothies in with the juices; sugar-packed iced teas alongside the unsweetened ones; flavored, sweetened milks in with the dairy; and sugary coffee drinks in with the regular coffee. There are even sodas in coolers by the checkout to tempt you as you're leaving.

LOOK HIGH AND LOW FOR HEALTH FOOD

Unless you watch Saturday morning cartoons, the cereal aisle is enough to make a grown-up feel out of touch with society. When did Chocolate Mud & Bugs hit the market? And Cinnamon Marshmallow Scooby-Doo? There's a reason these high-sugar, practically fiber-free products stand out. Sasson notes that all those cereals are lined up at our waist level, which corresponds to where the average kid's line of vision is centered. We almost have to get out the binoculars to spot the reduced-sugar or no-sugar-added cereals, such as Grape-Nuts, relegated to the nosebleed shelves.

In any store, some products are right in your face, and others are harder to find. Many of those easy-to-spot products are paying to be there: Twelve percent of supermarket profits come from so-called placement fees, money that manufacturers pay grocers for premium positioning. But what's in your face shouldn't necessarily go into your cart. "Heavily promoted items are more likely to be unhealthy," asserts Brownell. So look high, low, and around corners for alternatives.

And watch out for those tempting cereal-to-go breakfast bars marketed mainly to women. Sasson picks up a few, starts scanning, and then sighs—a bad sign: "Breakfast bars are all high in sugar and rarely have more than 2 grams of fiber per serving." In other words, these bars aren't health bargains.

AVOID HEALTH FOOD THAT ISN'T

ShopRite's organic section is large and attractive, filled with everything from pesticide-free canned goods to pristine, kettle-cooked-by-someone's-grandma potato chips. Sasson quickly points out that organic does not equal healthy. She's fine with organic fruits and vegetables, because they may be lower in chemical pesticides than other produce. Buying organic cupcakes and chips, though, is another matter: "When you're buying a high-calorie, low-nutrient product and it's organic, you shouldn't be consuming so much that the difference becomes significant." Organic, shmorganic; if it's cake, it's still cake.

DITCH "DIET" FOODS

Ditto for the diet aisle, where I optimistically steer the cart to load up on energy bars. Sasson pipes up: "Don't bother buying those unless you're a marathon runner or you want to gain weight. Most of this stuff is low-carb, not low-calorie," she explains, and can undermine your diet. "Studies show that you might even be in danger of overeating and packing on pounds because of what they call the SnackWell's phenomenon: You eat more because you think it's healthy," she says.

SHOP LIKE A WOMAN

We head to the freezer section last so those foods spend less time melting in our cart. When we get to frozen entrées and meals, Sasson explains that this is one area in which you should use your feminine ways to snoop out healthy products. The reason? There's so much variation here: "If you're trying to find the frozen pasta sauce without added sugar, the frozen pizza with the most veggies, or the entrée with the most fiber, you have to read labels carefully to make good choices." For example, Sasson warns that some companies are trying to get men to buy more frozen meals—by making the portions (and the calorie count) bigger. That's fine, unless you're a woman watching her weight.

CHECK YOURSELF OUT

While waiting in line to pay for my purchases, I can't help but notice the racks of candy and soft drinks in my path. They're there for a reason. A whopping 20 percent of customers succumb to last-minute impulse buying while they're in line—and, no surprise, there is no Brussels sprouts display here. So bury yourself in a magazine instead. Or try a new alternative: the self-checkout station, where only 12 percent of customers make those last-minute, indulgent food buys. We went that route and a few minutes later were driving away with a car full of healthy whole foods—and a very clear conscience.

CHAPTER 10

GOOF-PROOF EATING

Here's how to avoid the 10 top food mistakes—
and what to eat instead

It was easier when the only thing on the table was what you could hunt and gather. Sure, the menu was primitive. But at least there weren't any experts hovering over the fire, wagging their fingers and saying, "Eat this. No, no, don't eat that." Ours is an age of unprecedented bounty and convenience— and almost nonstop nutritional advice, much of it subject to change as new research findings come along or scientists change their minds. You try to keep up with the latest and make the smartest choices—but are they as healthy as you think? Here's a reality check, with tips from experts on how to make the very best of your good intentions.

MULTIGRAIN BREAD OR CEREAL

Foods labeled seven-grain or multigrain may seem like the healthiest choices—especially with new findings showing that a diet rich in whole grains protects against heart disease, cancer, and other ills. A recent study by Swedish researchers found that women who consumed generous amounts of whole grain foods had a 33 percent lower risk of colon cancer than women who consumed the least. The Nurses' Health Study, conducted by Harvard Medical School scientists, documented lower rates of heart disease and stroke among whole grain eaters. Experts don't know all the reasons behind the benefits, but they do know that intact grains are rich in fiber and nutrients—including vitamin E, B vitamins, and magnesium—that are stripped away when grains are refined into flour.

Unfortunately, many foods are only posing as rich in whole grains. "Take a closer look at the labels, and you may find there's not a single whole grain in them," says Cynthia Harriman, director of food and nutrition strategies for the Whole Grains Council, a nonprofit consumer group in Boston. The rea-son: Labels can claim that products contain grains even if they're highly processed and stripped of most of their nutrients and all of their fiber. "White flour is made from grain, after all," says Harriman.

Smarter move: Learn the lingo of food claims. Bread that's 100 percent whole grain means just that; it contains no refined flour. Cereal that's made with whole grain may have a little or a lot. Crackers labeled multigrain may not have whole grains at all. To be sure you're getting the grains you want, check the ingredient panel. Whole grains should be the first or second ingredient listed. Luckily, finding whole grain products is easier now that manufacturers supplying at least 16 grams of whole grains per serving—considered an excellent source—are stamping their packaging with the Whole Grains Council's logo.

Surprise!

A slice of multigrain bread has more calories—and the same amount of fiber—as two chocolate chip cookies.

BOTTLED WATER LACED WITH VITAMINS

It's a measure of how health conscious we've become that water is now fortified with nutrients and even medicinal herbs. But when asked for the l'eau down on so-called enhanced water, *Prevention* advisor and nutritionist Elizabeth Somer, RD, counseled: "Save your money." Many are bloated with unnecessary calories. The label of one leading brand, for example, reports that it supplies half the daily requirement for some nutrients. But to get that amount, you have to drink the whole bottle, which contains 125 calories. And for that, you get just six of the 40-plus essential nutrients provided by most supplements. An entire bottle, notes Somer, supplies no more vitamin C than you'd get from eating two strawberries.

Smarter move: Drink plain, refreshing, calorie-free water when you're thirsty, and take a multivitamin daily to make sure you get balanced levels of the essential vitamins and minerals.

VEGGIE CHIPS

You'd think you were at a farmers' market when shopping the snack aisle these days. Dozens of munchies are made from carrots, spinach, kale, and even exotic tropical vegetables. But scrutinize their ingredients, and you'll find that vegetable coloring is all most of them have in common with produce.

What could sound more virtuous than a brand called Veggie Booty—especially when the packaging advertises kale and spinach? The ingredient label reveals, however, that vegetables are at the bottom of the list (meaning they contribute less, by weight, than ingredients at the top of the list, like oil). Many of these seemingly healthful snacks are still loaded with calories: A 4-ounce bag of Hain Carrot Chips contains 600 calories—as much as Lay's Classic Potato Chips.

Smarter move: When you simply must have chips, look for brands with vegetables at the top of the ingredient list. Terra Chips, for instance, contains decent amounts of taro, sweet potato, parsnip, and other vegetables. A tip-off to a snack's healthfulness is its fiber content. One ounce of Terras contains 3 grams of fiber—not bad for a snack food. They're no bargain in the calorie department, however: At 140 per ounce, they're almost the same as regular

Surprise!

One-third of a cup of banana chips has as much fat as a Big Mac.

chips. If you're counting calories, baked potato chips—at 110 calories per serving—are a better choice. An even healthier alternative? A handful of nuts, loaded with fiber, healthy oils, and vitamins and minerals; they'll satisfy your urge to nibble. And if you want to be truly virtuous, go for the real thing: carrot sticks, jicama slices, lightly salted radishes, or roasted sweet peppers chilled in the refrigerator.

SNACKS "MADE WITH REAL FRUIT"

Pictures of luscious-looking fruit adorn the packaging, and the labels claim there is real fruit inside, but don't think you can count these snacks as one of the four to five daily servings that the new dietary guidelines recommend. Because current law doesn't require labels to specify how much fruit is in the product, manufacturers can brag on their packaging that the food is made with

real fruit if it contains only small amounts of fruit juice. "Concentrated white grape juice or pear juice may sound healthy, but all that really means is fruit sugars and water," says Gail Rampersaud, RD, of the food science and human nutrition department at the University of Florida in Gainesville.

Other downsides: Few of these snacks provide any fiber; by contrast, an unpeeled pear packs 5 grams, or about 20 percent of the 22 to 28 grams recommended daily for women. Some faux-fruit munchies even contain small amounts of artery-choking hydrogenated fats. And often they have as many calories—almost all from sugar—as candy does. For example, a 25-gram serving of Fruit Gushers has 90 calories, just about equal to a handful of Willy Wonka's Everlasting Gobstopper jawbreakers.

Smarter move: Treat these snacks as candy, which is what they really are, and eat them sparingly. Satisfy your sweet tooth with real fruit instead. If you're looking for convenience, pack a single-serving box of raisins or other type of dried fruit.

LOW-SODIUM PRODUCTS

Almost all of us could do with less salt, which has been shown to increase the risk of high blood pressure. Americans consume an average of 3,375 milligrams of sodium a day—way over the recommended maximum of 2,300 milligrams for healthy people (1,500 milligrams for the one in three among us who has hypertension).

Because processed foods represent one of the biggest sources of hidden sodium, it's great news that manufacturers are making low-sodium alternatives. Problem is, many still contain more salt than the 140 milligrams most of us should get in a single serving. A 1-cup serving of a leading chicken broth labeled with less sodium, for instance, contains 554 milligrams; 1 tablespoon of reduced-sodium soy sauce has 600 milligrams.

Smarter move: "Be wary of products labeled 'less sodium,'" says Rampersaud. The law requires that the sodium level be only 25 percent less than the original product. But if that product happens to be very high in salt to begin with—like many soups and broths—you may still be getting a lot of sodium. "To ensure that you get 140 milligrams or less per serving, look for products marked 'low in sodium,'" says Rampersaud.

FAT-FREE MILK

Smart move. But if you buy milk in glass or translucent containers, you may not be getting all the nutrients you expect. Although calcium in milk is relatively stable, vitamins A, B_2, C, D, and E and amino acids all break down gradually when milk is exposed to light. Milk is especially susceptible because the ribo-

Surprise!

Fruit leathers have about the same amount of calories and nutrients as 24 jelly beans.

flavin (vitamin B_2) it contains acts as a photosensitizer, says Donald McMahon, PhD, an expert in dairy foods processing at Utah State University. In a study at Cornell University, levels of vitamin A fell as much as 32 percent when milk in plastic containers was exposed to fluorescent light for just 16 hours. Other studies have found that up to 60 percent of the riboflavin is lost under similar conditions. Light also oxidizes fat and diminishes the flavor of milk.

Smarter move: Buy milk in opaque containers, which eliminate as much light exposure as possible. "A container that blocks light will maintain vitamin A, riboflavin, and other nutrients in milk for about 10 days," says Dr. McMahon.

WINE OR BEER

More than 100 studies have found that moderate drinkers have about one-third lower risk of heart disease than those who abstain. But excessive drinking— three or more alcoholic beverages a day, most studies agree—has been proven to send blood pressure climbing.

New evidence shows that light to moderate drinking on an empty stomach can contribute to high blood pressure risk. In a 2004 study that looked at data from 2,609 men and women ages 35 to 80, Saverio Stranges, MD, an assistant professor of preventive medicine at State University of New York at Buffalo, found that the risk of hypertension was almost 50 percent higher in people who drank alcoholic beverages without food than in those who imbibed only with a meal.

Smarter move: Enjoy that drink over dinner. "Consuming alcohol with a meal slows the rise of alcohol in the blood and speeds its elimination from the body," says Dr. Stranges. Together, those effects may help prevent increases in blood pressure. Drinking small amounts of alcohol with a meal is a good idea for another reason. Alcohol is known to help prevent the formation of small blood clots that might clog arteries and cause a heart attack— and which form most often after a big meal. One more advantage: Alcoholic beverages enjoyed with a meal are usually sipped, not chugged, which means you're less likely to become inebriated. The risks of regular overindulgence include weight gain, depression, and liver and kidney problems. Clearly, there are plenty of good reasons to save your drinking for dinner.

GRANOLA BARS

Snatching an on-the-go breakfast is better than skipping it altogether; numerous studies show that people who eat a morning meal are slimmer and have lower cholesterol levels and better memory recall than those who don't. But many of those seemingly healthy breakfast bars so great for eating on the run are basically candy bars in disguise, says nutritionist Christine Gerbstadt, MD, RD, a spokesperson for the American Dietetic Association. "Even though they may contain granola or fruit, some bars are full of high fructose corn syrup and trans fats to keep them soft and sweet," she says.

A top-selling granola bar contains nearly the same amount of sugar—14 grams—and fewer nutrients than a strawberry Pop-Tart or a slice of chocolate cake. A leading breakfast multigrain bar packs 15 grams of sugar as well as heart-harming trans fats. "That rush of sugar will leave you feeling drained and hungry by mid-morning," says Dr. Gerbstadt.

Smarter move: Check labels and choose a bar with less than 11 grams of sugar and no partially hydrogenated oils (that's code for trans fats). Also, choose a brand that has at least 3 grams of fiber, which slows digestion and provides sustained energy. For a healthier—and cheaper—option, do a little preparation over the weekend. Bake your favorite oatmeal-raisin cookie recipe with half the sugar and half the oil and pop the cookies into individual plastic bags; you'll get all of oatmeal's goodness without the mess. Or better yet, hard-cook a half-dozen eggs and grab one each morning along with some fruit and an English muffin for a portable breakfast.

AFTER-DINNER MINTS

The cooling taste of mint may sound like just the thing after a heavy meal, but it could spell trouble. According to the National Digestive Diseases Information Clearinghouse, mints are high on the list of foods that can cause heartburn, the telltale burning in the lower chest that occurs when juices from the stomach creep up into the esophagus. Mint seems to relax the muscle that keeps the valve at the top of the stomach clamped down, increasing the odds of reflux. Other surprising culprits: caffeine-containing food and beverages, such as chocolate, soda, and coffee.

Smarter move: Skip the mints (and the Mississippi mud cake and cappuccino) and have a piece of fruit instead. If you're prone to heartburn, drink a tall glass of water after meals to flush out the esoph- agus. And then take a stroll. Walking keeps you upright and enlists gravity to keep acids from splashing up the esoph- agus. And it can help in another impor- tant way: "Being overweight increases the risk of reflux," says gastroenterolo-

Worth Fretting Over?

Food alarms sound with clockwork regularity. Here's the scoop on three potential threats.

The overfortification of foods: With cereals, breads, sports drinks, and even beer now fortified with vitamins, minerals, and herbs, some researchers wonder if there's a risk of exceeding safe levels. "There's reason to be concerned," says Richard Wood, PhD, who directs the mineral bioavailability lab at the USDA Human Nutrition Research Center on Aging at Tufts University. "If a refrigerator is stocked with all kinds of foods that have been fortified with calcium—orange juice, cereals, cheese—it's easy for someone with a big appetite, such as a 16-year-old boy, to con- sume 3 to 4 grams of calcium a day, which is way over the upper limit of 2.5 grams."

Such high doses could lead to headaches, nausea, fatigue, constipation, even depression. And while most surveys show that the vast majority of people are more likely to fall short on vitamins and minerals, now that so many foods are fortified, it's harder to know how much you're getting, says *Prevention* advisor and nutrition- ist Elizabeth Somer, RD. Her advice: "Take a multivitamin to get balanced levels of the vitamins and minerals you need, and don't go overboard on products just because they're fortified."

A sticky situation for nonstick pans: Concern over toxic fumes from nonstick pans heated up recently when a class-action suit was filed against DuPont, the manufac-

gist Hashem El-Serag, MD, a heartburn expert at Michael E. DeBakey VA Medical Center in Houston. Getting into the habit of walking after a meal could help you keep the pounds off—and lower the risk of heartburn.

RESTAURANT LEFTOVERS

If you stop for a movie after the meal, your health may be in jeopardy. The food needs to be in your fridge or freezer within 2 hours (1 hour if it's over 90°F

turer of Teflon. "When nonstick pans are heated, they release a gas called perfluorooctanoic acid, or PFOA, which can cause a flulike condition," says Lauren Sucher, a spokesperson for the Environmental Working Group.

Under dispute is how hot the surface of the pan has to become before it releases the fumes. EWG says pans heated to just 325°F, the equivalent of a medium flame, pose a risk; industry representatives say cookware has to be heated to 600°F or higher before PFOA is released. The EPA and FDA are investigating. Until more is known, the EWG recommends using nonstick pans only over low heat. Never heat a pan without food or liquid in it.

Cooking oils under fire: Every home cook knows that overheated cooking oils can smoke and develop an unpleasant taste. But there's been some concern that toxic substances, including some carcinogens, may develop in the high heat. Home cooks needn't fret, says Fadi Aramouni, PhD, a professor of food science at Kansas State University in Manhattan. "Home cooking doesn't usually reach high enough temperatures, and even in restaurant kitchens the risk is low."

One small drawback to any heating of cooking oil: the loss of vitamin E, a key antioxidant. Cooking oil also oxidizes over time when exposed to sunlight, which can make it turn rancid. Dr. Aramouni's advice: Buy oil in small quantities to ensure freshness, and if you cook over high heat, use oil that has a high smoke point, such as canola.

outside) or you're risking food poisoning.

Another concern: microwaving leftovers in take-home food bags, pizza boxes, microwave-popcorn containers, and fast-food wrappers, and even on some paper plates. These can leach dangerous chemicals into the food when heated, reports Lauren Sucher, a spokesperson for the Environmental Working Group, a nonprofit consumer organization in Washington, DC. The chemicals include phthalates and bisphenol A, which are known to cause reproductive damage in animals, as well as fluorotelomers, which can release fumes that cause a flulike sickness. The seriousness of the danger remains controversial. "But why take a chance when it's easy to reduce your exposure?" asks Sucher.

Smarter move: When nuking food, place it in microwaveable containers, preferably glass or ceramic. And make sure you reheat those leftovers to at least 165°F to kill off any nasty bugs; bring soups and gravies to a boil.

MEDICAL BREAKTHROUGHS

What's new in the food arena? Read on!

PASS ON THE BURGERS

Can't go by a burger joint without stopping? Try reminding yourself that each time you give in, you may increase your odds of worsening type 2 diabetes. In a study of 37,000 women done by Brigham and Women's Hospital in Boston, women who ate red meat at least five times a week had a 29 percent higher risk of type 2 diabetes than those who ate it less than once a week. And eating processed meats such as bacon and hot dogs at least five times a week raised diabetes risk by 43 percent, compared with eating them less than once a week. The culprits? The scientists suspect the cholesterol in red meat and the additives in processed meat.

SKIP REFINED CARBS

A spare tire and rising insulin levels are often the first signs that your risk for heart attack, stroke, and diabetes is taking off. You may be able to head off a third serious risk factor, high blood triglycerides, simply by choosing healthful complex carbohydrates over refined ones, French researchers found. Nine obese people with excess belly fat and insulin resistance (but no diabetes) ate a breakfast based on complex carbs similar to whole grain cereal on one day. On another day, they breakfasted on "bad" refined carbs such as those in Danish pastry. Their blood levels of triglycerides rose 50 percent less following the good-carb meal than the bad-carb one.

Bonus: Sticking to complex carbs may also boost blood levels of heart-healthy HDL cholesterol, other research suggests.

STEER CLEAR OF THE DRIVE-THRU

You might get away with an occasional fast-food splurge, but become a regular "fast feeder" and your risk of diabetes zooms, according to University of Minnesota scientists. They studied 3,000 people, initially of normal weight and ages 18 to 30, for 15 years. Those who ate fast food more than twice a week gained 10 more pounds and developed twice the rate of insulin resistance—the two major risk factors for type 2 diabetes—as those who indulged less than once a week. Besides the jumbo portions, fast food is loaded with trans fats and refined carbohydrates, which may raise diabetes risk even if your weight remains stable.

JUST SAY *NON* TO FRENCH FRIES

Women who splurged on french fries just once a week were 21 percent more likely to get diabetes than those who ate none, according to a 20-year Harvard School of Public Health study of 84,500 women. Eating five servings per week of any white potatoes—including mashed and baked—raised the risk by 14 percent over those who ate less than half a serving per week. Blame it on spuds' high glycemic index (GI); potatoes break down quickly in your stomach, creating a fast, steep blood sugar rise. Over time, blood sugar spikes damage your insulin-regulating system, leading to diabetes. Obese women were even more likely to get diabetes from high potato intake. Makes sense, because they're more likely to have insulin resistance, a precursor to diabetes that high-GI foods may exacerbate. If you're overweight and/or sedentary—and that's most of us—switch to sweet potatoes.

GET TOUGH ON YOUR DIET

"Beating type 2 diabetes by getting tough about your diet (and exercising) works better than drugs," says researcher Christian Roberts, PhD. In his small, controlled 3-week study at UCLA, six out of 13 overweight or obese men with type 2 diabetes finished diabetes free, with normal blood sugar levels. How? With meals that were low in fat (12 to 15 percent of calories), moderate in protein (15 to 25 percent), and high in carbs (65 to 70 percent). Participants also walked 45 to 60 minutes a day. Eating low-fat foods and no refined carbs—absolutely no toaster pastries or brownies—was critical to their success, says Dr. Roberts, who predicts that sticking to the diet long-term may undo heart damage already started by earlier diabetes.

START WITH SALAD

May we recommend the salad? Eating greens with a vinaigrette before a starchy entrée, such as pasta, may help control your blood sugar. In an Arizona State University study, people with type 2 diabetes or insulin resistance had lower blood sugar levels if they consumed about 2 tablespoons of vinegar just before a high-carb meal. "Vinegar contains acetic acid, which may inactivate certain starch-digesting enzymes, slow-

ing carbohydrate digestion," says lead researcher Carol Johnston, PhD.

In fact, vinegar's effects may be similar to those of the blood sugar–lowering medication acarbose (Precose). Before you eat that fettuccine, enjoy a salad with this dressing: Whisk 3 tablespoons vinegar, 2 tablespoons flax oil, 1 clove crushed garlic, $1/4$ teaspoon honey, 3 tablespoons yogurt, and salt and freshly ground black pepper to taste. This recipe makes four 2-tablespoon servings.

BREAKFAST TO BEAT DIABETES

A daily bowl of high-fiber flakes and milk can help tame blood sugar and insulin resistance—good news for the one in four Americans on the fast track for diabetes.

When 77 men munched on various cereals, blood tests revealed that those with insulin resistance had elevated blood sugar and insulin levels after eating low-fiber cereal but had normal levels when fiber was a sky-high 35 grams per bowl, say University of Toronto researchers. Pour on fat-free or 1 percent milk for added protection; research suggests that a daily serving can slash insulin resistance risk by 20 percent, thanks to its vitamin D.

"A healthy high-fiber breakfast could cut your risk for insulin resistance by 30 to 50 percent," says Jo-Anne Rizzotto, RD, a nutritionist at the Joslin Diabetes Center in Boston. "If you need something sweet, add some berries to your high-fiber cereal."

Here are some fiber all-stars from top cereal makers, with the number of grams of fiber in 1 $^1/_2$ cups.

Diabetes Saved My Life

Nearly 21 million Americans now have diabetes. But there's a startling silver lining. Some newly diagnosed people actually credit this life-threatening illness with saving their lives. They are finding ways to thrive by harnessing the newest, most powerful tools for controlling this killer: better medications, faster and easier blood sugar tests, insurance coverage for sessions with diabetes educators, and more research-based info about the blood sugar–lowering benefits of nutrition, exercise, and stress reduction.

Carol Guber, 57, is one of those people. Spurred by her diagnosis and the healthy lifestyle it prompted her to adopt, Guber lost 52 pounds and gained new reserves of spiritual and physical energy. She's healthier, calmer, and fitter than she was 30 years ago. At 57, she looks a decade younger, the result of regular yoga sessions and morning workouts.

At first, Guber hid her diabetes from colleagues in New York University's food and nutrition department. "I was so embarrassed," she says. "Nutrition and food is my profession. Somehow, I thought knowing all about nutrients and healthy food preparation would keep me from getting diabetes. I couldn't believe it happened to me."

Food was more than a job: It was Guber's life. She had owned a café in Philadelphia, was retail sales manager for a caviar company, and had studied cooking with (and worked for) the renowned American chef James Beard.

When Guber was diagnosed with diabetes, she was married to a restaurant con-

- Quaker Crunchy Corn Bran: 10 grams
- Kashi Good Friends: 18 grams
- Kellogg's All-Bran: 39 grams
- Post 100% Bran: 35 grams
- Barbara's Bakery GrainShop: 24 grams
- General Mills Fiber One: 42 grams

CHECK OUT A MORE ABLE LABEL

Coming soon to labels near you: glycemic index (GI) values on foods containing carbohydrates. Under development for a decade by scientists at the University

sultant; together, they socialized with friends over lengthy and lavish meals. She was at least 50 pounds overweight.

Knowing that weight control and exercise would help control her blood sugar, Guber switched to a lower-fat diet with well-timed, balanced meals; watched portion sizes; and began exercising. And by testing her blood sugar daily, she learned how to balance diet, exercise, and stress so that there was room for a carefully chosen restaurant meal. "Once I knew that I needed to integrate diabetes into my life, I realized that the big thing for me was being out with my friends," she says. "That made it easier to enjoy smaller portions and to turn some foods down."

The lightning-bolt moment? "One day I said to myself, 'Wait a second, I'm not losing weight now to get into a particular dress for a big event. Diabetes is for the rest of my life.' There weren't going to be any quick fixes. That's a huge shift." It brought with it a new freedom to appreciate small, sustainable lifestyle changes— and to see their power.

Tiny changes led to enormous ones. Guber left her stressful marriage and went to work for herself as a writer and speaker specializing in health and wellness. Her first book, *Carol Guber's Type 2 Diabetes Life Plan*, was published by Broadway Books in 2002. "Putting my health and well-being as a top priority has been a key for me," she says. "Stress, for me, leads to negative behaviors. If I don't watch it, I'll overeat, stop exercising, and feel guilty about the whole mess. I'm not doing that anymore."

of Sydney, Australia, the GI ranks carbohydrates—including bread, crackers, vegetables, and fruits—for their effect on your insulin-regulating system.

The index compares the speeds at which carbs are broken down into sugars—and how fast those sugars are released into your bloodstream—against a standard: table sugar. It enters your bloodstream almost instantly, causing a fast spike in your blood sugar level, requiring a big jolt of insulin to stabilize it. High-GI foods—primarily the cookies and cakes we love—have almost the same effect on the body as table sugar does. Low-GI foods, on the other hand, release their sugars into your bloodstream more slowly and steadily, so insulin pulses out at a healthy, even rate.

Eating low-GI foods may cut your risk of type 2 diabetes and heart disease, recent Harvard studies show, and lower your cancer risk as well, University of Michigan research suggests. So, although controlling blood sugar is key to low-carb plans such as Atkins, there's more than just a slim waist at stake.

GO NUTS

If you're one of the 21 million Americans with diabetes, you need extra heart-protecting omega-3 fats. But most people don't know where to find them. A new Australian study included 35 adults with type 2 diabetes: Nineteen added omega-3s on their own; the other 16 ate 1 ounce of walnuts (14 halves) daily. The walnut eaters met their omega-3 targets, while those who chose their own omega-3s ate mostly saturated fats.

REDUCE INFLAMMATION

Chronic, low-grade inflammation is like a fever in the blood that precedes type 2 diabetes. A Harvard study of 124,700 women found that those who ate the most inflammation-promoting foods had a $2\frac{1}{2}$ to 3 times higher risk of developing diabetes, compared with those whose diets were rich in foods that reduce inflammation.

Diabetes promoters:

- Sugar-sweetened soft drinks
- Diet soft drinks
- Refined grains
- Processed meats

Diabetes fighters:

- Wine
- Coffee

- Cruciferous vegetables
- Yellow vegetables

WARN YOUR FAMILY

A new Canadian study has found that saturated and trans fats could trigger diabetes in people with a common genetic trait that governs insulin production. The gene slows insulin production when these bad-for-you fats are present, say University of Alberta pharmacologists.

If you've got type 2 diabetes, other family members may have this gene. Protect them by helping them steer clear of fatty meats, full-fat dairy products, and commercial fries and baked goods containing partially hydrogenated fat.

PART III

LOSE WEIGHT

CHAPTER 11

DIET PREP 101

Read this before you start any diet

The first day of the New Year. Bathing suit season. After your birthday passes. Next Monday. When you finish the last Dove Bar. Like most people thinking about dieting, you probably have a "start time," a day when you're sure you'll be ready to dive in. But is that ready enough to guarantee success?

"A lot of people say, 'I'm ready to take off the pounds,' but that's a lot different from being willing to make the lifestyle changes necessary to actually lose the weight," says John Jakicic, PhD, director of the Physical Activity and Weight Management Research Center at the University of Pittsburgh. The difference between the two is the difference between dropping those pounds and struggling but not succeeding.

With that in mind, take our quiz before you take the leap. By the time you get to the end, you'll have a better idea of whether you're prepared to face the challenges ahead of you. And if you're not, we'll equip you with what you need to do to make sure you're truly good to go.

1. YOUR LAST ATTEMPT TO LOSE WEIGHT WAS:

a. A disaster. You couldn't stick with the diet for more than a few days, so you'll never try that plan again.

b. A learning experience. Some things worked and others didn't.

c. A success—at least for a while—so you'll give it another try.

Studies show that most people who lose weight and successfully keep it off are hardly diet novices—they've lost the same 10, 20, or more pounds many times before. What finally turned things around? They learned from their mistakes. "You need to look at past attempts as a learning experience, not a failure," says Timothy Lohman, PhD, a professor of physiology and director of the Center for Physical Activity and Nutrition at the University of Arizona in Tucson. "Say to yourself, 'I've done this three or four times—what's the pattern here?' If you can see it, then you don't have to repeat it."

If a particular weight loss approach doesn't work for you, there's nothing wrong with starting from scratch. However, think about why the last strategy didn't work and let that guide you. For instance, did you choose a diet that required you to eat foods you don't particularly like while giving up your favorites? Was it impossible to drag yourself out of bed for morning workouts? Consider tossing out whatever tripped you up the last time.

As for the diet that worked for only a while, it probably won't work again because it clearly wasn't one you could stick with over the long haul.

Give yourself 3 points for answering b, 2 points for a, and 1 point for c.

2. YOUR MAIN REASON FOR WANTING TO LOSE WEIGHT IS:

a. You feel like your life is out of control because you're doing things (like eating badly and sitting on the sofa way too much) that you don't want to be doing.

b. You have a wedding, high school reunion, or other big event coming up and want to look great.

c. Someone—your spouse, your mother, or an acquaintance—made a remark about your weight, and you feel mortally embarrassed.

Trying to lose weight to gain someone else's approval rarely leads to success. But doing it because you want to feel in control of your life often does. Each time you turn down a piece of chocolate cake or step on the treadmill, you are taking control of your life, and that continual stream of positive reinforcement will help you stay motivated over time.

That's what Diane Berry, PhD, a researcher at the Yale University School of Nursing, found in a small but telling study. Berry interviewed 20 women, ages 33 to 82, who had lost an average of 52 pounds and kept it off for 7 years (two participants who were unable to maintain weight loss were also included in the study). Berry found that the feeling of regaining control of their lives through exercise and learning new skills such as portion control gave the women who were successful a sense of empowerment that helped them stay the course to long-term weight loss.

That doesn't mean that you should never try to lose weight to look great for a high school reunion, says Dr. Lohman. Meeting a short-term goal often can give you the incentive you need to keep going.

Give yourself 3 points for answering a, 2 points for b, and 1 point for c.

3. BEFORE YOU START YOUR DIET, YOU PLAN TO:

a. Keep doing what you've been doing—eating too much and exercising too little.

b. Get rid of the junk food in your cupboards and refrigerator.

c. Have one last blowout with all of your favorite foods.

Cleaning out your kitchen does reduce temptation. But the chips in your cupboard and the Häagen-Dazs in your freezer aren't the only things that can trip you up. A much better way to prepare is to go about life as usual and document it for a week or so. Keep a food diary, chart the events and emotions that lead you to eat, and log your workouts—even wear a pedometer to see how much incidental activity you get each day. You'll learn what triggers you to overeat and the shortcuts you're taking to cheat yourself on physical activity. Once you do that, have one last blowout if you must. Just don't fool yourself into thinking that treating yourself to a gastronomic swan song is all you need to do to prepare.

Give yourself 3 points for answering a, 2 points for b, and 1 point for c.

4. YOUR BOILED-DOWN VERSION OF WHAT IT TAKES TO LOSE WEIGHT IS:

a. Eat a lot less and exercise a lot more.

b. Cut out sweets, exercise an hour a day, and stick to steamed vegetables and lean proteins for dinner and salads for lunch.

c. Change how you think about yourself.

Most people will need to eat less and exercise more. But it's more important to be willing to change the behaviors and thought patterns that set you up for failure. If you think you're going to fail, you will be more likely to do so. It's a self-fulfilling prophecy. "You need to say, 'That's not me,' and consistently practice that," says Dr. Lohman. For instance, tell yourself, "I'm the kind of person who can turn down food in social situations and who enjoys the feeling I get from exercising." You know that woman: Fresh from her gym workout, she orders the healthy meal while everyone else is downing chips and margaritas. From here on, that's going to be you.

But you don't need to adhere to a rigid set of rules. Though many stock weigh-loss rules have merit, you'll be breaking them left and right unless they work in the context of your life. "You might start out by saying, 'I'm going to go to the gym six times a week,' when the reality of your home and work life makes that impossible," says Martin Binks, PhD, director of behavioral health at the Duke Diet & Fitness Center. It's important to be flexible, so hit the gym three times a week and walk with friends the other days, for example, if you want to make the new you the real you.

Give yourself 3 points for answering c, 2 points for a, and 1 point for b.

5. SOMETIMES YOU BINGE ON A BOX OF COOKIES OR A PINT OF ICE CREAM. THE REASON IS:

a. Certain emotions or events in your life trigger your binges.

b. You love sweets and have no willpower.

c. You don't know.

"When you're angry, what else could you do besides eat?" asks Dr. Lohman. "Or when you're bored, fearful, or tense? It's a good idea to make a list of options. It could be journaling, calling a friend, reading a book, taking a walk, pounding a pillow, or nurturing yourself in other nonfood ways."

If you don't know why you binge, follow the advice in number 3 to help you figure it out.

Give yourself 3 points for answering a, 2 points for c, and 1 point for b.

6. YOU'LL OVERCOME THE TIME BARRIERS TO EXERCISE BY:

a. Not even trying. There is simply no wiggle room in your schedule, so you'll just focus on your diet.

b. Breaking up workouts into short segments throughout the day.

c. Carving out a half hour to an hour a day for yourself without fail.

Figure out how to fit exercise into your day. Your success may depend on it. In an 18-month University of Pittsburgh study that tracked 104 women, ages 25 to 45, Dr. Jakicic found that those who combined diet with physical activity lost more weight than the women who tried to drop pounds using either alone. What's more, exercising seemed to help the women in the study stick to their diets: As their activity levels went up,

their calorie intakes went down.

Does it matter if you break it up or do it in one shot? That depends on you. Another study by Dr. Jakicic found that 20 to 40 minutes of exercise daily in 10-minute bouts, 5 days a week, helped some women become more steadfast exercisers (while experiencing the same calorie-burning and cardiovascular-improving benefits they would if they did longer workouts). But even Dr. Jakicic admits that method isn't for everybody: "For some people, finding three or four 10-minute bouts of time is more of a hassle than finding 30 to 60 minutes."

Determine what works best with your schedule. It sometimes takes creativity, Dr. Berry says. "My daughter would stand with her music and violin at the end of a lane and practice while I swam laps."

Give yourself 3 points for answering c, 2 points for b, and 1 point for a.

7. RESTAURANT FOOD CAN MAKE OR BREAK A DIET, SO:

a. You'll go to places that have only low-calorie choices.

b. You'll go to your favorite restaurants, but order more healthfully: dressing on the side, fish that's broiled instead of fried, and so on.

c. You'll eat out less often.

Limiting your dining out to restaurants that serve low-calorie meals or ordering food "your way" can be risky. "There are so many hidden calories in restaurant food," notes Dr. Jakicic. Veggies are usually tossed with butter (50 calories in $1/2$ tablespoon), tomato sauces can be loaded with olive oil (120 calories in 1 tablespoon), and grilled fish may be brushed with fat before cooking. "And when you go to a restaurant, you may be tempted with 'Just try a bite' or 'What about some wine or dessert?'" he adds.

In his research, Dr. Jakicic has found that the more people eat out during the week, the harder it is for them to shed pounds. Your best strategy: Limit restaurant meals to no more than one a week.

Give yourself 3 points for answering c, 2 points for a, and 1 point for b.

8. YOUR SIGNIFICANT OTHER:

a. Doesn't involve himself much in the things that you do.

b. Sticks his nose in everything you do.

c. Is easy to talk to and respects your wishes and decisions.

In 2001, Richard Stuart, DSW, a professor emeritus in the department of psychology at the University of Washington and a former Weight Watchers advisor, surveyed 25,000 married women to see how their relationships influenced their attempts to lose weight. To no one's surprise, Dr. Stuart found that half the women failed when their spouses weren't supportive. Less expected was his finding that many women succeeded when their spouses stayed completely out of it. The divide was about fifty-fifty. "It just shows that there is no 'correct' way," says Dr. Stuart. "Each couple has to negotiate their own terms."

If you need the support of your spouse or kids, ask for it and be explicit. "Tell them exactly what they can do to help you succeed," says Dr. Lohman.

Give yourself 3 points for answering c and 2 points for a or b.

9. THE WEIGHT THAT WILL MAKE YOU HAPPY IS:

a. The exact same weight that you were back in high school.

b. The weight that lowers all the predictors of disease—such as cholesterol and blood pressure—to a healthy level.

c. Okay, not supermodel skinny, but low enough to be considered very thin.

This is a trick question because all the answers could be right. Common wisdom is that "dreaming big" about getting small leads to failure; in fact, some research shows that women who have modest goals end up taking off more pounds than women with loftier expectations. But a recent study found a link between having "dream" weight loss goals and successfully shedding pounds. Researchers at the University of Minnesota School of Public Health found that women with an unrealistic goal—to lose 30 percent of their body weight—lost significantly more weight after 18 months than women with less lofty goals. Though they didn't actually hit their dream weight, they felt inspired to keep going because they were confident they could stick to an eating plan and had relatively high self-esteem—all predictors of weight loss success.

While there may be no "correct" goal for everyone, there are correct attitudes, says Jennifer Linde, PhD, lead author of the study: "It's okay to believe that you can lose a lot of weight as long as you're prepared to put in the time and effort it takes to change what you eat and get enough exercise each day."

Give yourself 3 points for answering a, b, or c.

10. A WRENCH HAS BEEN THROWN INTO YOUR WORKOUT SCHEDULE. YOU:

a. Give up on it. You'll start again when everything calms down.

b. Get up at the crack of dawn so you can get your workout in.

c. Just do more "incidental" activity, such as taking the stairs and parking farther from your destination.

It might be easier to lose weight if your life were regimented, but let's face it: Stuff happens. "That's why it's so important to have a contingency plan in place for those tough weeks," says Dr. Binks. Instead of giving up until the problem passes, try to figure out a way to continue. For example, you could go to bed an hour earlier in order to get up earlier for your morning walk. If that doesn't work, set a reduced goal, such as getting more incidental exercise. But don't get too comfortable with a trimmed-back workout. It's just a temporary solution. Get back to your original activity goal ASAP.

Give yourself 3 points for answering b, 2 points for c, and 1 point for a.

YOUR SCORE

26 to 30 points: Ready, set, go. You're prepared to change not just how much you eat and exercise but also your daily patterns. Most important, you know how to fit these changes into your life. You've taken into consideration your job, your family, and your other commitments—as well as the ups and downs of life—and have made a workable plan to achieve your goals. Keep in mind that you don't have to change everything at once. "Look for things that are the easiest for you to change and that will give you the most benefit. Then add in other changes as you go," advises Dr. Binks.

20 to 25 points: Although you're willing to take on many of the challenges of weight loss, you're not all the way there. To better prepare, develop some strategies to deal with the inevitable hurdles. How can you find time to exercise when, for instance, your schedule changes because your kids are out of school or it's too dark to walk at night? What can you use instead of food to deal with stress or disappointments? How can you avoid overindulging in your favorite foods? Have some support in place before you get started, whether it's friends, family, or an organized support group. "This is especially important for physical activity," says Dr. Lohman. "If you have someone to meet and hike or walk with, it can make a big difference."

Below 20 points: You know what it takes to lose weight but not to keep the weight off. You need to start planning—what you're going to be eating, when you're going to be exercising, who you're going to turn to for help when your resolve is low. To help you set an agenda, revisit other times you've tried to lose weight (or, if it's your first time, look critically at your life to see why you're overweight in the first place). Look at the barriers you've faced and how you responded to them.

How did you handle family meals? Were you able to eat lightly, or did the pressure from your family make you pile your plate too high? Why did you stop going to the gym even after paying for a membership? Did you hate the place or the exercise you were doing? Was it too hard to get there on time for classes? (For advice on finding a gym that you'll actually use, see page 177.) In the long run, losing weight—and keeping it off—is about creating a lifestyle you can maintain for the rest of your life.

If you aren't sure what's tripping you up, consider talking to a professional, such as a psychologist, nutritionist, or, if your downfall is exercise related, a fitness trainer. Once you know the obstacles you're likely to face, you can develop a game plan for success. Losing weight is never easy, but you can help yourself succeed at it if you do some of the work ahead of time.

CHAPTER 12

YOUR DIET DATEBOOK

Win the battle of the bulge
with a year's worth of strategies

You're cruising along on your new diet when you run up against the year's first really big test of your will: an invitation to a party that will surely feature irresistible puff pastry hors d'oeuvres, flowing cocktails, and a lavish dessert selection. The challenge will make bypassing the supermarket bakery look like a cakewalk. What's for certain: If you make it past this party, there will be another on its heels. There are national holidays, birthday parties, and scores of other impromptu celebrations—a promotion, a good report card, even making a deadline—coming this year. "Because we don't have established patterns of eating in these circumstances, every occasion offers different temptations," says Brian Wansink, PhD, a Cornell University food psychologist who has studied guests' eating patterns at festivities such as Super Bowl parties and office celebrations. "You need to go into the event with a strategy."

And what might that be? *Prevention* called upon leading experts for advice on how to handle 26 of the most common diet-busting social situations that crop up throughout the year. Consider this your weight control calendar.

JANUARY

New Year's Brunch: Enjoy a toasted whole grain waffle with berries and low-fat yogurt immediately after you wake up. "The slightest bit of hunger will wear away your ability to stick to your resolution," says Arthur S. Agatston, MD, author of *The South Beach Diet.* Why waffles? If you have them for breakfast, you'll be less tempted by the ones dripping with butter and syrup at the brunch.

First Friday: Don't weigh yourself this Friday—or any other. If you like what you see on the scale, you might be tempted to splurge on Saturday night. (One-quarter of resolutions don't make it past the first week.) A better time for a weigh-in is Monday morning, when you'll see the results of your weekend behavior.

FEBRUARY

Super Bowl Sunday: Develop a game plan for this day, which ranks first in snack foods consumed. On offense, bring a bowl of air-popped popcorn sprinkled with a little Parmesan cheese; it'll satisfy your craving for a crunchy and salty snack, and 4 whole cups have the same number of calories that just 14 potato chips have. On defense, don't eat anything—even finger foods—without putting it on a plate, and sit where you have to walk in front of the TV to get food. (Imagine the embarrassment of blocking your friends' view of the big play.)

Valentine's Day: Ask for strawberries dipped in dark chocolate. They're festive, tasty, filled with antioxidants, and 40 calories apiece. If you absolutely must have the box of chocolates, instead of hinting for chocolate truffles (70 calories each), slip your honey the phone number for Gayle's Miracles (800-572-4139; United States only). Each of the truffles in the 18-piece heart-shaped box has just 30 calories and is made without artificial sweeteners.

Snowstorm: Have a pizza party, but don't make the delivery guy drive in the snow. Make your own healthy pie with Boboli's 100% Whole Wheat Thin Crust, $3/4$ cup of your favorite tomato sauce, $3/4$ cup of shredded reduced-fat mozzarella cheese, and $1/2$ cup of sliced mushrooms.

Eat one-third of the pie—a larger portion than two Pizza Hut slices—and save 137 calories.

MARCH

Oscar night: Use the trick that New York City weight loss psychologist Stephen Gullo, PhD, gives his celebrity clients: Suck on a menthol-flavored lozenge instead of grazing on hors d'oeuvres. It'll keep your mouth busy for up to a half hour for a mere 15 calories.

St. Patrick's Day: Trade one green beer (8 ounces of light beer has about 70 calories) for an iced green tea. Not only is green tea virtually calorie free, but preliminary research suggests that it's a metabolism booster, too.

APRIL

Easter: Lay off the chocolate eggs in favor of a beautifully decorated hard-cooked egg. One is just 78 calories, and it's a terrific source of choline, an important brain chemical.

Tax Day: Breathe deeply between bites, and when you do nibble, pay attention to the food's taste and feel. Otherwise, in your frenzied state, you'll mindlessly shovel in food, says Ann Pardo, director of behavioral health services at Canyon Ranch Health Resort in Tucson.

MAY

Mother's Day: On the country's most popular day to dine out, make your reservation at a gourmet restaurant that serves reasonably sized portions of ultra-satisfying food, suggests Carrie Wiatt, a celebrity clinical nutritionist based in Culver City, California. By way of comparison: The sea bass with potato and leeks at Daniel, an acclaimed restaurant in New York City, has about 630 calories; a platter of fried shrimp, scallops, clam strips, and fish fillets at Red Lobster, up to 1,100 calories.

Memorial Day: Because creamy picnic side dishes damage a diet much more than the main course does, skip the calorie-dense potato and macaroni salads in favor of a 59-calorie ear of corn on the cob, advises Robyn Flipse, RD, author of *Fighting the Freshman Fifteen*.

JUNE

Father's Day: Serve Dad's dinner in courses rather than presenting it all at once, says Will Clower, PhD, author of *The Fat Fallacy*: "Eating more slowly will give your body the 15 or so minutes it takes to register that it's full." A suggested menu of 511 calories: Start with salad, move on to shrimp cocktail, follow it with a small steak with mushrooms and steamed veggies, and end with fruit and pudding.

Graduation party: Bring a camera and act as the "official photographer" (it can be part of your gift to the guest of honor) so your hands won't be free to pick up food.

Baby shower: Have a bowl of satisfying soup—hot or cold—before attending. In a recent Pennsylvania State University study of nearly 150 dieters, those who consumed 200 calories' worth of soup before lunch and dinner every day lost 5 pounds more after a year than those who ate 200 calories in low-fat but salty snacks as an appetizer.

JULY

Independence Day: Lay off the lemonade. We know the weather's hot, but a recent study at Penn State showed that when women consumed 156 calories' worth of nonalcoholic caloric beverages with a meal, they only slightly adjusted their food intake and ended up 104 calories in the hole. Better choice: sparkling water with a few raspberries dropped in.

AUGUST

Wedding reception: Eat two fat-free hot dogs without the buns at home and carry a clutch purse when you head out the door. Together, they will wipe out your desire and ability to stuff yourself with hors d'oeuvres. Think about it: Who wants pigs in a blanket after polishing off two franks? You won't have a hand free for food anyway, what with a purse in one hand and a drink in the other (go for a 50-calorie wine spritzer).

Summer vacation: Request that the minibar in your hotel room be emptied, and stock it yourself with water, milk, 100 percent juice, low-fat yogurt, and fruit. You can enjoy breakfast in your room every morning and avoid the temptation to eat your money's worth in pancakes, French toast, and omelets at the hotel's overpriced buffet.

SEPTEMBER

Labor Day: Be among the last of the picnickers to begin eating, so when it's time to jump back in the lake or play volleyball, you'll have finished only one plateful.

Back to school: Buy your kids' snacks in preportioned bags and store them out of sight to resist reaching for them. Distance makes a difference: In one study, when women had to walk 6 feet for a chocolate kiss, they ate five fewer of them than when the bowls were on their desks.

OCTOBER

Birthday party: Pop a strong breath strip in your mouth when you arrive to stave off a taste for nibble foods. Spare yourself at least 100 calories by opting for a slice from the middle of the sheet cake rather than an overly frosted (and undoubtedly overly sweet) end piece.

Halloween: Give trinkets as treats and you won't be haunted by chocolate. The kids won't mind as much as you may think. When Yale researchers allowed 3- to 14-year-old trick-or-treaters to choose between a piece of candy and a small toy such as a pencil or ball, half took the toy. But if Halloween just isn't the same without candy, handing out fun-size packs of Raisinets (67 calories) or rolls of Smarties (25 calories) are your best bets. Don't buy the assorted packages of candy because you'll be tempted to try one of every kind.

NOVEMBER

Thanksgiving: Don't eat the veggies! If the green beans are buried under that creamy mushroom sauce and the sweet potatoes are oozing with glaze or marshmallows, fill half your plate with skinless turkey breast, top it with cranberries (an antioxidant powerhouse), and take mini portions of other items you love and get only once a year, suggests New York City culinary consultant Jackie Newgent, RD. Total calories for 6 ounces of turkey; 2 tablespoons each of cranberry sauce, stuffing, and mashed potatoes; and a sliver of cornbread: 471.

Black Friday: As you kick off the holiday shopping season, skip the high-cal, high-fat mall snacks. Instead, order a kid's meal with fruit rather than fries. You'll get a better portion size for an adult, plus you can use the toy as a stocking stuffer.

DECEMBER

Holiday parties: Don't put more than two foods on your plate at one time. "The variety of foods at holiday parties prompts you to overeat. This plan forces you to decide early on what you most want to try," says Wansink. "Chances are, you'll be satisfied after just one refill."

Christmas: Don't waste 300 or 400 calories nibbling on food while you're cooking. Before you prepare the meal, make yourself an 80-calorie plate of crudités—four whole wheat crackers, one large celery rib, five baby carrots, and a teaspoon of ranch dressing. For sipping, fill your wine glass with sparkling water and a slice of lime.

New Year's Eve: Ring in the New Year with champagne. Each 90-calorie glass is a diet bargain, compared with a margarita (327 calories) or any other sugar-filled mixed drink.

CHAPTER 13

THE DIABETES WEIGHT-LOSS EXERCISE CIRCUIT

Lose your belly, drop pounds, control diabetes: This easy workout does it all

There's not enough time in the day to get in all the fitness mandates being thrown at you to both lose weight and handle your diabetes. You're being asked to do at least 30 minutes of cardio to blast fat and build fitness, lengthy strength-training routines to develop lean muscle, and arduous spot-toning moves to get rid of that stubborn belly fat.

That's why Jeff M. Reynolds, a former boot camp instructor in Kansas City, Kansas, developed this simple circuit workout that encompasses everything you have to do to get lean and healthy. It combines cardio, strength training, and tummy toners all in one 30-minute routine.

This workout will save you time, and it will also double your results. In a Montana State University study of 10 people, those who did a 20-minute strength-training circuit burned nearly twice as many calories as those who did a traditional weight routine in which they did three sets of each exercise and rested between sets.

The reason for this success: All exercises in circuit workouts are done back-to-back without resting between moves. Because your heart rate stays elevated, you burn more calories and train your heart and cardio system.

THE ESSENTIALS

Do this workout 3 or 4 nonconsecutive days a week.

Beginners: Choose low-intensity cardio moves and go through the circuits in the order in which they appear for a 30-minute, fat-blasting, body-firming workout. Sprinkle in the high-intensity cardio moves as you progress.

Advanced: Select high-intensity cardio moves and do the routine twice for a 60-minute workout that burns about 500 calories.

Equipment: You'll need an exercise mat and one or two sets of dumbbells, about 3 to 8 pounds each. Choose a weight that leaves your muscles feeling fatigued after each exercise. As you become stronger, you should increase the amount of weight you're lifting by a pound or two at a time.

Warmup: March or jog in place for 3 to 5 minutes. Do the same to cool down at the end of the workout, along with some stretching.

YOUR CARDIO MOVES

Start each circuit with 3 minutes of aerobic exercise. If you have a treadmill, stationary bike, elliptical machine, or other cardio exercise equipment, use it. If not, here are some moves that you can mix and match to crank up your heart rate.

Low Intensity

• March in place
• March forward and back
• Step side to side
• Kick front
• Grapevine
• Hamstring curls (kickbacks)
• Knee lifts

High Intensity

• Jog in place
• Jog forward and back
• Side-to-side jumps
• Kick front with hop
• Jumping jacks
• Jump rope
• Knee lifts with hop

CIRCUIT ONE

3-MINUTE CARDIO

Mix and match from the list on page 109.

2-MINUTE STRENGTH DOUBLE, SINGLE SQUATS

Stand with your feet about 3 inches apart, with your arms at your sides. Bend your hips and knees and sit back. Keep your knees behind your toes and let your arms rise in front of you. When your thighs are almost parallel to the floor, stop and lift your left foot off of the floor. Balancing on your right foot, straighten your right leg and stand back up. Lower your left foot and repeat, balancing on your left foot. Continue alternating legs.

1-MINUTE ABS STANDING CRUNCH

Stand with your feet together and your arms overhead. Contract your abs and raise your right knee as you pull both of your arms down to meet your knee. Lower your knee and extend your arms overhead. Repeat with your left knee. Continue alternating knees.

CIRCUIT TWO

3-MINUTE CARDIO

Mix and match from the list on page 109.

2-MINUTE STRENGTH
BALANCING PUSHUP

ASSUME a pushup position on your knees with your hands slightly wider than shoulder-width apart and your body in a straight line from your head to your knees. Bending your elbows out to sides, lower your chest toward floor, and then push back up. When your arms are almost fully extended, raise your right arm in front so you're balancing on your left hand as you complete the move. Hold for a second, then lower your right hand. Repeat the push up, this time lifting your left arm. Continue alternating arms. For an easier version: Do pushups on your knees without the arm lift.

1-MINUTE ABS FROG

LIE on your back with the soles of your feet together, your knees dropped out to the sides, and your hands behind your head. Curl your head, shoulders, and upper back off of the floor. Hold for a second, then slowly lower.

CIRCUIT THREE

3-MINUTE CARDIO
Mix and match from the list on page 109.

2-MINUTE STRENGTH
TWISTING ROW

HOLDING a 5- to 8-pound dumbbell in each hand, stand with your feet shoulder-width apart and bend forward from your hips so your arms hang beneath your shoulders, with your palms facing your legs. Bend your elbows toward the ceiling, rotate your palms up, and squeeze your shoulder blades together, pulling the dumbbells toward your chest. Hold for a second, then slowly lower.

1-MINUTE ABS PLANK WITH SIDE KNEE LIFT

BALANCE on your hands and balls of feet so your body forms a straight line. Raise your left foot and bend your left knee toward your left shoulder. Hold for a second, then lower. Repeat with your right leg. Continue alternating legs.

The Perfect Plan

Here are three great reasons why this workout is perfect for you and your diabetes treatment.

- It specifically targets belly fat—also known as visceral fat. It's this type of fat that's packed around your internal organs, and it's been linked as a dangerous risk factor for diabetes. A study of 678 Hispanic and African-American people with a family history of diabetes found that regardless of age, gender, or weight, visceral fat was the most powerful factor determining who had insulin resistance.
- This workout helps you achieve weight loss fast. And just a modest drop in weight—even 10 pounds—can lower your blood sugar level.
- In a Japanese study of 35 healthy-weight adults, those who did a similar cardio/strength-training circuit lost 16 percent of body fat, decreased "bad" LDL cholesterol by 19 points, and increased "good" HDL cholesterol by 11 points—all of which lowers your risk of heart disease. This is important for people with diabetes, as they have a five times greater risk of developing heart disease.

CIRCUIT FOUR

3-MINUTE CARDIO

Mix and match from the list on page 109.

2-MINUTE STRENGTH
CRISSCROSS CURLS

STAND with your feet hip-width apart. Hold a 5-
to 8-pound dumbbell in each of your hands with
your arms down at your sides, palms facing forward. Bending your right arm, curl the dumbbell
up and across your body toward your left shoulder. Hold for a second, then slowly lower. Repeat
with your left arm. Continue alternating arms.

1-MINUTE ABS TWISTING
CRUNCH WITH LEG DROP

LIE on your back with your legs up and your knees
slightly bent and your hands behind your head.
Curl up off the floor and twist your torso to the left,
bringing your right shoulder toward your left knee.
At the same time, lower your right leg to just above
the floor. Hold and then, without lowering your
head and shoulders, twist to the right and switch
legs, bringing your left shoulder toward your right
knee. Continue alternating sides while keeping
your head and shoulders off of the floor.

CIRCUIT FIVE

3-MINUTE CARDIO

Mix and match from the list on page 109.

2-MINUTE STRENGTH
CRISSCROSS EXTENSIONS

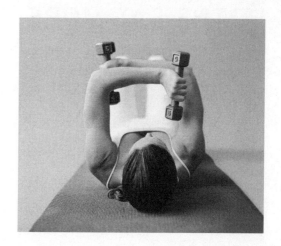

LIE on your back with your knees bent and feet flat on the floor. Hold a 3- to 5-pound dumbbell in each of your hands and extend your arms straight up over your chest, with your palms facing your toes. Bending your elbows and keeping your upper arms still, lower the dumbbells toward your chest so the left dumbbell is closest to your face. Hold for a second, and then straighten your arms. Continue, alternating the dumbbell that is closest to your face.

1-MINUTE ABS BOXER
CRUNCH

LIE on your back with your knees bent, your feet flat on floor, and your arms in front of your chest. Tuck your chin and roll up one vertebra at a time until you're sitting up. Hold and twist left and punch with your right arm, then twist right and punch with your left arm. Slowly roll back down and repeat.

CHAPTER 14

THE EAT-MORE, LOSE-MORE DIET

This diet is so simple, you'll never need to cheat

Prevention's Eat-More, Lose-More Diet is a plan you can—and should—stay on for the rest of your life. We've combined cutting-edge nutrition research with the latest findings on successful weight loss to create the smartest, healthiest diet possible. And if you're watching your weight, this plan has endless slim-down potential: It painlessly slashes empty calories while supplying all the nutrients you need to look and feel your best. We'll also help you tailor it so you can lose a pound a week, no matter what you weigh now.

The plan is broken down into 10 easy-to-follow principles, followed by a promise for each, so the payoffs will always be top of mind. We've used the federal Dietary Guidelines for Americans, but only as a jumping-off point. While the government bases its advice on research along with input from the food industry, *Prevention* reaches into the future for nutrition tips gleaned from emerging science—and from scientists who put your health first.

If you fall off the wagon for a day or two, don't worry about it. Just get back on track when you can. This isn't a diet in the punitive sense. It's a way of life. Think progress, not perfection, and you will succeed.

PRINCIPLE: EAT FRUITS AND VEGETABLES EVERY FEW HOURS

Promise: If you have a piece of fruit or a serving of vegetables every 2 to 3 hours, you'll maximize your body's disease-fighting ability, and you may even lose a pound a week without noticing. That is because phytonutrients—the health-promoting, disease-preventing substances abundant in plant foods—need to be replenished in your system often to keep their potency high. "In our studies, we find that blood levels of certain phyto-nutrients can drop rapidly 2 to 3 hours after consumption of produce," says Susan Bowerman, RD, assistant director of the UCLA Center for Human Nutrition.

Strive for four servings of vegetables and three servings of fruit daily, but remember, more is better. How many more? Well, the new Dietary Guidelines have a surprise: The daily target is now 13 total for the most active people (teen boys) in the population. We're suggesting a more doable range for women: 7 to 10 servings of produce a day to offer you the ultimate in disease protection and help you get the best nutrition bang for your caloric buck. (The servings are small: one cup of romaine lettuce counts, as does half a grapefruit.)

If you snack on produce instead of soda and chips three times each day, you can also expect to lose about 1 pound per week. A produce-packed diet also arms your body against diabetes, heart disease, and possibly some cancers and may keep your bones strong by helping them retain calcium. Include at least one serving a day of "potent" produce, preferably in whole, not juice, form: red (tomatoes), deep green (kale or broccoli), orange (carrots or squash), or citrus (grapefruit or oranges).

PRINCIPLE: EAT MORE FIBER-RICH WHOLE GRAINS

Promise: *Prevention* recommends that you get three to four servings of whole grains a day—up from the American average of 1—to boost your energy and heart health, possibly prevent cancer, and stay full longer so you don't overeat. First, a definition: Whole grain foods include oatmeal, whole wheat bread, brown rice, and wheat germ. Many processed cereals are made with whole grains, but check the package ingredient list to be sure. Best rule of thumb: "Whole grains contain at least 2 grams of fiber per serving, and you can find that on the label," says Joanne Slavin, PhD, a professor of nutrition at the University of Minnesota in St. Paul.

Whole grains may also be slimming, especially if you up your intake of fiber to at least the recommended 25 to 35 grams a day. According to Tufts University researchers, weight loss potential is higher in people who eat whole rather than refined grains, probably because high-fiber foods keep you feeling full longer. There are other benefits as well: "Dietary fiber accounts for 80 percent of the heart protection you get from whole grains," says James Anderson, MD, a professor of medicine and clinical nutrition at the University of Kentucky in Lexington, adding that fiber is emerging as both a preventive and a treatment for diseases such as diabetes and obesity.

PRINCIPLE: EAT TWO SERVINGS OF PROTEIN A DAY

Promise: The news on protein is that an amino acid—namely, leucine, found in meat, poultry, dairy, and fish—is essential for developing lean muscle mass and regulating hormones that control your appetite and help you burn calories. And the amount you get matters. The old thinking on protein was that if you were getting enough calories, you were getting enough protein, period. The new thinking is much more specific: While most Americans get double the protein they need, others get too little. You should be getting a 2- or 3-ounce serving (the size of a deck of cards) twice a day.

Studies support protein's slimming benefits. Researchers at the University of Illinois at Urbana-Champaign found that women who ate more protein—but the same number of calories—lost more weight and retained more lean body mass, compared with those on a lower-protein diet. Here's the catch: Eating larger amounts of protein will backfire—big time. Too much won't allow your body to use protein's amino acids efficiently, and if that big steak dinner (some restaurant cuts are 32 ounces!) pushes you over your calorie count for the day, that excess protein is more likely to be stored as extra fat than as muscle. Take-home message: More than about 6 ounces of protein a day is protein without purpose.

Beans are another healthy way to add protein to your diet, as well as potassium, folate, and iron. But which ones should you stuff in your burrito? The darker the beans, the better, conclude researchers at the University of Guelph in Ontario. Their study found that beans are loaded with the same heart-healthy, cancer-preventing compounds found in red wine, berries, and tea. But black beans had the most, followed by red, brown, yellow, and white. For comparison's sake, $1/_2$ cup of black beans had the same anthocyanin content as two glasses of red wine.

But don't discount good-for-you yellow legumes such as soybeans. "In addition to preventing heart disease, soy foods and soy protein appear to protect against breast, prostate, and colon cancer," says Dr. Anderson.

PRINCIPLE: EAT SWEETS WITH OR AFTER MEALS

Promise: You don't have to give up your favorite treats—just eat them at the right time to keep pounds off. That also means cutting down on sugar, eliminating high fructose corn syrup, and enjoying sweet treats only with or just after a meal, not as a snack. The reason: New research at Columbia University's College of Physicians and Surgeons found that subjects given a sugar-only drink got hungrier sooner than others given a sugar-protein drink. This suggests that eating sugary treats alone rather than with or after a meal may cause weight gain.

And how much sugar should you be eating? The Dietary Guidelines suggest "moderation," but *Prevention* prefers the World Health Organization's more specific recommendation: 10 percent of total calories. That means if you're eating a 1,600-calorie-a-day diet, you can enjoy 10 teaspoons of sugar a day. (If you're on a 2,000-calorie diet, you can increase that to $12^1/_2$ teaspoons.) That translates into a few teaspoons of sugar in iced tea or coffee, a dollop of honey on a piece of toast, a few sips of soda—and you're pretty much at your daily limit. According to the Economic Research Service, Americans eat an average of 31 teaspoons of sugar daily. Bottom line: Don't be average when it comes to sugar.

PRINCIPLE: KEEP SALT IN BALANCE

Promise: Staying in balance means you'll have a healthier heart and stronger bones, without feeling deprived. Yes, most Americans consume twice the 2,300 milligrams of sodium recommended by the Dietary Guidelines. But these same people probably skimp on potassium-rich fruits and vegetables and don't get enough calcium. Here's why that matters: The new thinking on sodium is that it's all about balance. You don't have to slash your salt intake to unpalatable levels if you boost your consumption of certain foods that contain the other minerals needed for optimal health. (Potassium in produce will help lower blood pressure and blunt the effects of sodium in your diet.)

So strive to keep potassium, calcium, magnesium, and sodium all in balance in your body. If you follow a diet abundant in produce, dairy, and whole grains (and thus potassium and other key minerals) and low in processed foods—2,300 milligrams of sodium is a smart ballpark figure that will help you maintain a healthy balance of sodium in your system.

PRINCIPLE: EAT SMALL-SIZE FISH TWICE A WEEK

Promise: You should eat at least two servings of fish a week because it's one of the best sources of omega-3 fatty acids, fats that help reduce the risk of heart disease. "The potential health benefits of fish can outweigh the risks of mercury toxicity if you eat a variety," explains Barbara Olendzki, RD, nutrition program director at the University of Massachusetts Medical School in Worcester.

Yet many women fear mercury and PCB contamination in some species, which may lead to birth defects (therefore, pregnant and childbearing-age women need to be especially vigilant). The good news is that if you stick to smaller "prey" fish—loosely defined as fish that are more likely to be eaten by other fish than to hunt them—you'll avoid unhealthy exposure. The reason? Long-lived fish tend to grow bigger, so toxins have more time and tissue in which to accumulate.

Here's a list of fish, in order of lower to higher contamination, that health experts say you can eat: scallops, clams, crab, oysters, shrimp, sardines, sole, tilapia, cod, haddock, mahi mahi, canned light tuna (limit albacore, which has higher mercury levels), salmon, pollock, and catfish. "There is preliminary evidence suggesting that diets rich in tropical fruits and vegetables may help prevent the uptake of mercury in the body," Olendzki adds. Alcohol and wheat bran in your diet may also reduce mercury absorption.

Olendzki also recommends trimming away the skin and fat, where much of the contaminants are stored. "When I eat fish, I enjoy it grilled or broiled without added fat," she adds. Alas, fish-and-chips lovers, fried fish doesn't count. University of Washington researchers reported that fried-fish eaters had none of the heart-health benefits of people who ate grilled, baked, or broiled fish. In fact, their risk for heart attack increased. Frying fish is tantamount to drowning

veggies in butter—the unhealthy fats negate the protective ones.

PRINCIPLE: EAT MIXED NUTS DAILY

Promise: Each type of nut offers a different nutritional benefit, from better sight to a slimmer waistline. Walnuts are a great source of omega-3 fatty acids, peanuts help curb your appetite, and almonds are rich in vitamin E and folic acid. "As a nutritionist, I always say 'Eat a variety of foods,' and that's really important when it comes to nuts," says Penny Kris-Etherton, PhD, a professor of nutrition at Pennsylvania State University in University Park.

For example, Brazil nuts are one of the best sources of selenium; walnuts contain those heart-healthy omega-3s; and pistachios have lutein and zeaxanthin, two carotenoids that help protect the eyes from harmful UV light. In addition, recent research shows that most varieties of nuts—including walnuts, almonds, peanuts, hazelnuts, and macadamia nuts—contain beta sitosterol and campesterol, two plant chemicals that have the ability to lower harmful blood cholesterol levels.

Your best bet for overall health is to choose unsalted nut varieties. It doesn't matter if they're dry- or oil-roasted or ground up as butter, because the benefits and calories are the same. Speaking of calories, nuts pack plenty of those, too—about 180 calories an ounce—so keep those portion sizes small.

PRINCIPLE:
EAT THE RIGHT FATS

Promise: For optimal heart function and overall good health, get rid of trans fats and keep saturated fats, found in meat and dairy, to a minimum. The majority of your daily fats should come from polyunsaturated and monounsaturated sources, although most of us get enough polys through processed foods made with corn, soybean, or safflower oils. Make an effort to consume more monounsaturated fats such as flaxseed and olive oils, which pack more heart-healthy lignans than other oils. This will help reduce the risk of heart disease, diabetes, and eye disorders; enhance bone health; and even make your skin more supple.

But we're not talking about drowning your bruschetta in olive oil. Limit yourself to about $1^1/_2$ tablespoons of these healthy fats out of a total of $4^1/_2$ tablespoons per day.

PRINCIPLE:
GO FOR DAIRY DAILY

Promise: Eating 3 servings of fat-free or low-fat dairy products is one of the best things you can do for your bones and belly, and it protects against heart disease and colon cancer, too. University of Tennessee researchers suggest that calcium in dairy foods increases the breakdown of fat—especially harmful belly fat—while suppressing fat storage.

And if you like yogurt, emerging research suggests that healthy bacteria in fermented dairy products may act as protective, anti-infection agents. Increased yogurt consumption might even help raise your resistance to immune-related diseases. "There is good evidence for the beneficial effect of yogurt in maintaining certain aspects of gastrointestinal health, and there is some evidence for colon cancer," concludes Simin Meydani, PhD, a professor of nutrition at Tufts University in Boston. Choose brands that have the National Yogurt Association's "Live & Active Cultures" seal to ensure you're getting all the benefits of healthy bacteria.

PRINCIPLE: QUENCH YOUR THIRST

Promise: Fluids can do wonders for your waistline. A recent study found that after men and women drank 17 ounces of H_2O, their metabolic rates increased by 30 percent within 10 minutes and peaked about 40 minutes later. But you don't need to drown in the stuff. A recent National Academy of Sciences report found that most women need eleven 8-ounce cups of fluid a day, but it doesn't all have to be water. A cup of tea counts, as does juice or the occasional cola. Just watch that sugar. Studies show liquid calories don't register on our hunger radar and can sneak up on your waistline.

Surprisingly, booze counts toward your daily fluid quota, meaning you can consume alcoholic beverages in moderation if you are not at risk for certain types of hormonal cancers (check with your doctor).

"I do not encourage nondrinkers to drink, but I also do not encourage women who enjoy a glass of alcohol a day to stop, because it may actually be good for your heart," explains cardiologist Holly S. Andersen, MD, an assistant professor of medicine at Weill Cornell Medical Center in New York City. She enjoys a glass of wine with dinner but sternly reminds her patients that there's no benefit to more than one a day: "And you can't have all seven drinks on a Saturday night."

CHAPTER 15

DIET WRECKERS AT YOUR DESK

Stay away from the desktop diner
with these diet makeovers

What was it today? A doughnut from the dozen you brought in for the whole crew? Candy from the vending machine? Microwave popcorn stashed in your desk drawer? Whatever you ate, you have company: Recent studies, including two from the American Dietetic Association, show that more than a third of office workers have breakfast alongside their keyboards; as many as two-thirds regularly munch on lunch in their offices; nine in 10 snack on the job; and 7 percent even have dinner desk-side. Corporate America seems to be turning into a giant kitchen, where eating on the job has become a necessity for the time-crunched and stressed. The average "lunch hour" has shrunk to 36 minutes, and chocolate has become a bottom-drawer staple. (Its feel-good endorphins make tension easier to handle.) But the number one reason for desk-side dining is hunger.

"Most office food isn't satisfying," says Baltimore nutritionist Colleen Pierre, RD. "Doughnuts, coffee, pastries, and candy give you temporary energy, but you're hungry a few hours later." It doesn't take long for the quick fix to become a pattern. So *Prevention* tried an intervention.

First, we found volunteers at four work sites who let us rummage through their desks, briefcases, office kitchens, and coat pockets, leaving no crumb uninspected.

Then Pierre gave the volunteers an office makeover—a corporate downsizing, if you will. Here's her analysis and habit-breaking strategies.

THE GROUP NOSH

The Haystack Group, Marietta, Georgia

Résumé: "A sweet tooth is a job requirement here," admits Stefanie Long, director of public relations, who shares this consumer research office with six others. Not a single one is on a diet, and all enjoy the same kinds of food. "When we chow down, we do it together. It's a social experience," says Holly Cline, an account manager.

Desk-side dining: Most of the crew eat breakfast and lunch at the office. Once a week, the company's founder, Bonnie Ulman, brings in a baker's dozen of mini Cheddar muffins. "I believe in taking care of the staff," she says. Other days might begin with sharing takeout Chick-fil-A Chicken Biscuits (buttermilk biscuits with a fried chicken patty) or bagels and cream cheese.

"Despite the fact that the coffeemaker is going all day, and we just got an espresso machine, one of us goes to Starbucks—sometimes twice a day—with an office order for tall mochas, lattes, and hot apple ciders," reports Cline. On stressful days, she says, they drink larger, 16-ounce cups of their caffeinated drink of choice with an extra shot of espresso.

At least three times a week, the group returns to Chick-fil-A for lunch, bringing back fried chicken sandwiches, fries, and Cokes. Alternatively, they might hit Taco Bell for Zesty Chicken Border Bowls and an occasional Nachos Supreme. Or they'll go for chips and sandwiches from a nearby deli. Occasionally, they organize a potluck lunch. "At the last one, the chocolate-covered strawberries were the biggest hit," recalls Long.

Between the sugar and caffeine highs and lows, the entire office usually slumps around 3 p.m. Their solution: chocolate. Last fall, to celebrate the completion of a book Ulman wrote, the group enjoyed two 3-pound bags of M&M's and a pound each of Hershey's Kisses, candy corn, and candy pumpkins. After 3 days, only a handful of Kisses remained. "Once someone brought in apples, but they rotted in the fridge," says Cline.

"Work is the place to be bad," says Long. "No one here judges anyone. When you mention to someone that you ate half a bag of Oreos, they tell you it's okay because they did, too."

Office overhaul: Pierre says: Everyone should agree to have a breakfast that delivers more nutrients and fiber in fewer calories than chicken biscuits, muffins, or bagels with cream cheese. The caffeine in all that coffee is increasing everyone's stress hormones. Reaching for candy is a natural response and, because chocolate is also a stimulant, it fuels hunger.

Ulman would do everyone a favor by passing up the Cheddar muffins and bringing in a fruit basket to put near the printer or wherever people gather.

For lunch, cut back the fast-food trips to once or twice a week—and make better choices at the restaurants. At Taco Bell, for instance, the Bean Burrito has about half the calories and a third of the saturated fat of the Zesty Chicken Border Bowl with dressing.

On the remaining days, try the soup and salad bar at a nearby supermarket, or organize a weekly potluck lunch and limit desserts to fruit.

If the Starbucks trips give people a much-needed break, skip anything topped with whipped cream and go for the steamed cider (180 calories) or decaffeinated, fat-free lattes (120 calories plus 35 percent of the calcium Daily Value).

THE OUT-OF-BALANCE EATER

Amy Brown, public relations manager and editor for a corporate communications firm, Chatsworth, California

Résumé: This 37-year-old mom starts her day at 5 a.m., when she shares a breakfast of raisin bread with her toddler daughter. Brown leaves the house by 6, is in the office by 7, and works through lunch, eating her midday meal at her desk so she can head home by 4:40 p.m.

"I do most of my eating at work," she

says. "I cook dinner for my family and have an artichoke myself because I'm too full from what I ate at the office."

Desk-side dining: "When I get to work, I usually take a scone or muffin from a tray that someone brings in for morning meetings," says Brown. When there are no pastries, she reaches into her desk drawer for her stash of almonds and crackers. Brown also keeps salad ingredients in the office fridge. To complete her lunch, she brings in chicken, barbecued salmon, or other leftovers from the previous night's dinner. Once or twice a week, she gets a salad from a gourmet grocery store along with a cookie or brownie. "I have two to three sweet snacks a day," admits Brown, who often raids a bowl of peanut M&M's in the office conference room.

Office overhaul: Pierre advises Brown: Stop starving yourself of real food. You eat a lot of desserts but no balanced meals. Improve your poor eating habits and set a good example for your daughter by having breakfasts and dinners that include the foods you want her to enjoy. Unsweetened instant oatmeal (with a little honey, if you need some

sweetener), milk, and fruit are fast and filling. Stir some chopped nuts into yours, too. The fiber in the cereal and fruit and the protein in the nuts will help keep you satisfied for several hours, so you won't need that scone. For a midmorning snack, keep your favorite lowfat yogurt in the fridge for a good dose of calcium and to quell your cravings for sweets.

Bringing lunch from home is a great idea, but your salad needs to be bulked up in fat or protein to keep you full throughout the afternoon. Also, if you choose chicken instead of leftover salmon or another oily fish in the salad, be sure to use an olive oil–based vinaigrette or sprinkle on some nuts. For fiber, have a small whole grain roll.

Instead of multitasking, give yourself 15 to 20 minutes to concentrate on your meal. You'll feel more relaxed and satisfied and therefore less tempted later by peanut M&M's. By dinnertime, you'll be hungry enough to enjoy a meal with your family. Keep dried fruit in your desk drawer and fresh fruit in the fridge for a midafternoon snack.

THE ONE-TRACK SNACKER

Vickie Spang, chief marketing officer for a law firm, Los Angeles

Résumé: The consummate professional, Spang, 53 and single, often works long hours. She tends to skip dinner unless she's invited out, because it's too much trouble to cook for herself at the end of the day: "If I'm really hungry, I'll microwave a bag of popcorn when I get home."

Desk-side dining: Spang stashes Skippy Super Chunk Peanut Butter in her desk drawer. (There's another jar in her car and a third in her apartment.) She helps herself to a heaping teaspoon for breakfast, another before lunch, and possibly another later in the day, if she works late. Come lunchtime, Spang turns the counter at California Pizza Kitchen into another office. While she's eating her usual—tortilla soup and barbecued chicken salad with extra sauce— she does her reading. "I sit at the counter, read the *Wall Street Journal,* and open interoffice mail," she says.

Spang mostly drinks bottled water, but on an occasional morning, she'll have a V8 before work. "I don't like vegetables much, so this helps," she says. One thing you won't find in her office is a candy dish. "I read in a professional magazine that it sends the wrong signal; you seem more like a mom than a professional," she says.

Office overhaul: Pierre tells Spang: You need to start your day with something nutritious and satisfying. Try a low-fat yogurt, drinkable yogurt, or a piece of string cheese with a few whole grain crackers or a small whole grain roll.

At lunchtime, since you're going to California Pizza Kitchen, how about eating pizza once in a while? Or pasta? Or a sandwich? You don't eat much food at home, so your on-the-job meals need more variety and have to provide more of the fruits and vegetables that are required every day. Some dishes to try: Vegetarian Pizza with Japanese Eggplant (any kid will tell you that veggies taste better when they're covered with cheese), Broccoli/Sun-dried Tomato Fusilli, or the Grilled Rosemary Chicken Sandwich (stuffed with tomatoes and romaine lettuce).

Peanut butter is one of the best foods to keep in your desk. But instead of eating it plain, spread some on a banana, apple, celery stalk, or carrot. Pick up ready-to-eat baby carrots or apple slices (sold in a bag of five small packages) and prewashed and precut celery sticks. To get more grains, stash some whole grain crackers in your desk to eat plain or with peanut butter.

Finally, have a late-afternoon snack if you're planning to skip dinner at home, or eat something for dinner if you're working late. You could reheat your leftovers from California Pizza Kitchen or buy frozen meals. (Tesoros makes a great Penne Toscana and a Chipotle de Azteca—rice with creamy pepper sauce plus grilled chicken, corn, and onions.) Or have a bowl of whole grain cereal with milk and berries. Smart, late-in-the-day snacks include the Athenos Traveler (hummus and pita bread packaged together), a premade fruit smoothie, and a package of sunflower seeds.

THE DORM-STYLE DINER

Lindsay Morgan, director of community affairs for a university, Denver

Résumé: A 30-year-old newlywed, Morgan recognizes that she rarely eats healthy foods in or out of the office. "I make a resolution, try it for 2 days, and then forget about it for 3 months," she says. Why? "I'm happy with my weight. I get good checkup reports from the doctor, and I play in a softball league," she explains. "I want to do better, but I can't get myself motivated."

Desk-side dining: Morgan starts her day at the office with two cups of coffee with cream and Sweet'N Low. Three times a week, she brown-bags her lunch—often a turkey sandwich with chips or Goldfish crackers and a can of cola. On the remaining days, she goes to Chipotle Mexican Grill, where she typically orders a chicken burrito with cheese, sour cream, and black beans, washing it down with a cola.

Then, midafternoon, she reaches into her desk drawer for a family-size package of Wonka Runts or Gobstoppers, hard candies that have been favorites since childhood. She's also fond of microwave popcorn. "Sometimes I polish off the whole bag for dinner when I work late," she says.

Office overhaul: Pierre advises Morgan: You're eating like a college student—skipping meals, drinking sodas, and noshing on chips, popcorn, and candy. You may be happy with your weight and health now, but this high-calorie, low-nutrient eating pattern will catch up with you. Instead of trying to make several changes at once and failing, choose one improvement and practice it for a month. That's about how long it takes for a new behavior to become a habit.

Start before you get to the office, with a breakfast that will keep you satisfied and energized. Try peanut butter on a whole wheat English muffin, or have a frozen whole grain waffle, toasted and topped with yogurt and fruit. Once you get adjusted to that pattern, work on lunch. Exchange your Goldfish and potato chips for a palmful of smoked almonds. Their healthy fats will sustain you throughout the afternoon. Next, bring in a piece of fruit to have after lunch.

Finally, try to cut back on your caffeine. Begin by replacing the cola with bottled water. Miss the bubbles? Try mineral water. Gradually decrease the coffee; replace one cup with decaffein-

---

Inside the *Prevention* Offices

What's lurking in the desks of the people at the nation's premier health magazine?

Pretty nutritious stuff, as you'd expect. Copy chief Joelle Junior has whole grain cereal and Planter's cashews, and research editor Karen Jacob keeps a Thermos of ice water atop her desk. Fitness director Michele Stanten doesn't keep any snacks on hand so she has to burn calories if she wants to eat them.

The staff does have a sweet tooth. In a common area, a basket of Hershey's Kisses sits out of sight on top of a filing cabinet.

Party time is the exception to the healthy rule at *Prevention*'s office. Cake, ice cream, and soda left over from a baby shower were spotted in the fridge. "If the staff has celebrations more than once a month, they may want to consider healthier choices," says nutritionist Colleen Pierre, RD. One option: a tea party with mini sandwiches, small cookies, a fresh fruit platter, and a selection of caffeine-free brews.

ated green tea for the antioxidants.

While you're making these changes, buy a few more items for your desk. Next to your candy, keep an assortment of dried fruits so sweets aren't your only option. Also stash a StarKist Lunch To-Go kit (which includes tuna, mayo, relish, spoon, crackers, and even a mint) in your drawer for nights when you're working late.

CHAPTER 16

FOOD ADDICTION

Science suggests that you can be
hooked on chocolate, cookies, and chips.
Here, the latest evidence, plus an eight-step
program for regaining control

For nearly 15 years, Dana Littleton ate chocolate practically all day long. "I used to drown myself in it," says the 34-year-old stay-at-home mom from Guntersville, Alabama. "I just couldn't get through my day without chocolate. I'd be positively frenzied if I didn't have it and feel calm and at ease when I did."

Littleton recalls a day a few years ago when she was home with her two girls. It was a punishing 20°F when she realized that she was out of Snickers, a favorite treat. So she bundled up 3-year-old Georgia and 4-month-old Caroline, put them in the car, and drove to the gas station. "I actually dragged a small baby out in the cold," Littleton says. "Anyone who knows me would say that it's out of character for me to do that. It was a sign that I was out of control. I wasn't even out of the parking lot before I had inhaled two candy bars."

Her habit had consequences, says Littleton, who started numbing herself with food after the death of her father at a young age. Her need for sweets helped drive her weight to 250 pounds; her back and knees hurt, and she had chest pains. "People tell me that at least I've never had an addiction like alcohol or drugs—something serious," she says. "But I tell them my addiction *was* serious."

ADDICTION—TO FOOD?

It seems that everywhere you turn—dinner parties, your best friend's kitchen, bookstores, even talk shows—someone is confessing to having a food addiction. For years, experts scoffed at the notion that you could be hooked on chocolate or chips. Some still do. But recently, high-tech medical scans have revealed surprising similarities in the brain chemistry of drug addicts and chronic overeaters—resemblances that have caught the attention of the National Institute on Drug Abuse (NIDA).

"We're involved in studies of brain changes associated with obesity," says Nora D. Volkow, MD, director of NIDA, whose 2001 study pioneered some of the food-addiction research. "We're doing it because many compounds that inhibit compulsive eating may also inhibit compulsive drug intake. The neurocircuitry overlaps."

The behavior of compulsive eaters also lends credence to the idea of addiction—the cravings and preoccupation with food, the guilt, the way these overeaters use food to relieve bad feelings, and the fact that binges are frequently conducted at night or in secret. Now some addiction and obesity experts have started to use the "A" word in connection with food and even to speculate that it may be partly responsible for America's rising obesity rate.

"Food might be the 'substance' in a substance-abuse disorder that we see today as obesity," says Mark Gold, MD, chief of addiction medicine at the University of Florida College of Medicine in Jacksonville. "If you ask some of the questions that are used to diagnose drug abuse—for instance, 'Do you continue to use the substance despite its negative effects?' or 'Do you have a preference for more refined substances?'—and then replace 'substance' with 'food,' it's not all that difficult to imagine that food addictions exist."

No one—Dr. Gold included—is suggesting that an addiction to food could be as strong as the one that drives people addicted to cocaine or heroin. Still, the research into the connection between overeating and addiction isn't just academic. It may finally put to rest the idea that anyone who eats excessively simply suffers from a lack of self-discipline. More important, the emerging evidence points to some very concrete steps that anyone can take to eat in a saner, healthier way.

BLAME IT ON THE BRAIN

People like Littleton have long been accused of lacking willpower. But research at the US Department of Energy's Brookhaven National Laboratory in New York suggests they may be missing something else instead: adequate brain receptors for dopamine, a chemical that is part of the brain's motivation and reward system. "Dopamine is the chemical that makes you say *aah*," says Gene-Jack Wang, MD, clinical head of positron emission tomography imaging at Brookhaven and leader of a series of studies investigating the brain chemistry of chronic

overeaters. "It gets us to go over and grab something that will make us feel good."

In 2001, Dr. Wang and his colleagues, Dr. Volkow among them, compared the brain scans of obese and normal-weight volunteers, counting up dopamine receptors. Obese people, Dr. Wang realized, had fewer dopamine receptors, and the more obese they were, the fewer of these crucial receptors they had. In fact, he says, the brains of obese people and drug addicts look strikingly similar: "Both have fewer dopamine receptors than normal subjects."

It's possible that drug use or compulsive overeating actually lowers the number of dopamine receptors. But it's also possible that some people are born with fewer, and if that's the case, say researchers, it could explain a lot. If overeaters or drug addicts are short on receptors for the "aah" chemical, they might not respond as readily to social interaction, art, sex, and other pleasures that ought to make them feel good. And that could be the reason they're driven to consume things that prompt dopamine's release— such as illicit drugs (the most potent activator) or foods high in fat, sugar, and possibly salt.

"If you have someone who is not responsive to natural reinforcers, that person may be more vulnerable to taking drugs," Dr. Volkow says. "If you get stimulated only by food, guess what happens? You can easily fall into patterns of compulsive eating."

WHAT THE COMPULSION FEELS LIKE

It doesn't take a brain scan to see the similarities between someone addicted to drugs or drink and a compulsive overeater. Like the alcoholic who continues to drink despite seeing her life crumbling around her, the overeater will consume food to the detriment of her social and family life. She may know that her eating is harming her health, but it doesn't matter, says Dr. Gold.

"I actually passed out once," says Terry Young, 40, of Cincinnati, who calls herself a sugar addict. "It was a total binge, with a gallon of ice cream, cookies, candy bars—like an alcoholic on a bender."

Young has struggled all her life to control her emotional eating, which she says she does almost as a way of medicating herself. She gorges to calm down after a hard day at work and fixes a big snack as a sedative before bed. It's gotten so bad that she's been known to steal her 7-year-old daughter's treats. "If it's in the house, it calls my name," she says. She went on antidepressants and says they helped.

"Like cocaine addicts who can't leave any cocaine behind, food addicts eat until no food is available," says Dr. Gold. "You might say, 'Yeah, I did that on Thanksgiving.' But food addicts do this all the time."

Patty White (whose name has been changed for this story) of Los Angeles can relate. Her "drug" of choice is cheese of any kind, from Brie to Cheddar. Two years ago, the 45-year-old saleswoman gave up cheese for Lent, but as soon as that period was over, she binged. "I went cold turkey when I quit smoking, but this time, going cold turkey was a disaster," she recalls. "I went wild. I gorged on cheese at every meal, gained 5 pounds in 4 days, and just felt disgusting."

Growing up, she saw family members go on similar binges, but they abused alcohol. "My grandfather was an alcoholic, and I see addictive behavior in other relatives," she says. "I'm a lot like them. But my excessive behavior is with food."

IS IT NATURE . . . OR NURTURE?

Addiction and obesity both run in families, and experts believe that genetic components account for at least some of a person's vulnerability. But animal research also suggests that the environment—mainly, how often you're exposed to an addictive substance—can shift brain neurochemistry, increasing the likelihood of addiction. One hint that environment plays a role comes from studies in which animals were repeatedly given cocaine: Frequent use actually decreased the number of dopamine receptors, says Dr. Wang.

If that's the case, we live in an environment perfectly designed to nurture food addictions. For decades, food-industry scientists have been working hard to figure out how better to hook people, claims David L. Katz, MD, MPH, director of the Yale-Griffin Prevention Research Center in Derby, Connecticut, and author of *The Flavor Point Diet*. Manufacturers now excel at hitting the sweet spot—making us crave more and more of a food.

"In a supermarket recently, I actually found a pasta sauce that, serving for serving, contained more sugar than a chocolate fudge sauce, though the sweetness was hidden because the pasta sauce was so salty," Dr. Katz says. "The question is, why would anybody pour a packet of sugar over their pasta? And the answer is that if you get used to that much sugar, another pasta sauce will taste too bland. The food industry wants us to need more and more of the substance to feel satisfied, so we'll go out and buy more and more of it."

Animal research at Princeton University has also shown that the way you indulge may have consequences. Bart Hoebel, PhD, a professor of psychology, placed rats on an alternating schedule of 12 hours with no food, followed by 12 hours of access to both rat chow and a solution of 10 percent sugar (about as sweet as a soft drink)—a pattern that results in binge eating. As the days went by, the rats began upping their intake of the sugar solution, drinking more and more at a time.

After about a month, he found the rats' brains were producing surges of dopamine during their binges. "In rats, binge eating promotes addiction just like binge drinking promotes alcohol addiction," says Dr. Hoebel. "It's possible that repeatedly bingeing on sweets could actually change the circuitry of your brain"—and make you want ever-increasing amounts.

GETTING STRAIGHT

Researchers aren't ready to declare the case closed on the causes of our collective weight problem. "The research is interesting, but I'd never say that people who struggle with food and weight issues are addicted in a clinical sense," says Martin Binks, PhD, director of behavioral health at the Duke Diet & Fitness Center. "The evidence just isn't there. And the implication is that if you have an eating problem, you're destined to lose control—there's nothing you can do."

Yet the notion of an addiction to food may help people like Dana Littleton. "At some point, I realized that I had hit bottom, just as an alcoholic or drug addict would," she says. Littleton took the same path that many have taken: "I prayed for strength to face what I had been running from. And for willpower—especially for chocolate. Then I got off my rear end."

Whether you look outside or inside yourself for the determination to stop your destructive behavior, researchers agree that it's important to recognize that you can change. High-fat, high-sugar foods may trigger some of the same brain effects as drugs like cocaine or heroin, but their impact isn't as powerful, say researchers, who point out that addicted rats, for instance, will choose cocaine over food. While it may feel at times like a runaway train, how you eat isn't out of your control, says Susan McQuillan, MS, RD, author of *Breaking the Bonds of Food Addiction*. Having a plan of action can help.

With that in mind, here are eight steps you can take to get back on track.

1. Don't go cold turkey. Although treatment for life-threatening drug or alcohol addiction generally requires abstinence, an all-or-nothing approach is impossible for food addicts. Everyone has to eat. Besides, some weight loss experts believe that such rigid thinking can make you crave the offending food more than ever. After Patty White's cheese bender, she realized that by banishing it entirely, she'd set herself up for failure. Now she lets herself eat cheese but in sensible amounts: "I sprinkle some on a taco instead of sitting down to a wedge of Brie."

Says Edward Abramson, PhD, professor emeritus of psychology at California State University, Chico, and author of the book *Body Intelligence,* "If someone told me that I could never eat another doughnut as long as I live, I would become so preoccupied with doughnuts that I'd probably gobble down a dozen by the end of the day. If I know I can have another doughnut sooner or later, I won't feel so desperate. I can eat just one."

2. Control your home environment. Just as someone with an alcohol problem shouldn't buy a magnum of champagne, you shouldn't overstock your kitchen, says Dr. Gold: "You have to assume that every food or drink you buy will end up in your mouth." Exercise purchase and portion control, he advises.

3. Temper temptation. Sometimes it's not just a food that sets you off but also the place in which you eat it. So putting yourself in a location where you used to eat excessively can be a recipe for trouble. Ex–drug addicts face this problem all the time, reports Marcia Levin Pelchat, PhD, a research scientist at Monell Chemical Senses Center in Philadelphia. "Going back to the old neighborhood often triggers a strong craving," she says. Similarly, the sight of the bakery

where you used to buy brownies might melt your resolve.

So shake up your routine. If tortilla chips are your weakness, don't go to Mexican restaurants. If you always have ice cream while watching TV, read a book instead (or knit to keep your hands busy as you watch TV).

4. Retrain your brain. In order to be satisfied with two cookies instead of an entire bag, you need to change the way your brain sees food on the plate, says Dr. Gold. First, switch to smaller plates and bowls to automatically reduce portion sizes. "This can make people very distraught because the brain looks at the smaller portions and decides they're not enough," says Dr. Gold. "But over time, the brain gets used to it."

Next, leave more space on the plate by again reducing the amount of food you serve yourself. Each step may take several weeks to feel comfortable, but stick with it: Consuming smaller portions will become second nature.

5. Adjust your tastebuds. One of the best ways to gain control over your eating is to restore your sensitivity to flavors, says Dr. Katz. You can do it without depriving yourself: If sugar is your downfall, keep sugar cookies in your diet, but when picking prepared foods that aren't supposed to be sweet—such as pasta sauce, bread, and chips—look for ones without added sweeteners.

Check ingredient labels for all the names that sugar goes by, including fructose, dextrose, and corn syrup. (For a list of sugar's aliases, go to www.prevention.com/sugarlist.) "By removing all that superfluous sugar from your diet, you'll soon reset the sensitivity of your tastebuds," explains Dr. Katz, who says that the same technique can be used to reduce your desire for salt or fat.

Be forewarned: You'll have to maintain vigilance. "Tastebuds are very adaptive little fellows," Dr. Katz says. "If you let extra sugar and fat into your diet, you could be lured back into your old patterns."

6. Exercise regularly. Milky Ways and Big Macs aren't the only things that satisfy the pleasure centers of your brain—so does exercise. In animals, at least, research has found that it increases dopamine levels and raises the number of dopamine receptors in the brain. Making a commitment to work out helped Littleton kick her chocolate habit. As a result of a vigorous exercise routine

and a more sensible diet, she's gotten down to 134 pounds in 3 years. "The feeling I get after I exercise is nothing like I'd get after eating chocolate," she says. "It's much better, and it doesn't come with guilt."

7. Learn to eat only when you're hungry. One classic tool that weight loss experts use to teach people how to better manage their appetite is the hunger scale. The scale ranges from zero to 10, with zero being ravenously hungry and 10 being overstuffed. "A food addict's goal is to stay away from either of these extremes," says McQuillan. Eat when you begin to feel hungry (2 or 3 on the scale) and stop when you feel comfortably satisfied (5 or 6).

Though it's obvious that you don't want to eat to an overstuffed 10, using the scale to gauge when you should start munching is important, too: If you wait until you're at zero, you may eat all the way up to 10.

8. Deal with your emotions. Even if a brain scan at Dr. Wang's lab were to show that you have a physiological basis for food addiction, it's likely that there would be an emotional element, too. It's important to stop using food to cope with your feelings, says McQuillan.

How Strong Are Your Food Cravings?

You might be a food addict if any of these descriptions fit: You continue to over-eat even though you know it's harming your health and possibly your family and social life; you hide out and eat alone; you feel compelled to finish all the food in your line of sight (or house); or you eat to the point of pain or discomfort.

Also consider the following four questions, suggests Mark Gold, MD, chief of addiction medicine at the University of Florida College of Medicine in Jacksonville. They're an adaptation of the CAGE questionnaire, a tool used to diagnose alcoholism. "You really need to answer yes to only two items to indicate that you may have a problem," he says.

Have you ever felt the need to Cut down on your eating? Many people overeat on occasion; the difference is that you feel that if you don't ration yourself, you will completely lose control.

Have you ever been Annoyed by criticism of your eating? If you get upset when anyone brings up what or how much you consume, it may mean that you are too attached to eating.

Do you feel Guilty about your eating? It builds up, because at every meal you say you're going to control yourself—and you fail.

Have you ever needed an Eye-opener? You may wake up in the morning and feel compelled to consume. "We have patients who get up in the middle of the night and eat," Dr. Gold says. "They say, 'I finished a cake. I don't know how I did it.'"

This can mean getting better at tolerating sensations of sadness, anger, or boredom, rather than rushing to soothe them with food. Sometimes it means asking what you need to make your life better.

"I failed when I tried to comfort myself with food after the death of my dad and after two miscarriages," says Littleton. "I had to turn around to face it head-on. Now I'm in control of my decisions."

MEDICAL BREAKTHROUGHS

Here's the newest research on the weight loss front.

HEED THE WEIGHT-DIABETES CONNECTION

If you're overweight, you're racing against time to shed the excess pounds before weight-induced type 2 diabetes catches up with you. Here's a reason why: A factory within each cell (the endoplasmic reticulum, or ER) gets overburdened by the extra influx of energy and nutrients. This triggers a signal that interferes with normal functioning of insulin receptors on the cell surface so the cell can't control glucose uptake and output. The resulting persistently high blood glucose levels are the hallmark of diabetes.

An increase of as little as 1 centimeter in waist size (that's less than $^1/_2$ inch) could raise the risk of developing type 2 diabetes by 28 percent for women and 34 percent for men, according to a Louisiana State University study.

STICK WITH YOUR DIET

A new study tracking 1,401 people with diabetes for 9 years found an encouraging fact: Simply trying to shed pounds could cut the diabetes-related death risk 20 to 30 percent. In fact, researchers at the Centers for Disease Control and Prevention (CDC) found that death rates were the same for both successful and unsuccessful dieters. Lead researcher Edward W. Gregg, PhD, thinks this might be because dieters have adopted healthier habits—eating more produce and exercising more—which have long-lasting benefits regardless of body weight.

BEWARE THAT BELLY BULGE

Life expectancy for Americans keeps rising: It's now 80 years for women and 75 for men, according to the latest CDC data. Make the most of those added years by getting your weight—especially what's around your waist—under control now. Wake Forest University researchers measured waist-to-hip ratios of 9,400 middle-aged people and found that those with spare tires—linked to disabling heart disease and diabetes—were up to 57 percent more likely to have diminished muscle strength and exercise capacity. A new Canadian study of 14,924 men and women concluded that even if your scale says you're healthy, a large middle could mean that you have dangerous abdominal fat.

This is the story of the apple versus the pear body type: Do you carry your weight around your hips or your waist and upper body? The difference is key, because as your belly measurement increases, so does your risk for heart disease, high cholesterol, high blood pressure, and diabetes—by up to 93 percent. (Hip fat does not seem to carry the same risk.)

How do you measure up? Current guidelines define high risk as a waist that's greater than 35 inches for women or 40 inches for men. But new, more detailed guidelines have been proposed by leading American obesity expert George Bray, MD, a professor of nutrition and chronic diseases at Louisiana State University in Baton Rouge.

And how do you measure? Place a tape measure just above your hip bones with the tape parallel to the floor and snug but not compressing your skin. And don't suck in your belly. That's cheating!

If your hips are 36", your waist should be no more than 29".

If your hips are 41", your waist should be no more than 33".

If your hips are 46", your waist should be no more than 37".

Here's how your waist size relates to your disease risk.

Low Disease Risk

Waist size: Women (28"–35")
Waist size: Men (31"–39")

High Disease Risk

Waist size: Women (35.5"–43")
Waist size: Men (39.5"–47")

Very High Disease Risk

Waist size: Women (> 43")
Waist size: Men (> 47")

MAJOR SURGERY, MAJOR RESULTS

According to a new study published in the *Annals of Surgery*, gastric bypass surgery may help treat diabetes. Of 191 overweight people with type 2 diabetes who had the surgery, 83 percent were able to go off their diabetes medication.

PART IV

MOVE IT

CHAPTER 17

PREVENTION'S ABC WALKING PLAN

Lose weight and look great with this special body-shaping plan

Imagine that your walks could deliver the results you want. Need to shed some winter weight? No problem. Want to slide into sleek new jeans? You can do it. Looking for a friendly, straightforward way to get back in shape?

It's all as easy as ABC—the *Prevention* ABC Walking Plan. ABC stands for Accelerated, Body Shaping, and Cardio—three types of walking routines blended into one plan. We scoured the best research to find moves that maximize calorie burn. You'll get intervals (to accelerate your results), circuit strength-training (for body shaping), and tempo workouts (to improve your aerobic fitness and heart health). These moves also keep your metabolism revved so you burn more calories after you're done. In just 4 weeks you'll be noticeably trimmer, faster, and stronger.

"Walking is great exercise," says exercise physiologist Len Kravitz, PhD, of the University of New Mexico in Albuquerque. "But if you always do the same walking workout, it may not keep you as fit as you'd like. You burn more calories and improve fitness faster when you surprise your body with a variety of workouts that include some higher intensity." A recent study of more than 15,000 men and women from the Fred Hutchinson Cancer Research Center in Seattle revealed that those who regularly walked fast or jogged were better able to keep off the pounds during middle age (when many of us gain) than those who stuck to the same slow pace.

The ABC plan rolls all these findings into one easy-to-follow program. Each day—except on rest days—you'll do a specific A, B, or C workout. The basic plan will help you slim down, tone up, and walk faster without fatigue. And you

---

Intervals for A Workouts

These A intervals assume that you've been walking regularly for at least a few months. If you're a true beginner, your joints and ligaments need conditioning to handle the intensity, so do intervals only once a week for the first 6 to 8 weeks.

A-Intense

Ratio: 1:4

Warm up for 5 to 10 minutes. Then increase your effort (if you're outside, walk faster or jog; if on a treadmill, you can walk faster or increase the incline) for 1 minute so your "work effort" is an 8 or 9+ on a scale of 1 to 10, with 10 being as hard as you can go. Ease your intensity to a 4 or 5 for 4 minutes of "active rest." Repeat for the number of times specified in each program. Always end this workout with "active rest" or a 5- to 10-minute cooldown.

Tip: "Because you have ample recovery time in this program, really push to keep the intensity high on the work effort," says fitness trainer and Walk Reebok Training member Leigh Crews. Be sure to maintain proper walking form.

A-Brisk

Ratio: 1:3

Warm up for 5 to 10 minutes. Then increase your speed for 1 minute so your work

can easily tailor the plan to meet your specific goals. *Prevention*'s ABC Walking Plan has all the workouts you'll need to deliver the results that will keep you going for years to come.

PICK YOUR PROGRAM

With *Prevention*'s new walking plan, meeting any health goal is as easy as, you guessed it, ABC. Simply choose from the following plans.

ABC Overall Shape-Up

For the walker who wants to boost performance, shed a few stubborn pounds, and tighten up flabby trouble spots, the best plan is an even blend of A, B, and C workouts. After 2 to 3 weeks, ramp up your A, B, and C workouts evenly by following

effort is an 8 to 9 on a 1-to-10 scale. Ease your intensity to a 5 or 6 for 3 minutes of active rest. Repeat for the number of times specified in each program. Cool down for 5 to 10 minutes at the end of the workout.

Tip: You will have less "active recovery" between work efforts in this workout, so each successive interval may feel harder, says Crews. If need be, lower the intensity of your recovery so you feel completely ready for your next work effort.

A-Steady
Ratio: 1:2

Warm up for 5 to 10 minutes. Then increase your intensity for 1 minute so your work effort is a 7 to 8 on a 1-to-10 scale. Ease your intensity to a 5 for 2 minutes of active rest. Repeat for the number of times specified in each program. Cool down for 5 to 10 minutes at the end of the workout.

Tip: This is a great interval for beginners; although you have less rest, you're not pushing the intensity as high. To make this more challenging, you can either increase your effort or extend the work portion to 90 seconds.

the advice in "Keep the Results Coming" on page 159. Or, once you're happy with your fitness and feeling comfortable, you may want to try another program.

DAY	WORKOUT
Monday	Rest
Tuesday	A workout Steady* 3 intervals (20–30 min)
Wednesday	B workout 1 time through circuit (30–40 min)
Thursday	C workout 30 min
Friday	A workout Brisk 3 intervals (20–30 min)
Saturday	B workout 1 time through circuit (30–40 min)
Sunday	C workout 40 min

*Rotate through the three interval workouts, performing two different types per week.

Beat the Blue-Jean Blues

A good walking workout burns fat and calories, but to really trim those stubborn lower-body trouble spots, you need more muscle-building B workouts. "Because you do these exercises during your walk,

your muscles are already warm and ready to work. And you're energized from the sunshine and fresh air," says fitness trainer and Walk Reebok Training Team member Leigh Crews.

After 2 to 3 weeks, ramp up your B workouts by following the advice in "Keep the Results Coming" on page 159.

DAY	WORKOUT
Monday	Rest
Tuesday	B workout 1 time through circuit (30–40 min)
Wednesday	C workout 30–45 min
Thursday	C workout 30–45 min
Friday	B workout 1 time through circuit (30–40 min)
Saturday	A workout Steady* 3 to 5 intervals (20–35 min)
Sunday	B workout 1 time through circuit (30–40 min)

*Rotate through the three interval workouts, performing a different type each week.

Walk Faster

Keeping pace with your speedy friends is good for more than an ego boost. "A lot of walkers get stuck at a 3.7 mph pace—or about 16- to 17-minute miles," says walking expert Mark Fenton. "By doing longer, fast intervals, you can break through that speed limit, hit 4 mph, or 15-minute miles, and reach a new level of fitness."

After 2 to 3 weeks, ramp up your A workouts by following the advice in "Keep the Results Coming" on page 159. Every 4th week, take a week off from intervals (sub in 30-minute C workouts instead) to give your body a chance to recover and rebuild your muscles.

DAY	WORKOUT
Monday	Rest
Tuesday	A workout Intense 3 intervals (20–30 min)
Wednesday	B workout 1 time through circuit (30–40 min)
Thursday	A workout Brisk 3 intervals (20–30 min)
Friday	C workout 30–45 min
Saturday	A workout Steady 3 intervals (30 min)
Sunday	C workout 30–45 min

Blast Fat

The three steps to weight loss are cardio, cardio, and cardio, says Dr. Kravitz.

"Every cell has fat-burning furnaces called mitochondria," he explains. "As you increase fitness through continuous aerobic exercise, those mitochondria increase their function dramatically to more effectively burn fat." That means plenty of C workouts.

After 3 to 4 weeks, start ramping up your C workouts by following the advice in "Keep the Results Coming" on page 159. After 2 months, consider adding time and intensity to your A workouts. Again, use the advice in "Keep the Results Coming."

DAY	WORKOUT
Monday	Rest
Tuesday	A workout Steady* 3 intervals (20–30 min)
Wednesday	C workout 30 min
Thursday	A workout Brisk 3 intervals (20–30 min)
Friday	B workout 1 time through circuit (30–40 min)
Saturday	C workout 45–60 min
Sunday	C workout 45–60 min

*Rotate through the three interval workouts, performing two different types each week.

THREE WORKOUTS ROLLED INTO ONE

Prevention's ABC Walking Plan combines the following three essential workouts.

A Is for Accelerated

As the name implies, these workouts include bursts of accelerated speed. "High-intensity exercise will increase your 'afterburn'—the number of calories you continue to use up after you've stopped exercising. It also strengthens your heart so all activity feels easier," says Dr. Kravitz. The end result: You move more, burn more calories, and melt more fat.

Intervals can be as simple as speeding up between every other telephone pole or so structured that you need a heart rate monitor and a stopwatch. Crews prefers something in between. "I like 'ratio' intervals, where you simply walk hard for 1 minute, easy for 2, and so on," she says. "They're easy to follow and very effective." See "Intervals for A Workouts" on page 148. It includes options that range from moderate to intense. The goal is to push your body's limits at different speeds; this will help improve its ability to recover and do it again.

To get started: Increase your walking speed by bending your arms so your elbows form 90-degree angles, and then pump them at a faster pace than your usual walking motion. Take quicker strides so your legs keep pace with your arms, and push off your toes at the end of each step. Keep your shoulders down, your eyes up, and your abs taut.

B Is for Body Shaping

These supersculpting moves are designed to challenge fast-twitch muscle fibers that walking doesn't typically engage. Your muscles are made up of slow- and fast-twitch fibers, and regular walking works predominantly the slow-twitch ones. You use fast-twitch fibers while strength training and during explosive movements such as sprinting or jumping.

"Fast-twitch muscles burn more calories and are the first to get out of shape from disuse," says Crews. "So if you have pencil calves or flabby thighs, these moves will shape them up fast." As a bonus, these exercises build strength and stability in your ankle, knee, and hip joints so you'll be less susceptible to injury.

To get started: Walk for 10 to 15 minutes at an easy to moderate pace (5 to 6 on a 1-to-10 scale). Then perform the following 10-minute Body Shaping circuit. At the end of the circuit, walk again for 10 to 15 minutes.

CURB LIFT-OFF

(calves, glutes, and thighs and improves balance and leg strength)

FIND a curb or small step. Stand sideways to the curb, one foot on the curb and the other foot down on street level. Keeping your chest lifted and your abs taut for support, bend your knees and lower into a squat so your legs are bent 45 to 90 degrees. Be sure to keep your knees behind your toes.

EXTEND your legs and stand and lift your lower leg out to the side. To make it harder, add a jump: Squat as before, then quickly straighten your legs and jump straight up. Land with your knees bent to absorb the impact. Repeat for 1 minute per leg.

DIP 'N' CURL

(triceps, abs, and shoulders for core and upper-body strength)

Sit on the edge of a bench and grasp it on either side of your hips. Inch your butt off of the bench and walk your feet out until your knees are bent 90 degrees. Extend your right leg with your heel on the ground and your foot flexed. Bend your elbows straight back and lower your butt toward the ground while pulling your right knee toward your chest. Don't bend your elbows past 90 degrees. Return to the starting position. Repeat for 1 minute, then switch legs. To make it easier, keep both of your feet on the ground while performing the dips.

BENCH PRESS

(chest, shoulders, triceps, and core for better torso tone and less upper-body fatigue)

STAND facing the back of a park bench or low wall. Place your hands wider than shoulder-width apart on the bench and walk back until your arms are extended and you're balancing on the balls of your feet. Position your feet wider than shoulder-width apart. Your body should form a straight line from your head to your heels. Bend your elbows and lower your chest toward the bench. Then push back up.

WHEN your arms are almost fully extended, raise your left arm straight out in front to complete the move. Pause for a second. Lower your left arm and repeat, this time raising your right arm. Repeat for 1 minute, alternating arms.

WALKING LUNGES WITH KNEE LIFT

(glutes and thighs and stretches hips)

On a level surface, stand with your feet hip-width apart. Keeping your chest lifted and your abs taut, step forward with your right foot and bend both of your knees to lower into a lunge position. Keep your front knee in line with your ankle.

Then straighten your knees and rise to standing. Draw your left leg forward; pause with your left knee lifted to hip level. Hold for a count of 3 before bringing your left foot all the way forward for the next lunge. Continue moving forward, with each step ending in a lunge, for 1 to 2 minutes.

PIVOT SQUATS

(glutes and thighs)

STAND with your feet wider than shoulder-width apart, your arms pointing straight ahead, and your palms together. Keeping your chest lifted and your abs taut, bend your knees and lower into a squat, so that your legs are bent 45 to 90 degrees, keeping your knees behind your toes.

PULSE three times, lifting and lowering your hips just a few inches. On the fourth pulse, turn your body to the right by lifting your left foot and pivoting on your right foot. Pulse three times facing right, then pivot on your left foot back to the front. Repeat, except this time turn to your left, and then back to the front. Perform for 1 to 2 minutes.

STANDING CROSSOVER

(quads and abs for a stronger core)

STAND with your feet a few inches apart. Bend your arms and hold them out to the sides so they form right angles, with your fingers pointing toward sky and your palms facing forward. Contract your abs and draw your right knee and left elbow toward each other. Pause and return to the starting position. Alternate sides for 1 minute.

C Is for Cardio

These walking workouts are the foundation of your program. "This is the solid aerobic training that burns fat and calories and keeps you fit," says Crews. "The key is to maintain a pace that lies between somewhat hard and hard—about a 6 on a 1-to-10 scale, with 10 as the hardest. You should feel like you can walk a fairly long time— 30 or 45 minutes—at this pace."

The best part: As you continue doing the A and B workouts, your C walks will get faster and burn more calories but feel easier.

Keep the Results Coming

As you become more comfortable with the program you choose (give yourself at least 2 weeks; you may need as much as a month), you can boost your results even further by ramping up your workouts as described here. Because most of the programs rely primarily on one of the three components—Blast Fat, for example, emphasizes C moves—you'll first want to increase that part of the workout.

A Workouts

Every other week, add one more interval to your A workouts, until you are completing a total of five. If you are following the Walk Faster plan, you can get even more dramatic speed improvement by increasing the interval work and rest time in the A-Steady intervals. Increase the work portion 1 minute each week for 3 weeks; you should end up walking hard for 4 minutes and recovering for 8 minutes.

B Workouts

Every other week, perform 1 more minute of one lower-body move and one upper-body move. After 6 weeks, you should be completing the entire circuit twice. Once you feel strong enough, try the more difficult moves for the Dip 'n' Curl and the Curb Lift-Off. Start slowly with these moves, and stop immediately if you feel any strain.

C Workouts

Every other week, extend your C workouts by 5 minutes. Your goal is to reach 60 minutes. Don't have the time? Once you can keep a steady pace for 30 minutes, try doing the distance in less time. Aim to shave 2 to 3 minutes off your time every other week. When you can do the workout in 25 minutes, add more distance to get back up to 30 minutes.

CHAPTER 18

PAIN-FREE WALKING

Solutions to the 10 most common walking injuries

We all know that walking is the safest, easiest form of exercise there is, so why should you bother reading this chapter? Because left ignored, an innocent niggle can easily become a chronic problem. In fact, each year, nearly 250,000 hoofers are hobbled, thanks to a walking-induced pain or a nagging old injury that walking has aggravated.

Take Roberta Smith, 37, an executive assistant in New York City. She started walking to and from work, only to find that the journey irritated the tendinitis she'd developed 10 months earlier from playing volleyball. "I thought I was safe with a low-impact activity like walking, but it was so painful I had to give it up."

As bothersome as the initial problem can be, the real damage is what happens next: You stop exercising, misplace your motivation, and soon gain weight and lose muscle tone. To make sure a debilitating injury doesn't prevent you from reaching your weight loss and fitness goals, *Prevention* asked the country's leading experts for their advice on avoiding and treating the 10 most common walking woes.

TENDERNESS ON YOUR HEEL OR THE BOTTOM OF YOUR FOOT

Could be: plantar fasciitis

The plantar fascia is the band of tissue that runs from your heel bone to the ball of your foot. When this dual-purpose shock absorber and arch support is strained, small tears develop and the tissue stiffens as a protective response. "Walkers can overwork the area when pounding the pavement, especially when they wear hard shoes on concrete, because there's very little give as the foot lands," says Teresa Schuemann, a physical therapist in White Salmon, Washington, and a spokesperson for the American Physical Therapy Association. Inflammation can also result from any abrupt change or increase in your normal walking routine. People with high arches or who pronate excessively (walk on the inside of the foot) are particularly susceptible.

You know you have plantar fasciitis if you feel pain in your heel or arch first thing in the morning (the fascia stiffens during the night). If left untreated, the problem can cause a buildup of calcium, which can create a painful, bony growth around the heel known as a heel spur.

What you can do about it: At the first sign of stiffness in the bottom of your foot, loosen up the tissue by doing this stretch: Sit with the ankle of your injured foot across your opposite thigh. Pull your toes toward your shin with your hand until you feel a stretch in the arch. Run your opposite hand along the sole of your foot; you should feel a taut band of tissue. Do 10 stretches, holding each for 10 seconds. Then stand and massage your foot by rolling it on a golf ball or full water bottle.

To reduce pain, wear supportive shoes or sandals with a contoured foot bed at all times. Choose walking shoes that are not too flexible in the middle. "They should be bendable at the ball but provide stiffness and support at the arch," says Melinda Reiner, DPM, vice president of the American Association for Women Podiatrists. Off-the-shelf orthotic inserts (by Dr. Scholl's or Spenco, for example) or a custom-made pair can help absorb some of the impact of walking, especially on hard surfaces.

Until you can walk pain free, stick to

flat, stable, giving paths (such as a level dirt road), and avoid pavement, sand, and uneven ground that might cause too much flexing at the arch, says Phillip Ward, DPM, a podiatrist in Pinehurst, North Carolina. If the condition worsens, ask a podiatrist to prescribe a night splint to stabilize your foot in a slightly flexed position, which will counteract tightening while you sleep.

SORENESS OR SWELLING ON THE SIDES OF YOUR TOES

Could be: ingrown toenails

Tender tootsies can develop when the corners or sides of your toenails grow sideways rather than forward, putting pressure on surrounding soft tissue and even growing into the skin. You may be more likely to develop ingrown toenails if your shoes are too short or too tight, which causes repeated trauma to the toe as you walk, says Dr. Ward. If the excess pressure goes on too long, such as on an extended hike or charity walk, bleeding could occur under the nail, and the toenail might eventually fall off.

What you can do about it: Leave wiggle room in your shoes. You may need to go up a half size when you buy sneakers because feet tend to swell during exercise. Use toenail clippers (not fingernail clippers or scissors) to cut straight across instead of rounding the corners. "People who overpronate when they walk can exacerbate existing problems in the big toes," says Dr. Ward, who suggests using inserts to reduce pronation. Especially if you have diabetes or any circulatory disorder, have your ingrown toenails treated by a podiatrist (find one at www.apma.org).

PAIN IN THE BACK OF YOUR HEEL AND LOWER CALF

Could be: Achilles tendinitis

The Achilles tendon, which connects the calf muscle to the heel, can be irritated by walking too much, especially if you don't build up to it. Repeated flexing of the foot when walking up and down steep hills or on uneven terrain can also strain the tendon.

What you can do about it: For mild cases, reduce your mileage—or substitute non-weight-bearing activities such as swimming or upper-body training, so long as these don't aggravate the pain. "Avoid walking uphill because this increases the

---

Quick Tip

See a specialist for pain that lasts longer than a few weeks. Good choices include orthopedic surgeons, physiatrists, podiatrists (for foot problems), and physical therapists.

---

stretch on the tendon, irritating it and making it weaker," says Schuemann. Regular calf stretches may help prevent Achilles tendinitis, says Michael J. Mueller, PT, PhD, an associate professor of physical therapy at Washington University School of Medicine in St. Louis.

In severe cases, limit or stop walking, and place cold packs on the injured area for 15 to 20 minutes, up to three or four times a day, to reduce inflammation and pain. When you return to walking, keep the foot in a neutral position by sticking to flat surfaces, and gradually increase your distance and intensity.

PAIN ON THE BONY SIDE OF YOUR BIG TOE

Could be: a bunion

A bunion develops when the bones in the joint on the outer side of the big or little toe become misaligned, forming a painful swelling. Walkers with flatfeet, low arches, or arthritis may be more apt to develop the problem.

What you can do about it: "Wear shoes that are wider—especially in the toe box," says Dr. Ward. If you don't want to shell out for new shoes, ask your shoe repair guy to stretch your old ones. Cushioning the bunion with over-the-counter pads can also provide relief, and icing it for 20 minutes after walking will numb the area. Ultrasound or other physical therapy treatments may reduce the inflammation. Severe cases can require surgery to remove the bony protrusion and realign the toe joint.

AN ACHE IN YOUR MID TO LOWER BACK

Could be: lumbar strain

Walking doesn't usually cause lower-back problems, but the repetitive movement can make an existing lower-back injury worse. It's easy to "throw out your back" when tendons and ligaments around the spine are overworked. Arthritis or inflammation of surrounding nerves can also cause pain in this region.

What you can do about it: For general back health, keep the muscles in your trunk strong. While you walk, engage your abs by pulling your belly button toward your spine as if you were trying to flatten your belly to zip up tight jeans. "Avoid bending over at the waist, a tendency when you are walking fast or uphill," says Schuemann. "Instead, keep your spine elongated and lean your whole body slightly forward from your ankles."

A shirt pull exercise might also prevent slumping by realigning your posture. You can even do it while you walk. Simply cross your arms at your wrists in front of your waist and raise your arms as though pulling a shirt up over your head. Grow taller as you reach up, then lower your arms, letting your shoulders drop into place. Tight hamstrings and hip flexors can also cause postural distortions that put pressure on the lower back, says Joel Press, MD, medical director of the Spine & Sports Rehabilitation

If the Shoe Fits...

When it comes to walking workouts, there's nothing more important than a good shoe. "Don't think that you can just go to the store and pick out cheap fitness shoes simply because you are a beginner or don't walk much," says Melinda Reiner, DPM, vice president of the American Association for Women Podiatrists. Different feet need different shoes. To find a perfect pair, keep these tips in mind.

Choose a walking shoe. Any old shoe may work, but a shoe designed for walking will decrease your risk of injury and boost performance. A good one will be flexible in the ball of the foot but not in the arch. (A shoe that bends in the arch will place increased stress on the plantar fascia.) The heel should be cushioned (you don't need a lot of padding in the forefoot) and also rounded to speed your foot through the heel-toe motion with ease.

Center of the Rehabilitation Institute of Chicago, so you want to be sure to keep those areas flexible, too.

PAIN IN THE BALL OF YOUR FOOT OR BETWEEN YOUR TOES

Could be: a neuroma

If tissue surrounding a nerve near the base of the toes thickens, it can cause tingling, numbness, or pain that radiates to surrounding areas. It may feel as though you're treading on a marble. This condition, known as Morton's neuroma, frequently develops between the base of the third and fourth toes. It's up to 10 times more common in women than men, possibly because women's feet are structured differently and because they tend to wear narrow, high shoes or very flat ones. "If you have Morton's neuroma, walking can irritate it," says Dr. Ward.

What you can do about it: Treatment varies from simply wearing roomier shoes to surgery, depending upon the severity of the neuroma. See a podiatrist at the first sign of pain because this condition can worsen quickly. Make sure that your walking shoes have a spacious

Go offline for a fit. This is one purchase that must be made in person. Whether you have low arches or tend to overpronate, the salespeople in a good, technical running store will watch you walk barefoot and help you choose the features you need. It's best to try a store that's independently owned.

Buy big. People—women especially—tend to buy shoes that are too small. Ask the salesperson to help you check the fit, and don't get caught up in thinking that you have to buy a size 8 because that's what you've always worn. Athletic shoes can be sized quite differently from your dress shoes.

Toss 'em often. Don't skimp on your feet. Once the interior padding has lost its spring, it's time for a new pair. Generally, that means replacing your shoes every 500 miles—sooner if you have foot, ankle, knee, or back problems.

toe box. Limit your time spent hoofing it in heels; if you must wear them, travel to work or a social event in comfy shoes, and then slip on a more stylish pair. Over-the-counter insoles or pads that relieve pressure and absorb shock may help, too.

STIFFNESS OR SORENESS IN YOUR SHINS

Could be: shin splints

Your shins have to bear as much as six times your weight while you exercise, so foot-pounding activities can cause problems for the muscles and surrounding tissues and create inflammation. The strain results from strong calves pulling repeatedly on weaker muscles near the shin. "Walkers who walk too much too soon, or too fast too soon, or who go up a lot of hills are susceptible to this injury because the foot has to flex more with each step, which overworks the shin muscles," explains Frank Kelly, MD, an orthopedic surgeon in Macon, Georgia, and a spokesperson for the American Academy of Orthopaedic Surgeons. Spending too many hours walking on concrete can

also lead to this sort of inflammation. Severe or pinpointed pain in the shin could also be a stress fracture of the tibia. (See the section on stress fractures on page 168.)

What you can do about it: Cut back on your walking for 3 to 8 weeks to give the tissues time to heal. "If it hurts to walk, avoid it," says Dr. Press. You might need an anti-inflammatory medication, such as ibuprofen, or cold packs to reduce swelling and relieve pain. In the meantime, keep in shape by cross-training with low-impact exercises such as swimming or cycling.

You should also strengthen the muscles in the front of the lower leg (anterior tibialis) to help prevent a recurrence. Use this simple exercise: While standing, lift your toes toward your shins 20 times. Work up to three sets and, as you get stronger, lay a 2- or 3-pound ankle weight across your toes to add more resistance. Once you're ready to start walking again, choose a dirt path and walk for 20 minutes at a moderate pace. Increase distance or speed slightly each week. "If your shins start to feel sore, rest for a day or two, and when you exercise again, take it even more slowly," says

Byron Russell, PhD, chair of the department of physical therapy at Eastern Washington University in Spokane.

SORENESS ON THE OUTSIDES OF HIPS

Could be: bursitis

Although there are many potential causes of hip pain, it's common for the fluid-filled sacs (bursae) that cushion the hip joint to become inflamed with repetitive stress. People who have one leg slightly longer than the other are more susceptible to this condition. Too much walking without building up to it can also be a cause.

What you can do about it: Instead of walking, ride a stationary bike, swim, or do some other non-weight-bearing activity for a few weeks, says Dr. Kelly, who also suggests an over-the-counter anti-inflammatory medication to lessen the discomfort. "When you begin walking again, don't just step back in where you left off. Start gradually: Walk every other day at first. Spend the first 5 minutes warming up by walking slowly, and do the last 5 minutes at a slower, cooldown pace," he says. In more severe cases, you

may temporarily need a cane or crutches to reduce pressure.

THROBBING IN THE FRONT OF YOUR KNEECAP

Could be: runner's knee

Every time your shoe strikes the ground, your knee feels it. Eventually, your kneecap may start to rub against your femur (the bone that connects your knee to your hip), causing cartilage damage and tendinitis. Walkers with a misaligned kneecap, prior injury, weak or imbalanced thigh muscles, soft knee cartilage, or flat feet—or those who simply walk too much—are at greater risk of runner's knee. The pain usually appears when walking downhill, while doing knee bends, or during prolonged sitting.

What you can do about it: Shift to another type of exercise until the pain subsides, typically 8 to 12 weeks. Do some quad strengtheners to help align the kneecap and beef up support around the knee. Sit with your back against a wall, your right leg bent with your foot flat on floor and your left leg straight in front of you. Contract your quads and lift your left leg, keeping your foot flexed. Repeat 12 times; work up to three sets per leg. While standing, place a looped band around both of your feet and side-step 12 to 15 times to the right, then back to the left. When walking or hiking downhill, take smaller steps and try not to bend your knees too much, or try walking sideways to give your side hip muscles a workout.

ACUTE PAIN IN YOUR FOOT OR LOWER LEG

Could be a: stress fracture

If you feel tenderness or pain when you press on a specific spot on your foot or lower leg, you may have a stress fracture—a tiny crack in a bone. Most common in the lower leg, they tend to occur when leg muscles become overloaded from repetitive stress because the bone, rather than the muscle, absorbs the shock.

This can happen if you ignore a shin splint, for instance; the continued strain on muscles and tissues will eventually shift to the bone. Walking is more likely to lead to a stress fracture if you walk too long without building up to it, especially if you have high arches or flat, rigid feet. Women may be more vulnerable because their muscle mass and bone density don't always act as adequate shock absorbers.

What you can do about it: Kick back and let the area heal for several weeks. "You need to get off your feet to avoid loading the bones," says Sheila Dugan,

Baby Steps

"It's all too easy to stress tissues by going a little too far, too fast," says Byron Russell, PT, PhD, chair of the department of physical therapy at Eastern Washington University in Spokane. "People think, 'I'm just walking,' so they don't try to build up gradually. But if you're not yet in shape, your body can't tolerate longer distances or fast paces, especially if you have an existing problem." If you're getting started, walk just 10 to 20 minutes on mostly flat ground five times a week; then increase the time by 5 to 10 percent each week.

MD, a physiatrist and an assistant professor at Rush Medical College. Try replacing walking with swimming, water aerobics, or upper-body weight training.

When you return to your regular regimen, stop before you feel any discomfort. "If you walk 1 mile and experience symptoms again, then start walking a quarter mile and take several weeks to build up to the longer distance," says Dr. Russell. Replace walking shoes when the interior cushioning has worn down, to ensure that you have adequate shock absorption.

To optimize bone health, do some lower-body strength-training twice a week, and eat calcium-rich foods like yogurt, cheese, and greens such as kale or take a supplement. Women should get 1,000 milligrams of calcium a day (1,200 milligrams if age 51-plus).

CHAPTER 19

THE MULTITASKER'S WORKOUT

These combination exercises will give you a speedy and powerful workout

It may not be a magical pill, but lifting weights can *significantly* reduce high blood sugar. In a 6-month study of 36 people ages 60 to 80, Australian researchers found that those who ate a healthy diet and followed a weight-lifting program saw blood sugar fall three times faster than those who simply dieted. Plus they lost body fat.

Crunched for time? Don't skip your strength-training—downsize it. By doing exercises that simultaneously target the muscle groups in your abs, rear, legs, back, and chest, you can spend less time sweating and still get the firming benefits of a full-length workout.

"Combination exercises that hit multiple body parts are great for allover body shaping because your muscles are constantly working," says *Prevention* advisor and exercise physiologist Kara Gallagher, PhD, of the University of Louisville in Kentucky. Since you work your upper and lower body at the same time, you also raise your heart rate and burn more calories for a mini–cardio kick. The result: "You're fitter and stronger, so you can power walk and play your favorite sports longer without getting tired," she says.

Here are Dr. Gallagher's secrets for a speedy and powerful workout.

WORKOUT BASICS

Do 10 to 12 reps of each move. Then repeat the sequence. The entire workout should take 15 minutes. Aim to do it on 3 nonconsecutive days a week.

You'll need 5- to 10-pound dumbbells. Combination moves are challenging, so start with a lighter weight than normal. Also, you'll need an exercise ball. This is a shortcut essential—just maintaining balance works muscles. Most women need a 55-centimeter ball; check the sizing chart on the package. You can find a ball for about $25 at sporting goods stores.

You should see results in 2 to 4 weeks. To squeak in even more aerobic benefits, jump rope, do jumping jacks, or jog in place for up to 2 minutes between exercises. "You'll get the fitness of a traditional aerobics routine and the lean muscle tissue of a weight-training program in half the time," says exercise scientist Gary A. Sforzo, PhD, of Ithaca College in New York. If you do this routine twice with a 2-minute burst of cardio between each set, you'll get 20 minutes of cardio and a full strength-training routine in just over half an hour!

CURTSY WITH FRONT RAISE

(glutes, quads, hamstrings, calves, abs, back, and shoulders)

STAND with your feet together, holding a dumbbell in your left hand. Take a giant step back and to the right with your left leg so that your left foot ends up at the 5 o'clock position.

BEND your knees and lower your body until your right thigh is almost parallel to the floor and raise your left arm to shoulder height. Return to the start. Do a full set on each side.

PLIÉ SQUAT WITH ARM CURL

(glutes, hamstrings, quads, and biceps)

STAND up tall with your feet wider than shoulder-width apart and your toes pointed out. Hold a dumbbell in each hand, with your arms down at your sides and your hands in front of your legs with your palms facing out.

BEND your knees and lower your butt until your thighs are almost parallel to the floor. Your knees should not travel past your toes. As you squat, bend your elbows and curl the dumbbells toward your shoulders. Pause and return to the start position.

BALL CURL WITH CHEST PRESS

(abs, chest, triceps, and shoulders)

HOLDING a dumbbell in each hand, lie on an exercise ball, supported from your upper back to your hips. Position the weights at either side of your chest, with the ends facing each other.

CONTRACT your 3abs and curl your head, shoulders, and upper back off of the ball. As you come up, extend your arms and press the weights over your chest. Pause and then reverse the move, going back to the starting position.

LUNGE ROW

(quads, hamstrings, glutes, back, and biceps)

HOLDING a dumbbell in your right hand with your arm at your side, take a giant step forward with your left leg. Bend your knees and lower until your left thigh is parallel to the floor. At the same time, bend from your hips and lower the dumbbell down to the inside of your left foot.

BEND your elbow and pull the dumbbell back toward your chest, and then straighten your legs and press back to standing, keeping your left foot in front of your right. Complete a full set, then switch legs and arms.

BALL PUSHUP WITH HIP HIKE

(chest, triceps, shoulders, and abs)

Lie facedown on an exercise ball with both of your hands on the floor. Walk your hands out, allowing the ball to roll beneath your body until it's under your thighs. Your hands should be directly beneath your shoulders. Tighten your abs and lower your chest toward the floor.

Press back up and immediately bend your hips and lift them up toward the ceiling as if you were going into a handstand. Pause, and then lower to the start.

CHAPTER 20

GYM SEARCHING

Here's how to find the right gym for you

Much more so than for men, for many women, stepping into a gym brings back a flood of memories—unflattering gym uniforms, smelly locker rooms, and being picked last for kickball, again. No wonder many women rank choosing a gym right up there with buying a swimsuit among their least favorite tasks. However, it doesn't have to be that hard, and the rewards of gym membership can be great.

"For years, I tried to exercise at home, but after feeding the pets, cutting the grass, cleaning the house, and helping my child with homework, the last thing on my mind was the treadmill in our family room," says Jane Duvall, 49, an office assistant in Iowa City. "Finally, after seeing my mom in the hospital with numerous health problems, I bucked up and joined a gym. The personal attention and the sight of other women getting in shape was exactly the motivation I needed. I lost 52 pounds in 3 years."

Duvall's story is remarkable, but research suggests that her success is far from unique. Recently, scientists at the University of Western Australia studied 126 women and found that those who exercised at a gym were four times more likely to stick with their routine than were those who worked out at home.

Although the women in the study were supervised while they exercised, you don't need a trainer by your side to get better results at a health club than at home, says Wayne Westcott, PhD, who has observed thousands of women's workout habits as research director for the South Shore YMCA in Quincy, Massachusetts. "Gyms offer a range of activities to keep you from getting bored," he says. "And you typically work out harder in a gym because you're less likely to get distracted by the phone, kids, or laundry."

GETTING WHAT YOU NEED

Health clubs are catering to women like Duvall more than ever before. The old gray and swampy weight rooms—once a bastion of no-neck jocks—have been scrubbed, shined, and stocked with women-friendly features such as saunas, stairclimbers, and even child care. The result: more personal attention and convenience and an emphasis on machines that trim and tone (cardio equipment and weight-training machines), as opposed to megapound free weights that build power and bulk.

Class schedules once dominated by standard-issue aerobic sessions now have jazzy new lineups including Cardio Salsa, Urban Yoga, and Pilates Strength. Plus, not a gym in the country can get away with omitting personal services such as customized fitness training and counseling in nutrition and weight loss. Having figured out that convenience and pampering (in addition to weight loss) are among women's most basic desires, clubs have begun offering a vast assortment of on-site extras: day care, hair salons, dry cleaning, gourmet take-out, massages, and facials.

With the types of services and facilities available today, there's no excuse for not finding a gym that's right for you. Still, in surveying our readers, *Prevention* heard over and over again that family responsibilities and lack of time and money were prohibiting them from making regular appearances at the gym. So we asked the leading experts how to turn these top excuses into get-to-the-gym solutions.

EXCUSE: "I HAVE NO TIME"

"I work 9- or 10-hour days—sometimes even longer—and I always think that if I'm going to make the effort to go to the gym, I'd better spend at least $1\frac{1}{2}$ hours there," says Meana Kasi, 26, a marketing manager in Silver Spring, Maryland. "Because I don't have that much time, I just never go."

Solution: Streamline your workout. Look for a gym—ideally, one within 15 minutes of your home or office—that has circuit training. These quick workouts mix short bouts of cardio with resistance training for a total-body workout in less than an hour. "I love that I can get in a complete workout in 30 minutes," says Melissa Coulstring, 28, a children's mental health counselor in Belleville, Ontario, who goes to Curves, the women-only fitness-club chain that popularized this trend.

EXCUSE: "I'M STRAPPED FOR CASH"

"I wish gyms would stop charging so much," says Edie Chow, 31, a retail sales associate in New York City. "I just can't afford to spend $250 on an initiation fee and then another $80 a month after that."

Solution: Look for the basics. You don't need a juice bar and Aveda gel in the locker room to get a great workout. Small, independent gyms may have fewer extras and luxuries, but they make up for it in price and service. Typically, small facilities charge $20 to $40 a month, depending on the region—often less than half of what you'd pay at a larger club. Curves gyms are also pared down (no pools, locker rooms, or classes), but at only $29 a month, their circuit training is a great bargain.

If you want a full-service facility, check out the local YMCA. Most have a weight room, pools, classes, racquetball, a track, and more. "I couldn't believe I'd get a gym with two pools for just $20.50 a month," says Kandi Schafer, 57, a housewife in Rome City, Indiana, who joined a Y. Other low-cost or possibly free options include church gyms (free), municipally run gyms (as little as $75 a year), and university gyms (often free or nearly free to neighbors).

EXCUSE: "I'M STUCK AT HOME WITH THE KIDS"

"My children are 7, 5, 4, and 2, and I homeschool my two oldest kids," says Jill Whipple, 27, of Navarre, Florida. "I can't drop everything to go to the gym, and I don't want to stick my kids in a playroom that's like something out of *Lord of the Flies*."

Solution: Put the kids in gym class. The International Health, Racquet & Sportsclub Association (IHRSA) reports that 70 percent of clubs offer child care, and more are adding it each year. Gyms generally charge $1 to $5 an hour per child, but many places will include several hours per week for free with your membership.

To make sure you're getting quality child care—not minimally supervised chaos—pick a gym that has a full-time daycare center manager and speak to her before joining. Also, ask what kinds of kids' programs they offer. Many places have special kids' fitness classes and craft sessions, which are much more fun for kids (and less worrisome for moms) than unstructured play-time.

EXCUSE: "I FIND THE GYM TOTALLY INTIMIDATING"

"In one gym I visited, the aerobics floor was positioned so that your rear end faced the exercise machines," says Cheryl Scott, 40, of Minneapolis, a former customer service representative. "Talk about uncomfortable!" Others say the thought of walking into a health club and not knowing how to use the equipment or perform the moves in classes such as Cardio Yoga and Pilates freaks them out. "I have this anxiety that everybody will be watching me do something wrong, and I will look like a complete idiot," says Rebecca Benitez, 33, an administrative assistant in Campbell, California.

Solution: Try a women-only club. Such a gym can be a haven if you're just getting back into a routine. "I'm much more at ease if I don't have to exercise around men," says Linda Pruneski, 43, an executive assistant in Willoughby, Ohio, who goes to Curves.

Another option is a more intimate, hands-on facility. "Small gyms are often more reassuring to the mid-thirties or mid-forties mom who has several kids, hasn't worked out in years, and doesn't want to deal with a bunch of 20-year-olds dancing around in spandex," says Todd Rotruck, a trainer in Greensboro, North Carolina, who has worked at several gyms in the past 12 years. "They're less of a meat market, and staff members pride themselves on learning members' first names and tend to dish out more personal instruction and individual attention than the big clubs will."

EXCUSE: "I KEEP STRANGE HOURS"

"I'm usually at the office until about 10 or 11 p.m.," says Audrey Henderson, 23, a public relations account executive in Venice, California. "I moved to LA in May and joined a gym, only to find that when I was ready to work out, it was closed."

Solution: Find an all-night gym. Health clubs are working overtime to accommodate early birds and night owls. Many large chains are open around-the-clock, such as Life Time Fitness, Crunch, and—no surprise—24 Hour Fitness.

Some small gyms are also willing to make special arrangements to fit your schedule if you ask. "My new facility allows me to let myself in at 5 a.m., which gives me time to work out and get to work before 8," says Rachel Reagan, 42, a banking assistant in Oklahoma City.

EXCUSE: "I'M ALWAYS ON THE ROAD"

"At my job, I log 110,000 miles a year," says Cynthia McKay, 49, a CEO for a gift basket company in Castle Rock, Colorado. "I'm sure some exercise would do wonders for my jet lag and sleepless nights, but I don't feel comfortable in hotel gyms, which tend to be isolated and too quiet and feel kind of iffy, especially for women."

Solution: Get a gym passport. Until airport gyms are commonplace—currently, only a handful of airports have them—joining a club that is a member of IHRSA's Passport program is a reasonable alternative. The program gives members of participating IHRSA clubs guest privileges (some clubs still charge a small guest fee) at more than 3,000 facilities worldwide. "At previous jobs, I traveled all over the United States and Canada," says Audrey Perry, 53, of Vernon, British Columbia, a former call center manager. "If I wanted to work out, I just went online and found a gym that was a member in the town where I was traveling and popped in with my Passport card." If you have a long layover, go to www.airportgyms.com for nearby facilities; most are within a 15-minute cab ride.

CHAPTER 21

THE TV-LOVER'S WORKOUT

Tune in and tone up

Channel surfing burns few, if any, calories, yet the average American watches nearly 5 hours of TV daily, reports Nielsen Media Research. And the risk of packing on pounds rises by 23 percent with every 2-hour increase in daily viewing, according to a Harvard study of more than 50,000 women.

But you can stay slim while you watch your favorite shows with this TV-friendly circuit designed by Cindy Whitmarsh, star of the exercise video *10 Minute Solution: Target Toning for Beginners*. The half-hour workout alternates between moderate cardio moves during the show and high-intensity cardio bursts and multimuscle strength exercises during commercials. To get started, you'll need 3- to 5-pound dumbbells, a sturdy chair, and a mat. Breaks can vary, so you may need to adjust the times slightly. Repeat the circuit if you're watching an hour-long show.

SHOWTIME CARDIO

MARCH

LIFT your knees to a comfortable height and march in place. Continue until the first commercial break.

COMMERCIAL BREAK #1

QUICK FEET

SPREAD your feet wider than hip-width apart, and take quick running steps for 30 seconds, barely lifting your feet off of the floor and keeping your hands in front of your body.

LUNGES WITH CURLS

STAND with your feet together, holding a dumbbell in each hand, your palms forward. Step your right foot forward about 2 feet. Bend your right knee and lower your left knee straight down toward the floor. (Keep your right knee over your ankle; if it's not, take a bigger step.) As you lower, bend your elbows and raise the weights toward your chest, keeping your elbows next to your body. Press into your right foot and stand back up, bringing your feet together and lowering the weights. Alternate legs for 2 minutes, taking breaks as needed.

SHOWTIME CARDIO

MARCH WITH A KICK

MARCH in place, right, left, right. Next, kick to the front with your left leg. March another three beats (left, right, left) and then kick with your right leg. Kick at a comfortable height so you don't hunch over. Continue, alternating left and right kicks between marches.

COMMERCIAL BREAK #2

HIGH KNEES

JOG in place, lifting your knees as high as you can for 30 seconds.

PUSHUPS WITH A ROW

HOLDING a dumbbell in each hand, kneel with the weights on the floor and your body extended to form a straight line from your head to your knees. Bend your elbows to your sides and slowly lower your body as close to the floor as possible. Keep your abs tight.

HOLD for a second, push back up to the starting position, and do a row with your right arm by squeezing your shoulder blades, bending your elbow, and lifting the dumbbell toward your chest. Hold for a second, then slowly lower the weight. Do another pushup followed by a row with your left arm. Alternate arm rows for 90 seconds, taking breaks as needed.

SHOWTIME CARDIO
STEP TOUCH

STEP your right foot to the side about 2 feet and tap your left foot next to your right foot. Then step your left foot out about 2 feet and tap your right foot next to your left. Continue stepping side to side.

COMMERCIAL BREAK #3
JUMPING JACKS

STAND with your feet together and your arms at your sides. Hop, spreading your feet apart and raising your arms overhead. Hop again, bringing your feet together and returning your arms to your sides. Continue for 30 seconds.

WALL SQUATS WITH SIDE RAISES

HOLD a dumbbell in each hand, press your back against a wall, point your toes forward, and slide down the wall until your legs form 90-degree angles, with your knees directly over your ankles. (Scoot your feet farther away from the wall, if needed.) Bend your arms at 90-degree angles so the dumbbells are about waist height in front. Slowly lift your arms out to the sides until the dumbbells are at shoulder height. Hold for a second, then slowly lower back to the starting position. Repeat for 45 seconds.

WALL SQUATS
WITH SHOULDER PRESSES

MAINTAINING the wall squat (you can stand if this is too hard), position the dumbbells slightly above shoulder height with your palms facing forward and your elbows out to the sides. Slowly press the dumbbells overhead until your arms are almost straight. Hold for a second, then slowly lower. Repeat for 45 seconds.

SHOWTIME CARDIO
KICKBACKS

STEP your right foot to the side about 2 feet and kick your left foot up behind you toward your butt. Then lower your left foot out to the side and kick your right foot up behind you. Let your arms swing forward and back as you alternate sides.

COMMERCIAL BREAK #4

SKI JUMPS

JUMP from side to side, as if you were hopping over a line. Keep your feet together and bend your knees when you land. Jump for 30 seconds.

TRICEPS DIPS

PLACE your hands on the sides of a sturdy chair with your feet flat on the floor and bend your knees 90 degrees. Bending your elbows behind you, slowly lower your body until your arms form 90-degree angles. Hold for a second, then press back up. Repeat for 45 seconds.

DUMBBELL TWISTS

Sit with your legs bent and your feet off of the floor. Hold a dumbbell in front of your chest. Rotate your torso (and the dumbbell) slowly from side to side for 45 seconds. (If this is too challenging, keep your feet flat on the floor with your knees bent.)

CHAPTER 22

THE NO-MORE-CRUNCHES BELLY-FLATTENING PLAN

This ultraeffective 20-minute workout will tone your tummy fast

In the endless quest for a flat belly, you've likely done hundreds (if not thousands) of crunches and balanced in plank poses for hours. And let us guess: You still don't have flat abs, right? Well, we have news for you: The latest research shows that it's not your fault.

"The way most people do crunches doesn't work the rectus abdominis [front abdominal muscle] effectively. That's why you can do thousands and not see much benefit," says abdominal activity researcher Gilbert M. Willett, a physical therapist at the University of Nebraska Medical Center in Omaha. Testing ways to put more punch in every crunch, Willett and colleagues monitored the muscle activity of 25 people while they did crunches following different sets of instructions, such as pushing the belly out or pulling it in, or no instructions at all. They found that when testers sucked in their abs before curling off the floor, they generated twice as much muscle activity as when they didn't prep their abs. "They not only worked their front abdominal muscles but also the oblique muscles on the sides, which help you look trimmer through the waist," says Willett.

FAB AB REVIEW

That simple yet potent tip got us thinking: What if we could find the best belly-flattening advice science had to offer and rolled it into one ultraeffective, easy-to-do program? After poring through research and scientific reviews, even we were surprised by all the tricks and tips that can maximize the belly-flattening power of exercise. The result is *Prevention's* best belly-flattening plan ever. Here are the key elements for going from flab to fab.

Cue before you crunch. By prepping your abs, you get more muscle activity out of every move. Before you roll up, pull your navel toward your spine. Keep the abs hollowed throughout the move, imagining your ribs flaring out to the sides. This activates the obliques and makes each rep more effective.

Hit your B-side. One recent study revealed that the lats (midback muscles) play an important role in performing core-based activities such as torso twisting and bending, yet they are often overlooked during core-strengthening routines, which tend to focus on the abs, obliques, and lower-back muscles alone. "Strong back muscles not only help you function better but also contribute to the overall appearance of your front because they help you stand straighter and balance your body," explains study researcher Wendi Weimar, PhD, an associate professor of biomechanics at Auburn University in Alabama.

Get off-balance. Another study found that single arm and leg exercises are good core challengers because your trunk acts like the "middleman," keeping you stable as you move your limbs, says Canadian exercise researcher David Behm, PhD, a professor of human kinetics at Memorial University of Newfoundland in St. John's. "Better trunk activation results in more toned muscles, which improves the appearance of loose, sagging tummy muscles and provides a slimmer, more compact waistline," he says.

Work the reverse. The rectus abdominis is one long continuous muscle running from your ribs to your hips. Though you can't completely isolate the upper (six-pack) region from the lower (belly pooch), you should exercise in a way that fires as many fibers as possible throughout the entire muscle. That means adding leg lift–type crunches to your repertoire. Another University of Nebraska Medical Center study of traditional ab exercises revealed that the "reverse crunch," where you keep your torso down and lift your legs, gets the lower portion of your rectus abdominis buzzing more than traditional crunches alone, and it's equally good at firing the upper abs.

THE FLATTEN FAST PLAN

Unlike traditional belly-flattening plans, this routine includes all the key elements we've just discussed to target your entire core—front, lower back, midback, and sides—from every angle to sculpt a tight, trim torso. The best part: You won't only look better, you'll feel better, too. "Back problems aren't just from major traumatic events, like picking up heavy objects," says Dr. Behm. "More frequently, they're from simply moving or flexing with poor posture and a tired, out-of-shape back." A strong core can prevent both.

Do the following 20-minute workout 3 nonconsecutive days a week. Perform two sets of the specified number of reps for each exercise, allowing 1 minute of rest between sets. On days you don't do the routine, keep your body moving with activities such as walking, swimming, or cycling to burn more calories and shed excess belly fat.

BELLY-BLASTING MOVES
DIAMONDS

Lie faceup on the floor with your knees open to the sides and the soles of your feet together. Clasp your hands and extend your arms over your chest. "Hollow" your stomach by pulling your navel toward your spine. Then lift your head and shoulders off of the floor, reaching as far forward as comfortably possible. Hold for a moment, slowly lower to the start position, and repeat. Perform 15 to 25 reps.

ONE-ARM BAND PULL

Stand with your feet hip-width apart. Hold an exercise band overhead with your hands about 18 inches apart. Position your right arm over-head and hold your left hand out to the side with your elbow bent about 90 degrees. (The band should be taut.) Keeping your right arm stable, contract your ab and back muscles and pull your left arm down until your left hand is in line with your chest. Hold for a moment, slowly return to the start position, and repeat. Perform 15 reps. Then switch sides and repeat. To further engage your core muscles, do the move balancing on one foot, then the other.

DOUBLE TWIST

Sit on the floor with your knees bent and your hands clasped just above your thighs. Keeping your back straight, lean back slightly, tighten your abs, lift your feet off of the floor, and balance. Rotate your upper body to the right, bringing your hands as close to the floor as possible, while simultaneously dropping your knees to the left (opposite) side. Return to the center and repeat. Perform 10 twists to the left, then repeat to the right.

T PLANK

Assume a full pushup position with your arms extended and your hands directly beneath your shoulders. Hold for 10 seconds. Rotate your body to the right, allowing your feet to naturally turn onto their sides, and extend your left arm toward the ceiling. Keep your hips lifted, so your body forms a diagonal T. Hold for 10 seconds. Return to the start position and repeat to the opposite side. That's 1 rep. Perform 2 or 3 reps.

KNEELING SIDE KICK

FROM a kneeling position, lean to the right and place your right hand on the floor directly beneath your shoulder. Extend your left leg out to the side so it's parallel to the floor with your foot pointed. Place your left hand behind your head.

CONTRACT your abs and bend your left leg, pulling your knee toward your chest. Straighten your leg and repeat. Perform 15 to 20 reps. Switch arms and legs and repeat.

ROLL AND REACH

Lie faceup with your legs bent, your knees pulled toward your chest, and your hands clasping your shins. Inhale and "hollow" your abs. Exhale as you roll up to a sitting position, balancing on your tailbone, and then extend your legs down to the floor. Bend forward from your hips and reach toward your toes.

Inhale, sit back up, and exhale as you slowly roll back one vertebrae at a time onto the floor, keeping your legs extended. Return to the start position and repeat. Perform 5 to 10 reps.

EXTEND 'N' CURL

KNEEL with your hands directly beneath your shoulders and your knees directly beneath your hips. Keep your back straight and your head in line with your spine. Simultaneously raise your left arm and right leg, extending them in line with your back so your fingers are pointing straight ahead and your toes are pointing back. Then contract your abs and draw your left elbow and right knee together beneath your torso.

EXTEND and repeat. Perform 10 reps, switch arms and legs, and repeat.

AB PIKE

Lie faceup with your arms at your sides. Bend your legs so your feet are off of the floor, your thighs are over your hips, and your heels are near your glutes. As you "hollow" your abs, straighten your legs and lift your hips up off of the floor. Hold for a moment and slowly lower back to the start position, bringing your hips down and bending your legs. Perform 10 to 15 reps.

MEDICAL BREAKTHROUGHS

Want the latest workout news? Look no further.

BEAT YOUR ENERGY CRISIS

Lack of go-power is one of the biggest barriers to working out, according to a study of 120 women by the Barnes-Jewish College of Nursing and Allied Health in St. Louis. (Two others are self-discipline and lack of time.) If inertia is your excuse, fuel up fast: Have a healthy carbohydrate snack about an hour before your walk or workout, advises Lona Sandon, RD, a nutritionist at the University of Texas Southwestern Medical Center in Dallas. Sandon's favorite pick-me-ups: a banana, a glass of fruit juice, peanut butter, or a granola bar.

POWER UP

Want more energy for your workouts? Start with aerobics—such as jogging, walking, or step class—and then do your weight lifting. In an 8-week study of 13 male athletes, University of Rhode Island researchers found that those who began their workout by running on a treadmill for 20 minutes and finished with a basic all-body strength-training session reported having more energy throughout than athletes who did the workout in reverse order.

Lifting weights breaks down muscle fibers—a good thing, but the researchers speculate this leads to a greater feeling of fatigue during the aerobic exercise that follows.

GET GOING

A 10-year study at the University of Western Ontario, in London, Ontario, discovered that you can cut diabetes and heart disease risk with exercise by 50 percent—even if you don't start until you're 55. All it takes is 30 to 45 minutes of walking, 3 days a week.

SUGAR UP?
GO DOWNHILL

If you worry that downhills are a waste of workout time, don't. Austrian researchers tracked two groups (45 people in all) for 4 months. The volunteers hiked 3 to 5 days a week in one direction on a long hill—either up or down. The downhill hikers had a 25 percent drop in blood sugar levels, compared with a 9 percent dip among the uphill crew. The reason may be that leg muscles demand more blood as they lengthen on a downhill, and more flow helps clear sugar.

No long hills to descend? Staircases in tall buildings are another option.

BURN BELLY FAT FASTER

A spare tire doesn't just make it harder to button your waistband; it can hurt your heart and boost the risk of diabetes and cancer. But you can flatten it fast by speeding up your workouts. In an 8-month Duke University study of 175 overweight 40- to 65-year-olds, two groups exercised and a third stayed sedentary. The couch potatoes' deep, organ-smothering abdominal fat spiked 8.6 percent. A group that did low-intensity workouts (such as walking at an easy pace) for 30 minutes a day, 5 days a week, kept their girth from growing—though they did gain $1^1/_2$ pounds.

The real rewards came with higher-intensity workouts: In the same amount of time, the third group shrank their waistlines and belly fat by 7 percent, and they lost 6 pounds. "All exercise helps prevent fat gain," says researcher William Kraus, MD. "But to lose abdominal fat, you have to work harder."

How hard? In the study, successful losers aimed for an effort of 6 to 8 on a scale of 1 to 10. That's what you muster for brisk walking uphill, jogging on flat terrain, or pedaling a bike about 12 mph. Beginners should start with

10 to 15 minutes and slowly work their way up.

STOP KIDDING YOURSELF

The heavier a woman is, the more she overestimates the amount of physical activity she gets, suggests a new study from the University of Alabama. "If these ladies were doing as much as they thought, they'd burn almost 1,000 more calories a day," says lead author Gary R. Hunter, PhD. He and colleagues asked 75 overweight and normal-weight women how much time they regularly spent on 63 daily activities, such as cleaning, gardening, climbing stairs, and walking.

After measuring the calories the women actually burned, the researchers found that both groups overestimated their activity, but the heavier women overshot it by more than 900 calories a day; women who weren't overweight missed by about 600 calories a day. The heavier women's misperceptions most likely stemmed from their lack of physical fitness, says Dr. Hunter. "If you're out of shape, you'll have more difficulty walking and climbing stairs, and thus you overestimate the time

it takes," he says. "If people already think they're physically active, then there's really no reason to do more."

LOSE FAT FASTER

Less is more—that's news you don't expect to hear from the gym crowd. New research presented at the American College of Sports Medicine's 2004 meeting found that, over a 2-month period, men who did one set of upper-body weight-lifting exercises had equal strength gains (21 percent) and better fat loss (19 percent versus 10 percent) than those who did three sets.

How can you gain strength and lose more fat with a third of the effort? The British researchers believe that the tiring three-set workout may cause exercisers to overcompensate with calories at their next meal. Women could expect the same results, these scientists say.

TREAT FEET RIGHT

It's a plus-size predicament: You need to exercise to lose weight, but your heaviness can lead to injury. "Joint and foot pain are common problems," says Baltimore orthopedist Stuart Miller, MD, who oversaw a recent survey of 6,000 adults that linked high body mass index with foot and ankle woes. What's a heavy exerciser to do?

Go slow. "Start with just 10 minutes a day," says Dr. Miller. As activity becomes more comfortable, aim for a half hour to an hour of activity every day.

Support your soles. Insoles such as Spenco or Superfeet help evenly distribute weight over your foot, easing impact.

Mix it up. Try non-weight-bearing activities such as cycling and swimming to give your joints a break.

Stretch it out. Stretching is the best way to avoid common heel pain known as plantar fasciitis. Stand an arm's length from a wall. Place one foot behind the other, keeping your heels down and your knees straight. Bracing with your arms, lean into the wall so that you feel your calf stretch.

PART V

STRESS LESS

CHAPTER 23

THE STRESS SURVIVAL GUIDE

Here are six stressed-out women's road-tested strategies for conquering the biggest threat to women's health

Researchers have linked dozens of physical symptoms to stress overload, from fatigue to weight gain. Add another symptom to that list: the risk for high blood sugar.

When you're stressed, your body is primed to take action. This "gearing up" is what causes your heart to beat faster, your breath to quicken, and your stomach to knot. It also triggers your blood sugar to skyrocket.

"Under stress, your body goes into fight-or-flight mode, raising blood sugar levels to prepare you for action," says Richard Surwit, PhD, author of *The Mind-Body Diabetes Revolution* and chief of medical psychology at Duke University. If your cells are insulin resistant, the sugar builds up in your blood, with nowhere to go.

What's more, one of the major responses to stress is depression, which is considered to be a primary risk factor for cardiovascular disease. This can be a particular problem for people with high blood sugar, who are already at higher-than-normal risk of heart disease. Stress raises blood pressure, which damages the lining of blood vessels. At the same time, substances that are released during times of stress, such as fatty acids, are trapped in these damaged areas. This leads to the development of plaques, fatty deposits that can block bloodflow, increase the risk of clots, and possibly lead to heart attacks.

To make matters worse, having diabetes is in itself a source of stress—one that's unlikely to go away. Still, there's plenty you can do to reduce the stress of living with this condition.

GOT STRESS?

Even if you were one of the few American women who don't occasionally feel like ripping their hair out, you'd probably be ashamed to admit it. Like it or not, stress has become a status symbol, the badge a woman wears to prove she has a full, active life.

But women may pay dearly for that stress—with chronic health problems or even their lives. Sure, some let stress roll right off them. Others just think they do. Over time, stress—and the parade of nasty chemicals it sends through the body when a deadline looms or a kid talks back—grinds away at your cells. That wear and tear triggers everything from insomnia to heart failure and exacerbates many other conditions, including headaches, digestive problems, and obesity.

Prevention found six women with significant stress-induced health issues who fought back, developing their own arsenal of stress-busting habits and weapons. Their experiences can help you get through each day stronger, calmer, and more in charge of your life than ever.

TERESA KAY-ABA KENNEDY

Stress problem: digestive troubles

36; single; yoga instructor; and entrepreneur, New York City

"In 1997, I spent 10 days in the hospital before I was diagnosed with Crohn's disease. I almost died." Although the precise causes of Crohn's—a painful inflammatory bowel disease (IBD) that affects about 1 million Americans—and IBD are unknown, stress may worsen the disease.

Knew she was in trouble when: "I read

what the doctor wrote on my chart; he called me a workaholic. Here I was, in my twenties, an MBA with a big job at MTV. I was always waving off my boyfriend when he tried to talk to me about balance. Working until 1 a.m. was normal—and fun. And here's a doctor writing, 'TV executive, high stress, never takes vacations.' In his eyes, I was a stress case. It was very humbling."

How stress fooled her: "I never felt stressed-out, even though I had some physical symptoms. I thought I was the picture of health; I even had six-pack abs." When she injured her back during a workout, the pain medication aggravated the Crohn's, putting her back at square one.

What saved her: Yoga. "For a year, I couldn't even lift myself out of a bathtub because of the inflamed disk in my back. At first, my approach to yoga was just to practice breathing." Over the next year, she gained strength and then began to train as a teacher. In 2002, she founded the Ta Yoga House in Harlem. "I know I'm a type A yogi, but my practice has given me a new sense of managing my energy. I've rebuilt my health from the ground up."

Why it works: Yoga diminished stress

symptoms in a 2004 Reed College and Oregon Health Sciences University study of 18 yoga students. And in a 2003 Spanish study, researchers found that when 42 people with Crohn's learned stress-relieving techniques, most had significantly less pain.

Early warning signs: "Mostly, my Crohn's is under control now. But when my joints start to ache—a symptom of a pending flare-up—I know I haven't been taking care of myself."

Emergency stress Rx: "I focus on breathing deeply. You can do it anytime, even if you're injured or too busy to do yoga."

Serenity strategy: "In addition to my daily yoga practice, I keep my mantra right on my computer: faith, family, and healthy food."

ALLISON WHAITE

Stress problem: obesity

30; divorced; development coordinator; home building company, San Diego

Two-thirds of Americans are overweight, and chronic stress is part of the cause. Elevated levels of the stress hormone cortisol have been linked to increases in body fat and a decreased ability to sleep, so the body has less energy to exercise and craves more quick-fix snacks.

Knew she was in trouble when: "I saw my reflection in the glare of the TV one night. I had always been a big stress eater, but I was in an unhappy marriage, which was making me eat more and more. My husband would go in one room and use the computer; I'd go in the other and eat. That night, I really saw myself, shoveling chips in my mouth while I was watching one of those home-decorating shows. I just said, 'What are you doing?' The next month, I signed up with Jenny Craig."

How stress fooled her: Research has shown that big-league stressors—like Whaite's lousy marriage and subsequent divorce—compound weight issues, regardless of what study subjects eat and how much they exercise. And in a 2003 study by the University of California, San Francisco, stressed-out rats went for foods that were high in sugar, fat, or both, instead of their normal rat chow.

What saved her: "Daily exercise. At first, I hated it. Then one day, I went walking with some friends in the park. People were there with their dogs; birds were singing; it was sunny. And I realized, this is what I need to handle my stress. When I hit my goal weight of 165 pounds, I bought myself a Tiffany bracelet that says I did it."

Why it works: Women who increase the intensity of their workouts (as Whaite did by cranking up her walking to running) reduce anxiety even more effectively, found a 2003 study.

Early warning signs: "M&M's. But as I've gotten used to eating healthy meals, it only happens every few weeks."

Emergency stress Rx: "Heading outdoors for a run or a walk, enjoying the fresh air and the scenery."

Serenity strategy: "Because stress makes me crave food, I've retrained myself to find other things that soothe me, like spending time with friends or getting manicures and pedicures."

MARLENE WELCH

Stress problem: anger

45; single; raising her 12-year-old nephew; marketing, Chicago

Women are especially vulnerable to the health risks that anger creates. A 2004 study of 1,500 women found a high correlation between needing anger management therapy and having heart disease symptoms. And women are more likely than men to take out their work-related stress and anger at home. Scientists still don't know whether women suffer more than men because they repress their anger. But they do think stress plays a key role: A study of rats found evidence of a fast-acting feedback loop, where the animal's stress and anger continually reinforced each other.

Knew she was in trouble when: "I felt like my life was falling apart. I'm a recovering alcoholic, and although I had taken care of that problem, everything was still a mess—my marriage was imploding, and I was always unhappy. I called a couples' counselor to make an appointment and over the phone, the therapist said to me, 'You sound angry.' I got mad and heard myself saying, 'I'm not angry!' I was that out of touch."

How stress fooled her: "I just didn't get the connection between stress and anger. And then it was hard for me to admit I was angry. If I admitted it, that meant I was not a nice person."

What saved her: Therapy. "Right after I started meeting weekly with Mitch Messner, the director of the Anger Clinic in Chicago, I had a really dramatic 'aha' moment. As I was telling him what was wrong, he told me I was in danger of living the rest of my life as a miserable woman. All of a sudden, it hit me. I was angry with everybody. But I had a choice. I could keep on playing the victim and be angry—or be happy. It was up to me." Though she and her husband eventually divorced, a year of regular therapy helped her see how directly her anger stemmed from the way she handled stress.

Why it works: While therapy isn't a Band-Aid for all emotional problems, researchers at Stanford University found that the coping skills learned in therapy are even more valuable for people with anger-management problems than for those with depression.

Early warning signs: "My heart pounds, I breathe faster, and I feel afraid."

Emergency stress Rx: "I'll sit down and write an 'anger letter'—a quick note to help me figure out who or what I'm really upset with or about. They aren't meant to be sent. I've written them to my ex, my parents, even myself. They clarify things. And taking 10 deep breaths helps a lot. When I do have an outburst with someone—which happens infrequently—I make sure we sit down and talk about it afterward."

Serenity strategy: "I still see the therapist from time to time, when I feel like I need to check in, and I've also run some anger-management sessions for women at the Anger Clinic. Helping other people with the same problem gives me perspective."

VALERIE SZABO

Stress problem: insomnia

40s; single; 6-year-old son; divorce lawyer, McLean, Virginia

Experts believe that the inability to get adequate sleep affects 60 million Americans, and more women than men. Stress is a primary cause, says the National Center on Sleep Disorders Research.

Knew she was in trouble when: "I once fell asleep at a meeting after winning an intense trial. The client was a doctor, and I woke up to find him taking my pulse, yelling out to my cocounsel, 'It's okay; she's not dead!'"

How stress fooled her: Szabo often has to work long hours, preparing for trials on a schedule she doesn't control. "But I was letting cases keep me up at night, often bringing files home."

What saved her: Aromatherapy. "The work I do is very emotionally draining because so often children are involved. And I'm trying to be a good mother,

trying to date. It's hard to shut those stresses out. Fragrance helps. I love roses—I planted 21 rosebushes in my backyard, just for the smell. And I like lotions and bath scents that smell pretty. Peach and orange and other citruses are energizing, but my favorites are soothing cinnamon and vanilla."

Why it works: There's a semblance of science behind the bubble-bath theory. In a study published in the *International Journal of Cosmetic Science*, researchers at the industry trade group International Flavors & Fragrances reported that the majority of the 100 women who took scented baths not only felt more relaxed but were more relaxed than those who took unscented ones. Scientists looked at electronic images of the trapezius muscles (the ones in your upper back that turn to stone when you're stuck in traffic) to measure tension levels. Another recent study found that the citrus smell of clementines made people feel happiest; vanilla made them feel most relaxed.

Early warning signs: "When I'm on the computer and it's 10:30 p.m., and then when I look up again, it's 2:30 a.m."

Emergency stress Rx: "I have a huge Jacuzzi—it's like the double-wide of

Jacuzzis—and I'll float vanilla candles in it and take a long bath before bed."

Serenity strategy: "Finishing up the day with a ritual of pretty smells, like face creams and herbal tea, helps me feel more ready for sleep."

MARY FARLEY

Stress problem: two major heart attacks, 8 years apart

54; married; two children; works part time for film production company, Mt. Kisco, New York

"When the first happened, I was in my forties, and because I was fit and had no family history of heart disease, my doctor told me it was a fluke. Eight years later, I had the second. After doing some research, my doctors and I were able to figure out that both heart attacks happened during very stressful periods. I did not have genetic or lifestyle risks, but in both cases, there was a lot of work stress, as well as a lot going on with taking care of the kids."

Heart disease is the leading killer of women in the United States, and stress is a significant contributor. Earlier this year, researchers at Johns Hopkins identified "broken heart" syndrome as a fairly com-

mon diagnosis: Stress chemicals literally stun the hearts—sometimes fatally—of those with no history or risk of heart disease. And people with elevated levels of a stress protein are seven times more likely to die within a month of their heart attack than those with lower levels, found researchers at Brigham and Women's Hospital in Boston.

Knew she was in trouble when: "My cardiologist explained that my heart problems weren't part of a chronic condition. In my case—and in many cases—stress causes an acute event inside the arteries. I have to constantly monitor my stress level, the same way a diabetic has to watch her diet."

How stress fooled her: Like many type A women, Farley imagined that because she had flexibility in her schedule, she had less stress. But a new analysis of the government's large-scale Framingham Offspring Study has shown that women who have a great deal of control over when, how, and what kind of work they do are 2.8 times more likely to develop heart disease than those who work at demanding jobs where they have little control.

What saved her: "My friends. I couldn't do without my family, but somehow, friends provide a whole different kind of support." Now she builds bonding time into her schedule: She walks and plays tennis with pals and calls an old college friend each week.

Why it works: Researchers from Duke University followed 322 heart disease patients for 2 years. Those with stronger social supports felt less stressed and had better health outcomes than those with fewer pals.

Early warning signs: "My last heart attack was 4 years ago, and I've gotten good about trotting myself over to the emergency room if I'm at all concerned. But I've also gotten more proactive about recognizing the signs of a stress buildup. I start to get twinges in my back that tell me it's time to relax."

Emergency stress Rx: "If it doesn't have to get done today, I jettison it."

Serenity strategy: "Relax. I'll sit down and read a newspaper or even do a crossword puzzle—something I hadn't done in a very long time."

KATHRYN PETRO HARPER

Stress problem: major depression

42; married; academic coach, Santa Clara, California

About 12.4 million American women (double the number of men) suffer from depression, and of those, 6.7 million have major depression, according to the National Institute of Mental Health. Research psychologists have found a direct chemical link between high levels of the damaging hormones produced by stress and depressive behavior in rats.

Knew she was in trouble when: "In 1994, I was sexually assaulted by an acquaintance. I didn't get help or support; I just avoided men for several years. I functioned but felt like I was under water. Then in 1997, I started graduate school, which was very stressful. I also started counseling, and although I gained some insights, I still felt numb all the time. In 1998, my beloved cat had to be put down, and that was the last straw. It was the darkest time of my life. I cried all the time. I felt hopeless. I had no energy."

How stress fooled her: "Eventually, I saw a psychiatrist who helped me see that although this stress-triggered major depression—started by the attack, then made much worse when my cat died— was bad, I'd had a milder form of depression for years. But I'd ignored many of the classic symptoms, like fatigue."

What saved her: Meditation and medication. Antidepressants helped get her head above water, and she continued with therapy. "I finally felt like I had an emotional skin," she says. But she wanted even greater control over the blues. When she heard about an informal class on seated Vipassana meditation, she took it. "I couldn't believe how much it helped. Meditation is so subtle and so powerful—it's not like there are any dramatic moments of enlightenment, but within a year of practicing, I was able to sit still, kind of turn off my brain, and detach from all the hubbub of my life. I'd say to myself afterward, 'Now, what was I so upset about?'"

Why it works: Researchers at the University of California, San Diego, found that meditation put people with mood disorders in a better mental state and decreased their "ruminative" thinking—chewing the same downbeat thoughts over and over.

Early warning signs: "Though I haven't had a major depression since 1998, stress can still set off a minor one. Feeling sad is fine, but when I start to feel numb, or like I can't take pleasure in all the little things, it's time to get serious."

Emergency stress Rx: "I practice mindfulness as much as possible. When I do a task, I try to be completely present in it. When cooking, for instance, I notice the colors, textures, and scents, rather than thinking about the next chore."

Serenity strategy: "I'm not shy about calling my doctor to change my medication levels if I need it. For example, my father-in-law was ill recently, so we made an adjustment. I also exercise regularly; it helps to make me tired, which makes me sleep better, which increases my energy."

CHAPTER 24

SECRETS FROM THE STRESS DOCS

23 anti-meltdown tips from top stress experts

The kids are down with the flu and so is the babysitter. And the presentation you've worked on nonstop for 3 weeks is set for 9 a.m. sharp, no excuses. We all know how debilitating stress can be when we're living through a big bad day. The corrosive hormones sent coursing through the blood during repeated bouts of aggravation can, over the years, raise your risk of heart disease, obesity, and depression. In December 2005, researchers at the University of California, San Francisco, discovered that stress triggers damage at the cellular level. Those anxiety-soaked experiences derail not only your day but your body.

To help you get through these dark days with less wear and tear, we consulted the best-known stress experts in the United States. Drawing on their own bad experiences, they talked about everything from minor annoyances to life-altering losses, revealing how they coped, what they learned, and the lessons for all of us.

KEEP YOUR PERSPECTIVE

Through her obstetrics-gynecology practice, Christiane Northrup, MD, has set new standards for treating female patients in a supportive environment. Her theories of how our mental outlook can affect our physical health have made her books runaway bestsellers. Her most recent title is *Mother-Daughter Wisdom: Creating a Legacy of Physical and Emotional Health.*

"One of the most stressful stretches of my life was a 12-city tour on public television in 14 days," says Dr. Northrup. "It was worse than being on call as a doctor. I was up late doing fund-raising for the stations, and then I'd have to get up at 7 or 8 the next morning to get to the next city by noon. The way I normally de-stress is to sleep, and I didn't really have time to sleep on this tour.

"I rushed out of my hotel at 4:30 in the afternoon to get to one station, and they told me the show wouldn't be on for another 2 hours. They had given me the wrong time—I was so angry. It was clear the producer wasn't going to fess up that they made a scheduling error. That was the most frustrating aspect." Dr. Northrup hadn't eaten, so she asked her driver to find a restaurant. "It was a downward spiral: The driver didn't know where anything was. I spotted a place, but she couldn't get off the turnpike."

When Dr. Northrup got back to the station, she told the driver to pick her up after the show, at 9:45. "I walked out, and the driver wasn't there. We had to call her cell phone, call her boss, and she said, 'I'll be there in 15 minutes.' At this point, 15 minutes would have made me insane, so someone at the station drove us to the hotel. We called the limo company and told them, 'Do not send this driver tomorrow.'" When she got back to the hotel, she immediately turned to her top stress buster:

Take a bath before bed. "I insisted on this every night. The water does something—it's very soothing. It just cleanses away the stress."

Breathe through your nose. "I perfected this technique long ago. It stimulates the parasympathetic nervous system, and it helps rest, restore, and expand the lower lungs. That helps me tremendously."

Remember to say no. "I very consciously said no to as many things as I possibly could on this tour. The schedule was insane."

Get perspective. "Ask yourself: How bad is this, really? First, did somebody die? If the answer is no, then ask, is someone deathly ill? No? We'll get over this. This is everyday stress, and these questions put it in perspective."

Use humor. "When I was in med school and things got really bad, a friend would joke that he could always drop out and join the Vermont truck driving school. You have to have a default setting in your brain. If it gets that bad . . . dah, dah, dah. Use humor to put things in perspective."

ESCAPE MOOD HIJACKING

Jon Kabat-Zinn, PhD, the author of several books on stress reduction, including the recent *Coming to Our Senses*, is the founder of the University of Massachusetts Medical School's Stress Reduction Clinic in Worcester. But even a master of calm can have a day derailed by minor annoyances: "Finding dirty cat-food dishes in the kitchen sink—this used to really upset me. I'm not sure why, but it did. I didn't have a pet growing up. Maybe I saw it as a bigger health threat than it is. Anyway, I would react right away when I saw the cat dish in with our dirty dishes."

Anger hit first. "I found myself getting upset with my wife, since she was often the one who put the dishes in the sink. I would take it personally—I had told her I didn't like it. Partly, she thought I was overreacting. This would become an argument in a hurry. As soon as I saw those dishes, my heart rate would go up."

It's a standard response Dr. Kabat-Zinn has studied in patients. "We all lose our minds when things don't go our way in the world. We very easily get triggered—I call them emotional hijacks. We spiral down into anxiety and just feel like the world has it in for us."

After years of fighting this, Dr. Kabat-Zinn realized his wife wasn't changing. This was his burden to bear—or unload. "I tried to see the whole thing differently, with more awareness and humor. When I saw the dishes, I analyzed my reaction as it happened. My initial feeling of revulsion wasn't that extreme; it was really the sense of my request being ignored, a sense of betrayal, that was most upsetting. If I didn't act but just stayed with the emotions, breathing through them and permitting myself to just feel them, they dissipated fairly quickly."

When annoyances threaten you, Kabat-Zinn's advice is to stay in the present moment and . . .

Analyze your emotions. "Try to be aware of what's going on in your body—that feeling of outright irritability, a contraction in your face, anger, or fear. Don't express it, just experience the emotions and try to see if they're worth acting upon. Respond mindfully. See if you can be comfortable not overreacting. Try to breathe into that tension, be open, and feel breath moving in your body."

Plan a wise response. "You can flip out, insult the person, or get depressed—but whatever happened is already over. Your expectations weren't met: Now what? Look for solutions that allow you to face bad situations. Then, as best you can, let go and move on with your life."

PRACTICE LAUGHING

Linda Richman is Mike Myers's mother-in-law (and the model for his memorable Coffee Talk Lady character on *Saturday Night Live*). Richman has shared her philosophy for surviving tragedy through humor in *I'd Rather Laugh: How to Be Happy Even When Life Has Other Plans for You.* She's developed her methods through too much practice—including her mother's mental illness, her father's death when she was 8, and her 11 years of agoraphobia. Richman calls herself a summa cum laude graduate of the school of hard knocks.

"Because of the demands of my work, I moved 11 times in 14 years," Richman says. "I move like other people change their underwear." But one move stands out: "May 25, 2000, from Tucson to Miami. I'm in the house when the movers begin to bring in the stuff." That's when Richman noticed that it wasn't her stuff. "I tell the guy, 'That's not my furniture,' and he argues, 'Yes it is. The boxes are marked.' I say, 'You're going to tell me that's my furniture when I'm telling you it's not?'

"He says, 'That's the way it's marked, lady.' And they keep bringing in cartons of stuff I've never seen before." He's hell-bent on delivering the load, and her stress meter is off the chart. "The guy just won't check the other loads. He just won't," Richman says. "Then this brilliant idea comes. I say to myself, 'Let the next people go crazy. Then the movers will have to come back, move out this stuff, and bring in mine.'" So Richman sat back on her "new" couch, put her feet up, and watched them deliver an apartment's worth of the wrong furniture. She called her sister, who lived three blocks away, and said, "Judy, you will die laughing when you hear what's going on."

Richman decided to move in with Judy, and they spent 3 delightful days together. "We went to a flea market, we went swimming, we went to Bloomingdale's." Then the owner of the moving company called, frantic, and delivered her things. How'd she stay so calm? Here are her chill-out rules.

Give up. "You can win 90 percent of the time; 10 percent, you can't. When you can't, give up. I figured out that I have no control over anything except how I react."

Learn resilience. This isn't easy. "I work at being happy the way young women work at being thin," Richman says.

Get the giggles. "Put on a funny video or read something that delights you every single day. It's hilarious, a great way to start the day. I call it practicing laughing. It's totally Norman Cousins, and it works."

EMBRACE ADVERSITY

Pamela Peeke, MD, an assistant clinical professor of medicine at the University of Maryland School of Medicine and an adjunct senior scientist at the National Institutes of Health, has done research linking stress, nutrition, and metabolism. Her most recent book is *Body for Life for Women: A Woman's Plan for Physical and Mental Transformation.*

Dr. Peeke was heading out from her home near Washington, DC, for a series of lectures, and looking forward to addressing an audience of 500 women at an American Heart Association fundraising lunch in Evansville, Indiana. "I get to Dulles Airport, and I'm feeling good. Then the counter agent tells me that there is no flight. They had canceled it months ago, but nobody told me." This kicked off the worst day of her frequent-flying career. "I'm running from one concourse to another in high-heeled mules. Finally, I find a flight and check my luggage, but by the time I get through security, they're closing the door." Her luggage made the flight, but she did not.

Two hours later, she caught a plane to Cincinnati, where she could get a flight to Evansville, but her worries were far from over. "I'm hungry, tired, and wondering where my luggage is. By this time, I'm feeling moderately homicidal." Her dinner was a couple of energy bars on the way to her connecting flight. "When you take one of these puddle jumpers, you have to go out on the tarmac, and there are five planes all lined up. Well, I ended up on the wrong one. The door closed, and as we started to roll, the captain came on the PA: 'I hope you're all going to enjoy your trip to Columbus.' I shot out of my seat, and they actually turned the plane around. I ran up the stairs just in time to get on the right plane."

Dr. Peeke pauses to deconstruct the stress: "I did everything right—booked the trip well in advance, got to the airport on time. When they told me there was no plane, they took away every ounce of my control. And it's always very stressful that the agent isn't as concerned as you are." Here's what Dr. Peeke does when things fall apart—and what you can try, too.

Embrace adversity. "When I heard there was no flight, I could feel the cortisol and adrenaline surge through me. You have to come up with a solution. I could bag the trip or rise to the challenge."

Avoid despair. "Fight the inclination toward those three bad boys: hopelessness, helplessness, and defeat. A woman behind me at the counter broke into tears, saying, 'They'll never get me on an airplane.' You have to regroup, keep focused, and make something happen."

Guard against distraction. "When you're stressed-out, you can let your guard down. That's how I got on the wrong plane."

Make your best effort. "Give it your all, but then you have to let go," Dr. Peeke says. "That's all you can do."

STICK TO YOUR ROUTINE

Alice Domar, PhD, is the director of the Mind/Body Center for Women's Health at Boston IVF, a senior staff psychologist at Beth Israel Deaconess Medical Center in Boston, and an assistant professor of obstetrics, gynecology, and reproductive biology at Harvard Medical School. She's done pioneering work on the effects of stress on fertility.

"After a recurrence of breast cancer, my mother went into a hospice around Labor Day 2004. She was a social worker, and for the first week, she was still going out to see patients. Then, boom—she died," Domar says. "The hospice called around 3:30 in the morning to say that they thought she was about to die. I went right to the hospice, and it happened at 6:40 in the morning. I was very close to my mother; it was such a blow, the most stressful day of my life.

"She went so fast that it was merciful for her, but it never gave us a chance to have the kind of conversations I would have liked to have had. I never thought beforehand, 'Hmm, how am I going to cope the day my mother dies?'"

As an expert who counsels other women facing serious stress, Domar was surprised by her reactions. "I cried when she died, and then I totally held it together for the next week while we sat shivah. I was stunned that I could think so clearly, by how focused and detail oriented I was." Coping became harder 6 months later, she says, when numbness had faded and grief hit hard: "Everybody else goes back to normal life, and you don't." Domar found that following her own advice—and instinct—was the best possible path through her grief.

Honor your needs. "I came home from the hospice and took a very long walk, which gave me time to be alone and do some thinking. And for me, exercise—specifically, long, vigorous walks—is by far the best way to deal with stress. It got me away from the house and phone."

Keep the routine going. "I stuck to my family's routine, getting the kids up and dressed and taking my older daughter to school, where her teacher kept her day as normal as possible."

Accept help. "At the funeral, three of my friends said, 'We'll skip the cemetery, and we'll set up the food.' Normally, I'd have said, 'No, I can do it myself.' But I thought, 'This is going to make my life a lot easier.' I said fine."

Stay informed. "Every month, the hospice my mom died at sent out a little sheet, saying this is what you may be feeling right now, and I remember a couple of months ago feeling really depressed. Then I got this sheet that said, 'This is the time when depression really peaks.' I felt a lot better knowing that this was normal. The same thing happened when I got anxious; it was nice to know the stages.

"When the father of a childhood friend died a few months ago, I began telling her what to expect. She'd tell me, 'This is how I'm feeling now,' and I'd say,

'Okay, that's exactly where I was. A couple of weeks from now, you're going to feel this and this.' I think knowing what to expect and having someone to talk you through it makes it easier."

COOK AWAY ANXIETY

Andrew Weil, MD, founder and director of the Program in Integrative Medicine at the University of Arizona, is a pioneer in integrative medicine. *The Healthy Kitchen: Recipes for a Better Body, Life and Spirit* is his prescription for eating well.

In 1968, Dr. Weil was spending a year as an overworked intern in a San Francisco hospital. "In those days, med students did 3-day rotations. I got into such awful mental states, never seeing daylight, being in unpleasant surroundings. And as a volunteer at the Haight Ashbury Free Clinic, I saw everything—psychological breakdowns, sexually transmitted diseases, injuries from street violence." One day stands out in a year that brimmed with stress: "During the San Francisco State riots, I was with a group of physicians sent in to help. There was a group that sent doctors into these things. I had the feeling that the organization's

ulterior motive was to have doctors photographed being victimized by the police. I felt I had been used by this group; the whole thing was so upsetting on so many levels. I went out there and was engulfed. I was shocked by the behavior of both the rioters and the police. It was impossible to treat people."

In that moment, managing stress wasn't possible or even appropriate. But afterward? "When I finally got myself out of there, I stopped at an upscale supermarket, bought ingredients, and spent several hours cooking in the kitchen. There was something about chopping vegetables, making order, creating something wonderful—that whole process neutralized my negative mental state. I made soup, vegetable lasagna, poached salmon."

Dr. Weil had yet to discover the techniques that he now champions and would advise anyone to use to calm down after an extreme encounter.

Learn relaxation techniques such as breathing exercises, meditation, and yoga. "I had not learned to meditate. I didn't know anything about practicing yoga or breathing exercises. I didn't have those skills or resources, which are the cornerstone of how I now reduce stress."

Exercise away the anxiety. "Physical activity is a very important part of my routine now. It keeps my moods even."

Whip up a good meal. Even after developing all these other calm-inducing techniques, Dr. Weil hasn't forgotten the first one. "I still like to cook. It's a very satisfying feeling."

GET BACK TO THE BASICS

Barbara De Angelis, PhD, is a writer and motivational speaker whose books on relationships, personal growth, and finding meaning in life have sold more than 8 million copies. Her most recent title is *How Did I Get Here? Finding Your Way to Renewed Hope and Happiness When Life and Love Take Unexpected Turns.*

"There's stress that's just uncomfortable, and there's stress that creates anxiety about your future, your well-being, and your stability," says Dr. De Angelis. "This story begins on 9/11, but it's not a 9/11 story. It's about the impact that day had on my career. I had spent 2 years on a book, *What Women Want Men to Know,* and a PBS special. They were the most important projects I'd ever undertaken. On September 11, I was in Nashville, 3 days into a tour for

my book. I wept for days in that hotel—for everybody, for the state of humanity. It was only later that I realized my entire tour had vanished and the TV special would go unnoticed. I knew I'd pay a severe price for these projects that had gone down."

Her stress, she says, grew from fear of the unknown, not knowing what to do, and tremendous isolation. She finally got a flight home to Santa Barbara, California, 6 days later. But her boyfriend, who was coming to live near her during a year's sabbatical from his teaching job in Rochester, New York, had no car and couldn't get a flight. In that moment, she decided to drive across the country and pick him up. "It wasn't logical. I was exhausted, and I have night blindness." But she knew she had to do it. "I drove 15 hours a day, because the only thing that mattered was being with the person I love.

"I didn't even listen to the radio; it was like meditation. I thought about what I was grateful for, what really mattered."

After Dr. De Angelis picked up her boyfriend, they began driving back. "On the way, we stopped at the Grand Canyon, which I'd never seen. As we stood there, the canyon gave off this sense of timelessness; it has endured so much—world wars, other disasters on the planet. There it was, silent, the wind moving through the trees, the animals, the rocks stubbornly in place. Unchanging. It was like a shrine. It was the best thing I could have done for myself, but I never would have chosen it consciously or logically."

The drive gave her more than she could have imagined. "It was a recommitment to love—not to my career, not to money, not to notoriety. In the most stressful time, what was my core value? It was love." The experience led her to the subject for her new book, and the heart of her advice.

Don't expect to dodge calamity. "We baby boomers were taught that if we did everything perfectly, we would get what we wanted. Our grandparents and parents were much better equipped for stress because they lived through wars and the Depression. We expect that if we do A, B, and C, we will get what we want, and we're shocked when we don't."

When the unexpected hits, get back to basics. "You have to remember what really counts in your life. For me it was love, and I drove cross-country for it."

CHAPTER 25

THE HEALING POWER OF HYPNOSIS

The latest research shows that it can ease pain, speed healing, increase fertility, even fight cancer

Wendy W. couldn't believe it: Her cycles had always been very regular, but the minute she decided to try to get pregnant, she stopped menstruating. After 4 months without a period, the 24-year-old nurse at Dartmouth-Hitchcock Medical Center in Lebanon, New Hampshire, consulted an ob-gyn who was a fertility specialist. He couldn't find the slightest thing wrong with her or her husband. Okay, she concluded, I guess my mind has stopped my period. She called the hospital's psychiatry department. "I want someone good," she said.

Da-shih Hu, MD, a psychiatrist and an assistant professor at Dartmouth Medical School, invited Wendy into his office. They talked about her life, marriage, and work but found no obvious reasons why her reproductive system had shut down. When Hu suggested that hypnosis might help,

Wendy bristled. "I thought he was literally nuts," she says. "I knew nothing about hypnosis, except that it's a bad Vegas act. And I hate magicians."

But two sessions later, with nothing to lose, she decided to give it a try. Dr. Hu asked her to close her eyes, take a deep breath, and imagine a wave of relaxation spreading slowly from her toes to the top of her head. "It was the feeling you get right before you go to sleep," she recalls. At the doctor's instruction, she took several more deep breaths, until she felt herself drifting off. Soon her head slumped toward her chest, and the straight-back chair seemed to morph into a comfortable recliner. Dr. Hu asked Wendy to imagine a safe, restful place to visit, and at her suggestion, they "walked" to a waterfall. "Do you hear the sounds of water?" Dr. Hu asked. "Do you feel a breeze?" A quiet fluidity entered her soul, instilling a sense of peace she'd never known.

"I was in the room, but I wasn't there," she says. "I was above myself, looking down, like a mom looking down at a child. And I had this amazingly powerful feeling: I felt like I could fix myself." Dr. Hu later asked Wendy to think of a day when she should start menstruating. On that very day, her period started. Soon afterward, she became pregnant, and 9 months later, her son was born.

A funny thing is happening to hypnosis, long a feature of vaudevillian routines: It's becoming respectable, working its way into the nation's premier research hospitals, medical journals, and doctors' offices. An increasing number of physicians are using hypnosis to ease patients through childbirth, angioplasty, chemotherapy, breast biopsy—even full-on surgery.

Hypnosis is helping people get over fractures, burns, migraines, asthma, fibroids, peptic ulcers, and skin disorders. The same techniques practiced by ancient Egyptians 2,000 years ago and "discovered" by Austrian physician Franz Anton Mesmer in the late 1700s are now scoring impressive results in medical experiments across the United States, Europe, and beyond. Mind, it seems, really can overcome matter.

"If somebody told you there was a medication that could treat 100 different conditions, didn't require a prescription, was free, and had no bad side effects, you wouldn't believe them," says Harvard Medical School psychologist Carol Ginandes, PhD. "I don't want to sound like a snake oil salesman, because hypnosis is not a magic wand. But it should be made available as a supplementary treatment for all patients who could benefit. Right now."

HOW HYPNOSIS WORKS

Contrary to popular folklore, a hypnotized person isn't asleep and can't be compelled to act against her own wishes—although anyone who's watched a Borscht Belt magician turn a middle-aged man into a squawking chicken might doubt that. While researchers can't fully explain what hypnosis is or why it works, they do know that 75 to 91 percent of people can be hypnotized.

Psychologists describe hypnosis as an altered state of mind in which one's normal skepticism is largely suspended, allowing a patient to focus attention on a single image and be open to suggestions posed by a trained guide. Some practitioners call it daydreaming with purpose. It's similar to the absorption you experience when reading a good novel, watching an engrossing movie, or listening so intently to the car radio that you arrive home without a clue as to how you got there.

New brain scan technology shows that hypnosis can alter the way sensory messages are received in the brain and experienced in the body. In a recent brain-imaging study conducted at the University of Iowa, researchers found that hypnosis actually blocks pain signals from getting to the part of the brain responsible for conscious perception of discomfort. PET scans—which reveal active areas of the brain—also indicate that hypnotized people process suggested sounds and images in the same part of the brain that registers real ones. That is, the brain accepts hallucinations as authentic. Simply imagining sensations, without hypnosis, doesn't have the same effect.

That, of course, is what makes hypnosis such a great stage act. In a trance, your senses can be tricked. You can be persuaded that a bottle of ammonia smells like perfume or that a large, fuzzy rabbit is sitting on your lap. But the brain effects also help explain why hypnosis has become so useful to modern medicine. It can make you conclude that chemotherapy isn't nauseating, for example, or that third-degree burns are not painful.

"Fantasy can preempt pain," explains Linda Thomson, PhD, a nurse practitioner and clinical hypnotherapist in Bellows Falls, Vermont. And because pain isn't good for you, reducing it can pro-duce profound benefits.

HELPING THE BODY HEAL ITSELF

Hypnosis appears to speed recovery from many types of trauma. In a 2003 pilot study, published in the *American Journal of Clinical Hypnosis*, Harvard's Dr. Ginandes and colleague Patricia Brooks, PhD, evaluated 18 women who'd just undergone reconstructive breast surgery. The patients were assigned ran-domly to one of three groups for 8 weeks. All groups received conventional follow-up care; the second also met weekly with a therapist for emotional support, while the third met individually with Dr. Brooks, who used hypnotic suggestion in a 30-minute session each week to reduce pain and inflammation and speed soft-tissue repair. An audiotape was made for each participant in the hypnosis group so she could practice self-hypnosis daily at home.

One week after surgery and again after 7 more weeks, a surgical team, which was "blinded" to the therapy assign-ments, assessed the incision sites. Their conclusion: The hypnosis patients healed much faster. The women also reported that they experienced less pain and quicker recovery. An earlier pilot study by Dr. Ginandes on hypnosis and bone fractures, funded by the National Insti-tutes of Health, found similar results: faster healing, greater mobility, less dis-comfort, and reduced use of pain medi-cation among orthopedic patients who used hypnosis.

Physicians have long been frustrated in their attempts to treat patients with irritable bowel syndrome (IBS), whose symptoms—sharp abdominal pain, diarrhea or constipation, bloating, gas, and backache—are compounded by stress, anxiety, and depression. In 2003, doctors in Manchester, England, released a study that had tracked 204 IBS patients for 5 years.

Patients at South Manchester Univer-sity Hospital attended up to 12 hypnosis sessions over 3 months and were encouraged to visualize soothing yet empowering scenes inside their colons. One woman imagined her gut as a flowing, colorful scarf. Another saw her colon as a runaway train whose driver had gone to sleep. She took over the controls and slowed down the train to a comfortable speed.

The results exceeded the researchers' expectations: More than 70 percent of the patients rated themselves "very much better" or "moderately better" after hypnotherapy. Five years later, 81 percent of patients who'd initially benefited from the treatment reported that the improvements had lasted. Their anxiety and depression were reduced by at least half, as were their reliance on pain pills and the number of doctor visits they made.

In another study, Olafur Palsson, PsyD, a clinical psychologist at the University of North Carolina at Chapel Hill School of Medicine, reported an 80 percent success rate among 18 IBS patients who were treated with hypnosis after conventional care failed. Those results, coupled with several other recent studies on IBS and hypnosis, are remarkable, says psychologist Arreed Barabasz, PhD, director of the Hypnosis Laboratory at Washington State University in Pullman and editor of the *International Journal of Clinical and Experimental Hypnosis*: "These findings show that benefits of hypnotherapy for IBS are long lasting and that continued improvement after hypnosis treatment ends is the norm."

Warts are uniquely vulnerable to hypnosis; it beats the usual treatment, salicylic acid, hands down. In a Tulane University study of 41 patients whose warts would not respond to other treatments, 80 percent were cured with hypnosis. Studies suggest that other skin conditions may also respond: In a trial of 18 patients, hypnotherapy cleared up eczema symptoms—itching, sleep disturbance, and stress—for up to 2 years.

Few examples of hypnotic healing are as dramatic as those that come from treating burns. Dabney Ewin, MD, a clinical professor of surgery and psychiatry at Tulane University School of Medicine in New Orleans, hypnotizes burn victims in the emergency room. Dr. Ewin's published case studies include a restaurant worker who burned his arm up to his elbow in a 370°F deep-fat fryer. The doctor induced a deep trance within 4 hours of the accident and provided a hypnotic suggestion—"all your injured areas are cool and comfortable"—to the victim.

Dr. Ewin and others have shown that such care can slow or even stop the inflammation and blistering that can cause permanent damage. In the worker's case, the injury healed in 17 days with relatively little scarring. Dr. Ewin uses a series of slides to show examples of burns in which early intervention prevented serious, lifelong injuries.

EASING PAIN

Work with burn victims demonstrates another benefit of hypnosis: It's an astoundingly powerful pain reliever, says David Patterson, PhD, chief psychologist at the University of Washington's department of rehabilitation medicine, who copublished an extensive review of the topic in the American Psychological Association's *Psychological Bulletin* in 2003. "Hypnosis seems to be useful for virtually every clinical pain problem imaginable," he says.

One of the biggest risks after a severe burn is infection, which can lead to scarring, amputation, or even death. To prevent that, nurses at burn units have to remove patients' dead skin every day for several weeks, even months, in a process called debridement. The pain is so severe, it can cause more anguish than the original burn. To ease it, patients are given morphine and other powerful pain relievers, but those drugs can be habit-forming and can cause confusion, gastrointestinal upset, and breathing trouble.

At Seattle's Harborview Medical Center, Dr. Patterson has been using hypnosis for 20 years to make that pain bearable. His team of 10 psychologists teaches the most severely burned patients, who appear to benefit most from hypnosis, how to induce a state of relaxation and comfort. The session includes an instruction—called a posthypnotic suggestion—that cues the patient to feel the same level of comfort days, weeks, or even months later. A simple touch on the shoulder by a nurse, for example, if suggested in the original session, can trigger a trance, enabling a patient to undergo wound care without pain. "Hypnosis is very well suited for burn pain treatment," says Patterson, "because the pain is intense but short-lived, and you know when it's going to happen."

Pregnant women, too, have a pretty good sense of when the pain is going to start, and hypnosis has proven helpful in easing labor. Several studies—including a new one out of the University of Adelaide in Australia that surveyed 77 women who'd been hypnotized during delivery—have shown it can shorten labor time, reduce pain and the use of pain medication, decrease the risk of complications, and speed recovery. In the Australian study, hypnotized mothers were less likely than others to need an epidural or labor-inducing drugs.

Some other reasons you might want to try it: Children born to hypnotized mothers scored higher on Apgar tests (a measure of health), and the mothers were less prone to postpartum depression. What's more, those who have previously given birth without hypnosis tell doctors that it makes labor a more pleasant experience.

People with peptic ulcers may not know when pain will strike, but they can still use posthypnotic suggestion. Patients in a British study were able to regulate their secretion of gastric acid, so that only 53 percent experienced further pain, compared with 100 percent relapse in a control group.

One in four Americans doesn't get regular dental care or avoids dentists altogether, simply because of anxiety. Some dentists and oral surgeons assume that hypnosis takes too much time to be useful in their busy offices, but most patients can benefit from just 5 minutes of hypnosis-related relaxation training, says Al Forgione, PhD, a psychology professor at the Craniofacial Pain Center of the Tufts University School of Dental Medicine in Boston. The technique won't eliminate the need for novocaine, but it takes enough of the edge off to allow fearful dental patients to get the care they need.

Finally, there have been more studies on the effect of hypnosis on headaches than on any other form of chronic pain. It helps reduce the frequency, duration, and intensity of migraines and other headaches by as much as 30 percent.

MAKING SURGERY SAFER

Robert Scott, 64, was hit by a truck when he was 4 years old, leaving him with a crushed bladder. Now, with a good-natured smile, the retired school custodian relies on hypnosis to cope with the minor but painful surgery he must routinely undergo. Scott comes to Beth Israel Deaconess Medical Center in Boston every 8 to 10 weeks to have a urinary catheter—which is attached to his kidney through a hole in his back—pulled out and replaced.

While a team of doctors and nurses in green scrubs gathers surgical equipment and readies the massive, whirring, x-ray–guided scope overhead, Scott lies on his stomach, listening to the softly delivered instructions of Gloria Salazar, MD, a radiologist and hypnotherapist. She sits by Scott's head, encouraging him to relax and imagine a place he'd rather be. "Your body needs to be here," she says gently, "but you do not." She reads to him from a script used on all hypnosis patients at the hospital. Scott closes his hazel eyes, takes a series of deep breaths, and seems to drift off to sleep. As doctors insert a long guide wire into his back, Scott doesn't flinch. When they fish the 12-inch catheter out of his kidney and guide a new one down in its place, he doesn't seem to even notice.

"With other patients, we use intravenous pain medication," says attending radiologist Salomao Faintuch, MD, as he pulls the tube out. "But we know Mr. Scott responds well to hypnosis, so we use only local anesthesia." Sedatives such as Valium and morphine prolong operations and can cause complications, Dr. Faintuch adds, so it's better to do without, if the patient can handle it.

Scott can handle it because he's whisked his mind far away from the doctors probing deep inside his body. "I have a meadow that I go to, and there's a pond, which I put ducks on," he says after Dr. Salazar guides him back to full consciousness with a reawakening cue. "I take my grand-daughter fishing. We talk and play." Five years ago, when he got intravenous sedation instead of hypnosis, Scott says, "it felt like someone took a piece of steel and stuck it right into my kidney." Now, he says, "I feel a lot of pressure, but no pain." Does the meadow really exist? "No." Does the grand-daughter? "Oh, yes," he says with a smile. "But she's only 2 months old."

This is no ordinary hospital ward, but then its director, Elvira Lang, MD, is not your average administrator. Dr. Lang, a radiologist and Harvard Medical School professor, has transformed the interventional radiology department at Beth Israel Deaconess—where MRIs, x-rays, and ultrasounds are used in unclogging arteries and shrinking tumors—into a 24-hour, hypnosis-on-request unit. Virtually any patient, undergoing nearly any procedure, can receive hypnosis-induced pain relief within minutes. ("We don't always use the 'H' word when we talk to patients," Dr. Faintuch confesses, "because they think of people on TV who do silly things. So we say 'relaxation exercises.'")

In 2000, Dr. Lang published a groundbreaking study on surgical hypnosis that many physicians credit with helping to legitimize the technique's role in the operating room. The study traced the outcomes of 241 patients randomly assigned to receive hypnosis, standard anesthesia, or sympathetic (but nonhypnotic) care while undergoing minor surgery.

Dr. Lang and her colleagues found that patients who were guided through hypnotic relaxation during surgery used 50 percent less pain and antianxiety medication, suffered 75 percent fewer complications, and left the operating room 17 minutes sooner than the other groups. In a follow-up study, Dr. Lang found that hypnosis is a cost saver, too—halving the $638 sedation costs of minor surgery.

Dr. Lang suspects that hypnosis helps patients tolerate operations by stabilizing heart rate and blood pressure. She's looking to see if it can substitute for sedation in women undergoing needle biopsies for suspected breast cancer, women having uterine fibroid surgery, and patients receiving chemotherapy for malignant liver tumors. The studies, funded by the federal government, are not yet complete, but Dr. Lang says the preliminary results are encouraging.

Elsewhere, doctors have recorded great success using hypnosis on patients undergoing complicated, high-risk surgery. At Dartmouth-Hitchcock Medical Center, doctors use hypnosis to reduce pain and nausea among epilepsy patients who have electrodes placed inside their skulls to detect the source of their seizures. At the University of California, Davis Medical Center, doctors didn't even need to formally hypnotize spinal surgery patients in order to limit their blood loss during the operation. They simply told 41 patients that blood would flow away from their backs during spine surgery. These patients lost roughly 650 cc of blood on the operating table; others on standard sedation lost nearly twice that.

RELIEVING CANCER SYMPTOMS

David Spiegel, MD, a psychiatry professor at Stanford University and a leading researcher on medical hypnosis, has found that the approach can help some patients with terminal cancer live longer and more comfortably. Dr. Spiegel studied 125 women with metastatic breast cancer. Those who learned self-hypnosis techniques had 50 percent less pain than women receiving standard care—and lived, on average, $1\frac{1}{2}$ years longer.

Part of the reason may be that the nausea, anxiety, and all-around lousy feelings induced by chemotherapy can be alleviated by hypnosis, several studies have shown. Boris Lavanovich, 51, a real estate consultant in Ludlow, Vermont, used hypnosis to cope with an experimental chemotherapy regimen he took to treat

Hypnosis for Beginners

Experts say it's time for hypnotherapy to be included in the tool belt of American medicine. Here's what you need to know to make it part of your care.

Who can be hypnotized? Nearly everyone, says Max Shapiro, PhD, director of education and research for the New England Society of Clinical Hypnosis and the former chief psychologist at Newton-Wellesley Hospital in Massachusetts. He has found that 91 percent of the population is susceptible to hypnotic suggestion. Other studies suggest at least 75 percent of people can be hypnotized.

For people who struggle with the technique because of pain—burn patients, for example—virtual reality may hold an answer. David Patterson, PhD, chief psychologist at the University of Washington's department of rehabilitation medicine in Seattle, has codeveloped software that uses a specialized helmet with a screen to display snowy canyons and icy rivers populated by penguins and snowmen. Hypnotic narration assures patients they'll feel comfortable.

Who should you see? Be sure you consult a licensed clinician. Contact the American Society of Clinical Hypnosis (www.asch.net) or the Society for Clinical and Experimental Hypnosis (www.sceh.us) for information about health care professionals in your area. Your treatment might be covered by insurance: Licensed providers often bill insurance companies for therapy that includes hypnosis to treat a variety of disorders, but it's still a bit of a tug-of-war.

What are the side effects? A small minority of people develop headaches, dizziness, nausea, anxiety, or panic under hypnosis. People struggling with major mental illness should consult a mental health professional before getting hypnotized.

The Limits of Hypnotic Suggestion

Ironically, the two uses for which hypnosis has gotten the most attention—smoking cessation and weight loss—are the areas in which its performance is weak.

Smoking: Hypnosis has helped people quit, with some impressive initial results: In two studies with 160 participants, 81 to 88 percent stopped smoking for 12 months. But other studies have failed to come close to that level of success, and the long-term failure rate appears to be the same as for other techniques.

Weight loss: Though people have trimmed down using hypnosis, it's been useful only in conjunction with other methods. In a University of Northern Colorado study of 109 participants undergoing behavioral modification, the group that also received nine weekly hypnosis sessions lost 15 more pounds. In another study, patients on a diet who also employed self-hypnosis lost more weight. But it's unclear whether hypnosis works well as a stand-alone treatment for losing weight.

chronic lymphocytic leukemia, a lethal blood cancer. "They told me I was stage 4, out the door," Lavanovich says with a dry chuckle. The mountain biker and skier needed medication to counteract nausea, convulsive shakes, and rapid temperature swings brought on by chemotherapy. Without the self-hypnosis training, Lavanovich doubts he could've tolerated the treatment or that he would have benefited.

Lavanovich's experience is one that hypnotherapists see time and again: A patient has only to try the technique to become a believer. That's what happened with Wendy, the skeptical nurse who used the therapy to conceive her first son. She had a second son without incident, but when she and her husband decided to try for number three, once again her periods vanished. This time, she didn't hesitate: She turned to hypnosis, imagining the waterfall and soft breeze that got her body back on track the first time around. It worked—she's now the mother of four sons.

MEDICAL BREAKTHROUGHS

Reducing stress, getting enough sleep, and boosting your energy are all important tasks for your overall health—and for your life with diabetes. Here's the latest research to help you do all three.

MEN: QUIT YOUR DAY JOB

Your job may be wreaking secret havoc with your blood sugar. Are you:

Stressed-out from 9 to 5?

Working in a shark tank?

Required to put in long hours with little financial reward or recognition?

If a man answers yes even once, his diabetes risk could be two to three times higher than that of a guy toiling under happier circumstances, a new University College London study of 10,000 British workers suggests. "The effect may be due to higher stress hormone levels," says lead researcher Meena Kumari, PhD, an epidemiologist.

Women's health wasn't affected by job status. "Close friendships and other strong sources of identity—children and families—may help to protect them," Dr. Kumari says. Ways that men can counter stress:

Stay active. Aim for 30-plus minutes 5 days a week.

Be social. Set up a regular night out with friends or join a sports league or organization that shares your interests.

Eat smart. Work stress can spoil even the healthiest eaters' diets, driving them to snack on fatty, sugary foods.

CHILL OUT TO BRING DOWN BLOOD SUGAR

Learning to melt your stress away may coax blood sugar down to healthy levels, suggests research from the Medical University of Ohio. The experiment followed 30 people with diabetes, half of whom practiced daily tension-taming exercises, such as muscle relaxation, and had their techniques monitored with weekly 45-minute biofeedback sessions. The others took diabetes education classes.

After 10 weeks, those who relaxed saw about a 10 percent drop in fasting blood sugar and in the level of HbA1c—a sign that their glucose had stayed lower around the clock for the previous couple of months. Such results mean lower risk of diabetic complications, such as heart disease, blindness, and nerve damage. Meanwhile, the education group's blood sugar and HbA1c levels actually rose slightly.

"Stress triggers hormones that raise blood sugar," explains lead researcher Ronald McGinnis, MD. "Reducing chronic stress switches this process off." If that's not motivation enough, the relaxation group also experienced a drop in depression and anxiety. To find a biofeedback therapist, check out www.bcia.org and click on Find a Practitioner.

EAT RIGHT, SLEEP TIGHT

One in three Americans is plagued by insomnia, the National Institutes of Health estimates, and 10 percent of them struggle for shut-eye every night. Atul Malhotra, MD, a Harvard Sleep Disorders Research Center physician-scientist, suggests these tips for welcoming the sandman.

Eliminate unusual suspects. Even decaf coffee and chocolate contain small amounts of caffeine. Purge all caffeine sources for 2 weeks. If you sleep better, make the change permanent. Some people are acutely sensitive to caffeine, and you may be surprised by how little can keep you awake and how long its effects last.

Avoid spicy or gassy foods and wolfing your dinner. Anything that challenges your tummy can cause indigestion, which will keep you awake.

Try lighter suppers. An overly full stomach may cause frequent waking. Have your largest meal at lunch, long before bedtime.

Ban late-evening alcohol. A glass of wine with dinner won't hurt, but a nightcap just before you hit the sack may disrupt REM (rapid eye movement) sleep. The result: waking up during the night or simply less restful sleep.

Have a bite before bed. A small snack about an hour before turning in may help you fall asleep. Going to bed with a growling, empty stomach can keep you awake.

REPEAT AFTER ME: I AM LESS STRESSED

Mumbling to yourself may not be as crazy as it seems. Repeating a mantra—a meaningful word or phrase said silently—can help you cope with the hassles of life, finds a new study from the Veterans Administration San Diego Healthcare System.

In it, 66 volunteers were taught to repeat a mantra (sometimes called a mantram) of their choice as often as possible during low-stress activities such as washing dishes or getting ready for bed. The goal was to train their brains to associate the phrase with calmness so they could employ it to counter turmoil. Mantras varied: Some chose words or phrases with religious meanings, while others went secular. One golfer repeated "fairways and greens."

Regardless of their choice, the returns were similar: Six months later, 83 percent had employed their mantras to help them stay calm, and 75 percent were able to ease stress, frustration, and tension. "Mantras are a Jacuzzi for the mind," says lead researcher Jill Bormann, PhD, RN. "And unlike many stress-reduction techniques, you can literally use this anywhere, anytime."

DABBLE IN KABBALAH

Have Madonna, Demi, and Roseanne made you curious about Kabbalah, Judaism's school of healing wisdom? A new book, *Matrix Healing* by Raphael Kellman, MD, can answer your questions. The premise is positive—that meditation, the sacred power of water, and compassion can dramatically improve health. Here are two of the book's hydrotherapy water treatments.

Energy-restoring bath: Fill a tub with

about 10 inches of cool water (about 60°F). Stay in the tub, dipping water all over your body, for a minute. Get out and vigorously dry off with a rough towel.

Anti-stress bath: Get into a tub that's filled halfway with water at body temperature. Gradually add cold water, so that after about 15 minutes, the water feels quite chilly. Get out and wrap yourself in a large, warm towel; rest quietly for an hour.

GIVE GINSENG A GO

While waiting for your change at the convenience store, you spy the exotic-looking vials of ginseng beside the cash register. Are they really the instant energy boosters they claim to be? Experts concede that Britney Spears may have known what she was doing when she was photographed sipping this Asian herb. Panax ginseng has a history in Chinese medicine for treating conditions related to excessive use of the voice, which practitioners believe can weaken you. Modern science backs some of the claims for ginseng: Studies suggest that it boosts energy, immunity, and the ability to withstand stress.

The best way to take ginseng is for a few days at a time, when you're feeling particularly exhausted. Look for the Pine Brand of Panax Ginseng Extractum from China. A typical daily dose of ginseng is 200 milligrams of a 5:1 standardized extract.

AVOID COMPLICATIONS

HEART DISEASE BREAKTHROUGHS

The latest research on the diabetes–cardiovascular disease connection

When you have diabetes, one of the most important things you can do, apart from controlling your disease, is to keep an eye on your heart health. People with diabetes have a very high risk of heart disease and stroke because of the circulatory problems caused by the excess glucose in the bloodstream. A high cholesterol level makes matters worse, further boosting your risk of heart disease and stroke.

Here we've pulled together the latest research on diabetes and heart disease to help you keep your ticker ticking.

DEADLY DIABETES GENDER GAP

Diabetes boosts heart disease risk to a greater degree in women than in men, a recent Finnish study finds. Women with diabetes, in fact, are 14 times more likely to develop heart disease than women without diabetes. Men with diabetes, by comparison, are three times more likely to develop heart disease than men without diabetes.

Why the gender gap? Diabetes appears to hit women's arteries harder than it does men's, say researchers at Finland's University of Kuopio, who followed 2,131 women and men for 13 years. A related study finds that women are less likely to get aggressive treatment for heart disease risk factors than men.

Despite this gender gap, a University of Michigan survey of 97,000 Americans found that there's also a gender gap in one simple component of heart disease prevention.

The percentage of women at high risk for a heart attack who take a daily, low-dose aspirin: 45

The percentage of high-risk men who take a daily, low-dose aspirin: 58

WHY YOUR BP MATTERS

Percent of people with diabetes with high blood pressure: 71

Number whose doctors are aggressively treating it: 4 in 10

Percent who don't even know they've got a problem: 29

Added heart attack and stroke risk caused by high BP: at least 100 percent

CHOCOLATE RX

Cocoa researchers and scientists from the candy conglomerate Mars Inc. are exploring the potential healing power of cocoa-based drugs for people with diabetes and heart disease.

A growing stack of research shows that flavanols in cocoa and dark chocolate can relax blood vessels and even improve the way the body metabolizes blood sugar—good news if you've got high blood pressure or high sugar levels. In summer 2005, the world's leading cocoa investigators and scientists from Mars held a summit in Switzerland to discuss the future of prescription drugs made from these flavanols. Mars says it is negotiating with several large pharmaceutical companies but declined to name them.

Cocoa flavanols seem to spur the body to produce more nitric oxide—a compound that relaxes the inner lining of your arteries. "The potential implications for a naturally occurring stimulant to nitric oxide activation are truly intoxicating," notes researcher Norman K. Hollenberg, MD, PhD, a radiologist at Boston's Brigham and Women's Hospital and a cochairman of the cocoa conference. If you indulge in dark chocolate while waiting for this "cocoa pill," be sure to watch your calorie and carb counts. The ADA advises carb limits of 45 to 75 grams per meal and 15 to 30 grams per snack.

MORE CHOCOLATE RX

On Valentine's Day, ensure that your lover's pulse quickens with the right gift: Dark, creamy chocolate. After 16 volunteers in a new study from Athens Medical School each munched a 3.5-ounce bar of extra-dark chocolate, ultrasound scans revealed better bloodflow for the next 3 hours.

Experts have long known that dark chocolate contains substances, known as polyphenol flavonoids, that are heart healthy. This research reveals that the sweet actually improves the functioning of the endothelium, a layer of cells in arteries (including those in the heart) that prevents plaque buildup and protects against high blood pressure.

"Our research suggests that flavonoids can directly act on endothelial cells and stimulate the production of nitric oxide, a substance that dilates arteries," says researcher Charalambos Vlachopoulos, MD, a cardiologist. Other research suggests that eating 3 ounces of dark chocolate per day could lower blood pressure.

Unfortunately, you still can't eat an entire box of Godiva guilt free. Chocolate's fat and high sugar content can lead to excess pounds, which is never a good thing for your heart.

TOMATO THERAPY

Healthy blood cells slip and slide over each other, lacking the clinginess that leads to artery-choking clots. However, Velcro-like cells are a hallmark of type 2 diabetes and are one reason people with diabetes suffer more heart attacks and strokes than average. Now, an Australian study of 20 adults with type 2 diabetes, ages 43 to 82, found that drinking a cup of tomato juice daily for 3 weeks had a blood-thinning effect, reducing the stickiness of platelets—the matrix of blood clots—by 27 percent.

More than just tomatoes' famous ingredient, lycopene, is involved, the researchers say—added proof that healthy foods beat supplements most of the time.

FISH FOR A HEALTHIER PUMP AND PIPES

Fatty fish guards your heart, brain, and circulatory system, new science shows.

Fixing jiggy heartbeats: A 12-year Brigham and Women's Hospital study of 4,800 people found that those who ate any fish one to four times a week had a 28 percent lower risk of atrial fibrillation (AF) than those who avoided fish. AF disrupts your heart's rhythm, causing fatigue and shortness of breath.

Blocking strokes: Northwestern University scientists analyzed eight studies, involving 200,575 people and concluded that eating fatty fish (such as salmon, mackerel, and herring) just once a week cut the risk of clot-caused strokes by 13 percent, though it had no effect on strokes from burst blood vessels.

Disrupting atherosclerosis: A Harvard study of 727 women found that those who ate fatty fish almost every day—compared with those who ate them only three times per month—had 7 to 10 percent lower blood levels of molecules that bind plaque-building cells to artery walls.

FAT-FREE MAY MEAN NUTRIENT-FREE

Feeling proud of your commitment to fat-free salad dressing? Reconsider. New research has found that none of the lycopene or alpha- or beta-carotene that fight cancer and heart disease is absorbed from salads with fat-free dressing. Only slightly more is absorbed with reduced-fat dressing. The most is absorbed with full-fat dressing.

In the 12-week study at Iowa State University, seven people ate salads of leafy greens, cherry tomatoes, and carrots, topped with Italian dressings containing 2 tablespoons of canola oil, 1 teaspoon, or none. Blood samples collected every 60 minutes for 12 hours documented nutrient absorption.

Exception: Choose fat-free dressings if you top salads with fatty cheese, bacon bits, egg yolk, or avocados, which all aid nutrient absorption.

CALCIUM HEART SCAN

To check for clogged vessels in the heart, a doctor wires the patient for an ECG (electrocardiogram) and then has the patient run on a treadmill. This imaging stress test is excellent for detecting blockages, but it misses life-threatening atherosclerosis at least half the time, suggests new research from Cedars-Sinai Medical Center in Los Angeles. Scientists found the flaw when they gave calcium scans—a newer test that detects calcium deposits inside artery plaque—to 1,119 people with normal imaging stress-test results.

The upshot: 56 percent had scores above 100, a sign of higher long-term heart risk, and 31 percent had scores over 400, putting them at superhigh risk and in need of an immediate medical intervention, says lead researcher Daniel Berman, MD, director of cardiac imaging at the hospital.

Doctors do the calcium scans with widely available computed tomography imaging equipment, but the $200 to $400 price tag isn't covered by insurance. It's worth paying for if your heart risk is above normal—there's a history of early heart attack in your family or you have high blood pressure, elevated cholesterol, or diabetes.

HEART-HEALTHY HORMONES

Despite hormone therapy's record of driving up cancer and heart disease risk in older women, there's tantalizing evidence that starting hormones before menopause may have heart-healthy effects. That's what the 5-year, $15 million Kronos Early Estrogen Prevention Study (KEEPS) will explore (as well as whether estrogen delivered through a skin patch is as effective as—and potentially safer than—estrogen pills).

The theory has support: Research suggests that younger women who use oral contraceptives have a decreased risk of heart disease and ovarian and uterine cancers. Recruitment for KEEPS is under way at eight research centers around the country. For information about enrollment, call (866) 878-1221 or go to www.keepstudy.org.

DEADLY QUIET HEART ATTACKS

A heart attack without crushing chest pain—the type often experienced by women—is three times more likely to kill than one with classic symptoms, finds an international study of 20,881 heart attack patients.

Among the 1,763 who didn't have chest pain, one in four was misdiagnosed in the emergency room. Doctors were less likely to give them treatments that bust clots, protect heart muscle, and save lives, says lead researcher and cardiologist David Brieger, PhD, of Concord Repatriation General Hospital in Australia.

Patients' symptoms included fainting, vomiting, nausea, shortness of breath, and heavy sweating. "In someone who's female, elderly, or diabetic, these symptoms could be a heart attack," Brieger says.

BIOFEEDBACK FOR BETTER BLOOD PRESSURE

Scientists at Chicago's Rush University Medical Center monitored the blood pressure of 149 people, 89 of whom tried the FDA-approved Resperate, a CD-player-sized gadget, for 15 minutes a day for 2 months. When they strapped on the machine's chest sensor and breathed in time to its music, they gradually slowed their breathing to a relaxed 10 breaths per minute. The result: an average 15-point drop in systolic blood pressure (top number) and a 9-point drop in diastolic (bottom number).

Slow breathing signals the brain, says Joseph Marek, MD, a cardiologist and hypertension specialist. "Muscles around blood vessels relax, and blood flows more easily." Talk to your doctor before using Resperate; it costs about $300 (usually not covered by insurance).

CHAPTER 27

THE DENTAL-DIABETES CONNECTION

Perfect pearly whites can protect against diabetes complications

Treat your teeth like gold: Your diabetes care—and overall health—depend on it.

What does your dental hygiene have to do with diabetes? Unhealthy mouths unleash bacteria into the bloodstream, where the bugs travel to vital organs. As a result, your chance of diabetes complications can go up, your stroke risk can quadruple, and your risk of a heart attack can spike up to 14 times higher.

Don't let it happen to you. Open up and apply these teeth-protector tips, and we practically guarantee you'll live longer and—an added benefit—do it without dentures.

PROTECT AGAINST PLAQUE

When you run your tongue over your teeth in the morning and feel that filmy substance, it's plaque—a mossy mix of germs, dead cells, and saliva. Left alone, it becomes a breeding ground for bacteria that cause cavities and gingivitis, a big word for inflamed gums. And gingivitis can lead to the ligament-destroying oral disease called periodontitis, says Marjorie Jeffcoat, DMD, dean of the school of dental medicine at the University of Pennsylvania in Philadelphia. "You can have an infection and not know it," she says.

Set up tea time. A recent Chicago College of Dentistry study showed that people who rinsed their mouths with black tea multiple times a day had less plaque buildup than those who swished water. "Polyphenols in tea suppress the bacterial enzyme that triggers plaque accumulation," says Christine D. Wu, PhD, the lead study author. "Drinking tea a few times a day could have the same effect." Choose iced or hot tea, but try to drink it during your meals.

Worried about staining? Go green. "Green tea contains the same polyphenols as black tea," says Wu, "but it isn't fully fermented, and fermentation contributes to the staining."

Pull strings. Flossing belongs to that special category of onerous chores that includes cleaning out the refrigerator, but it has to be done. The key is matching floss to teeth. "If you have rough fillings, use waxed floss," says Dr. Jeffcoat. "If you have bigger spaces between the teeth, consider braided floss." And for average teeth? Go with unwaxed floss—the friction will pull out more plaque. In terms of technique,

Quick Tip

What about the well-publicized research stating that rinsing with Listerine or a similar product is as good as flossing? A study in the *Journal of the American Dental Association* found that swishing with Listerine and flossing are most effective of all.

Dr. Jeffcoat says to listen as you slide the string. "When it squeaks, you know the plaque is gone."

PROTECT YOUR ENAMEL

Your enamel is both a shield and a showcase. Its enemies: erosion and abrasion. Erosion is the breakdown of enamel by acids, while abrasion is wear from brushing. Either way, worn enamel sabotages smiles and lets bacteria tunnel into teeth.

Blow bubbles. Sugarless gum is powerful medicine for your mouth. Numerous studies have shown that chewing the sticky stuff stimulates the delivery of building-block minerals into damaged enamel. Most recently, researchers in Japan showed that people who chew sugarless gum fortified with the ingredient casein phosphopeptideamorphous calcium phosphate (or CPP-ACP) can patch up twice as much enamel as those chewing gum minus CPP-ACP. Look for sugarless gums, such as Trident White, that list Recaldent as an active ingredient.

Pick a soft brush. Pair heavy hand pressure with a firm-bristled toothbrush and you're all set—to clean grout in your bathroom tile. "Some people actually brush grooves in their teeth," says Bruce Reuben, DDS, an oral surgeon in Chicago. To protect and polish your enamel, pick up a soft-bristled brush with tapered tips, such as the Colgate 360. Researchers at the University of Pennsylvania compared this type with a soft brush with rounded tips and found that the former removed more plaque while remaining gentle on teeth.

PREVENT TARTAR

Tartar is created when excess calcium in your saliva combines with plaque. The result is a brownish-yellow deposit above the gum line that provides a microscopic toehold for even more bacteria.

Choose the right paste. Fluoride fights cavities, but it can't touch tartar. For that, you need a toothpaste containing pyrophosphate, a chemical that disrupts the calcification process. Start using a tartar-control toothpaste now, and your dental hygienist will do less scraping later.

And in case you're tempted to stick with your regular toothpaste and just use a tartar-control mouthwash, consider this: "One place that mouthwash does not clean is where the teeth touch each other," says Richard Price, DDS, a consumer advisor for the American Dental Association.

Reach the hard spots. "You see your biggest tartar buildup where the saliva ducts enter the mouth," says Price. "It's like a river laying down silt." Unfortunately, these hot spots—the backs of your lower front teeth and the outer sides of your top molars—are difficult to reach with a full-size toothbrush. Choose one with a small head. And when you tackle the backs of your lower front teeth, turn the brush perpendicular to the floor, then scrub up and down.

Say Cheese

Eating anything sugary (which you can only have in limited moderation with diabetes) causes the pH level of your saliva to plummet, transforming plaque into tooth-dissolving acid. But follow your occasional sweet treat with a piece of cheese and your pH level will stay steady. A study review published in *Nutrition Reviews* that looked at the pH-boosting properties of 12 cheeses shows that while provolone is pretty good, Cheddar's better. In fact, aged Cheddar, Gouda, Monterey Jack, and mozzarella raised pH levels highest. And one bite is all you need; the study subjects ate less than a quarter ounce.

CHAPTER 28

THE NEW DIABETES-CANCER LINK

New research shows a connection between diabetes and cancer. Here's how to protect yourself.

With so many other complications from diabetes to worry about, no one needed one more. Yet a study of more than 1.2 million South Koreans found that those with type 2 diabetes ran a 25 percent higher risk of getting cancer and a 30 percent higher risk of dying of it compared with people without diabetes.

Insulin, the hormone that enables the body to use sugar, may explain the link, says researcher Jonathan M. Samet, MD, chairman of the epidemiology department at Johns Hopkins Bloomberg School of Public Health. In type 2 diabetes, either the pancreas doesn't produce enough insulin or the body can't make efficient use of it. In an effort to compensate, the pancreas ramps up insulin production. But insulin also spurs cells to divide, and rapid cell growth can open the door to cancer.

Great.

In the study, the pancreas and liver were the most likely cancer targets; that's not too surprising because these organs are particularly stressed by diabetes.

CANCER-PROOF YOUR LIFE

Knowing that, more than ever you likely want to do all that you can to protect yourself from cancer. So we've combed through research, interrogated experts, and found cutting-edge strategies to help keep you safe.

Worship a wee bit of sun. People who get the most vitamin D, which lies dormant in skin until ultraviolet rays activate it, may protect themselves from a variety of cancers, including colon, breast, and non-Hodgkin's lymphoma. Ironically, it even improves survival rates of melanoma, the most serious skin cancer. But 10 to 15 minutes a few days a week is all it takes to benefit. (Or you could try a supplement—aim for 400 IU a day.) If you're out any longer than that, slather on the sunscreen.

Eat an orange every day. It just may zap a strain of the *H. pylori* bacteria that causes peptic ulcers and can lead to stomach cancer. Researchers in San Francisco found that infected people with high levels of vitamin C in their blood were less likely to test positive for the cancer-causing strain.

Listen to Katie Couric. Though colonoscopies are about as popular as root canals, if you're 50 or older, get one. Colorectal cancer is the second leading cause of cancer death in the United States. Don't think you're off the hook because you got a digital fecal occult blood test at your last checkup. Research by the Veterans Affairs Cooperative Study found that the test missed 95 percent of the cases. (Schedule your first colonoscopy before your 50th if you have a family history of colon cancer.)

Steam a little green. Piles of studies have shown that piles of broccoli help stave off ovarian, stomach, lung, bladder, and colorectal cancers. And steaming it for 3 to 4 minutes enhances the power of the cancer-fighting compound sulforaphane, which has been shown to halt the growth of breast cancer cells. (Sorry, microwaving doesn't do the trick; it strips out most antioxidants.) Get more protection by sprinkling a handful of selenium-rich sunflower seeds, nuts, or mushrooms on your greens. Researchers are discovering that sulforaphane is about 13 times more potent when combined with the mineral selenium.

Pick a doc with a past. Experience—lots of it—is critical when it comes to accurately reading mammograms. A study from the University of California, San Francisco, found that doctors with at least 25 years' experience were more accurate at interpreting images and less likely to give false positives. Ask about your radiologist's track record. If he or she is freshly minted or doesn't check a high volume of mammograms, get a second read from someone with more mileage.

Drink joltless java. Downing 2 or more cups of decaf a day may lower the incidence of rectal cancer by 52 percent, finds a study from two large and long-term research projects—the Nurses' Health Study and the Health Professionals Follow-Up Study from Harvard University. One theory is that coffee increases bowel movements, which helps to reduce the risk. Why decaf reigns supreme, however, remains a mystery.

Drop 10 pounds. Being overweight or obese accounts for 20 percent of all cancer deaths among women and 14 percent among men, notes the American Cancer Society. (You're overweight if your body

mass index is between 25 and 29.9; you're obese if it's 30 or more.) Plus, losing excess pounds reduces the body's production of female hormones, which may protect against breast, endometrial, and ovarian cancers. Even if you're not technically overweight, gaining just 10 pounds after the age of 30 increases your risk of developing breast, pancreatic, and cervical cancer, among others.

Make like a monkey. Or a bunny. Women who ate four to six antioxidant-laden bananas a week cut their risk of kidney cancer by 54 percent, compared with those who didn't eat them at all, found an analysis of 61,000 women at the Karolinska Institutet in Sweden. Gnawing on root vegetables such as carrots did the same.

Get naked with a friend. You'll need help examining every inch of your body—including your back, scalp, and other hard-to-see places—for possible changes in the size or color of moles, blemishes, and freckles. These marks could spell skin cancer. Women, take special note of your legs: Melanoma mainly occurs there. For the guys, the trunk, head, and neck are the most diagnosed spots.

While you're at it, check your fingernails and toenails, too. Gray-black discoloration or a distorted or elevated nail may indicate the disease. And whether you see changes or not, after age 40, everyone should see a dermatologist yearly.

See into the future. Go to www.your diseaserisk.harvard.edu to assess your chance of developing 12 types of cancer, including ovarian, breast, and colon. After the interactive tool estimates your risk, you'll get personalized tips for prevention.

Pay attention to pain. If you're experiencing a bloated belly, pelvic pain, and an urgent need to urinate, see your doc. These symptoms may signal ovarian cancer, particularly if they're severe and frequent. Women and physicians often ignore these symptoms, and that's the very reason that this disease can be deadly. When caught early, before cancer has spread outside the ovary, the relative 5-year survival rate for ovarian cancer is a jaw-dropping 90 to 95 percent.

Get calcium daily. Milk's main claim to fame may also help protect your colon. Those who took calcium faithfully for 4 years had a 36 percent reduction in the development of new precancerous colon polyps 5 years after the study had ended, revealed Dartmouth Medical School researchers. (They tracked 822 people who took either 1,200 milligrams of calcium every day or a placebo.) Though the study was not on milk itself, you can get the same amount of calcium in three 8-ounce glasses of fat-free milk, along with an 8-ounce serving of yogurt or a 2- to 3-ounce serving of low-fat cheese daily.

Sweat 30 minutes a day. One of the best anticancer potions is a half hour of motion at least 5 days a week. Any kind of physical activity modulates levels of androgens and estrogen, two things that can protect women against estrogen-driven cancers such as ovarian and endometrial, as well as some types of breast cancer. The latest proof comes by way of a recent Canadian study that found that women who get regular, moderate exercise may lower their risk of ovarian cancer by as much as 30 percent. Bonus: All that moving might speed everything through your colon, which may help stave off colon cancer.

Stamp out smoking—all around you. Lung cancer is well known as one of the main hazards of smoking. But everything the smoke passes on its way to the lungs can also turn cancerous: mouth, larynx, and esophagus. The fun doesn't stop there. Smokers are encouraging stomach, liver, prostate, colorectal, cervical, and breast cancers, as well. The good news: If you give up the cigs today, within 15 years, your lung cancer risk will drop to almost presmoking lows. Share that news with the people who puff around you, too, because exposure to someone else's smoke can cause lung cancer, and it may boost your chances of cervical cancer by 40 percent.

Step away from the white bread. If you eat a lot of things with a high glycemic load—a measurement of how quickly food raises your blood sugar—you may run a higher risk of colorectal cancer than women who eat low-glycemic-load foods, finds a Harvard Medical School study involving 38,000 women. The problem eats are mostly white: white bread, pasta, potatoes, and sugary pastries. The low-glycemic-load stuff comes with fiber.

Have your genes screened. Do you have a strong family history of any kind of cancer or multiple cancers? Talk with your doctor about genetic counseling. For instance, nearly everyone born with familial adenomatous polyposis (the genetic predisposition to colon cancer) develops the disease by age 40 if preventive surgery isn't done. Knowing this

early can aid in prevention and early detection.

Request a better breast scan. If you're at high risk of breast cancer—you have the BRCA1 or BRCA2 genetic mutation, for example—ask your doctor to pair your routine mammogram with an MRI. A recent study found that together, the two picked up 94 percent of tumors; mammography alone detected 40 percent and MRI, 77 percent.

Grill smarter. Cooking your food over an open flame is a great way to cut calories. Unfortunately, it can also raise your cancer risk: The grill's high temps can trigger substances in muscle proteins to form cancer-causing compounds called heterocyclic amines, or HCAs. But avoiding this potential hazard is easy: Simply keep gas jets low or wait until the charcoal turns into glowing embers before you start cooking.

Protect yourself even more by lacing your burgers with rosemary (and perhaps other antioxidant-rich herbs such as basil, oregano, or thyme). The herb helps reduce the amount of some HCAs in meat, a Kansas State University study found. Also helpful: Microwaving meat ahead of time helps disable HCA formation and cuts down on grilling time.

Keep your house clean. Yet another reason to love your Swiffer: Active postmenopausal women who got most of their exercise from housework cut their risk of breast cancer by 30 percent, Canadian researchers say.

Let garlic lie. Thanks to this bulbed wonder, you can ward off vampires and stave off cancer. To preserve the potential cancer-fighting power of garlic, chop it up and let it sit a bit. Research suggests that heating garlic can block 90 percent of the activity of alliinase, the enzyme that helps to form a cancer-fighting compound. Alliinase is activated when the cloves are crushed or cut, but if cut garlic cools its heels for 5 to 10 minutes before heating, enough compounds are formed to survive cooking.

Check for radon. Exposure to this odorless, radioactive gas that's produced by the natural decay of uranium is the second leading cause of lung cancer in the United States, according to the EPA. Test your home to see if you're safe. The National Safety Council's National Radon Hotline (800-767-7236) offers low-cost test kits; they're also available at hardware stores.

Play hot tomato. Red fruits (watermelon, tomato, pink grapefruit) are loaded with lycopene, a substance that has been proven time and time again to be a potent cancer fighter. It seems that heating said fruits makes the lycopene easier for the body to use, which explains why men who eat a lot of ketchup, pizza (it's in the sauce), and spaghetti (ditto) are far less likely to get prostate cancer. As for men who eat warm grapefruit, they need their tastebuds examined.

Ditch the wieners. You can smother 'em in all the ketchup you want, but you can't negate a hot dog's, well, negatives. A new study of 190,545 people finds that eating a wiener daily may boost your risk of pancreatic cancer, which is nearly always fatal, by 67 percent. Same goes for sausage and other processed meats.

CANCER'S LONG REACH

But even if you do everything "right," you still have a risk for hearing those dreaded words: *It's cancer.*

Three out of four families.

One in two Americans.

These are the lives that will feel cancer's touch. Not a pleasant thought, but of the children who will contract the disease, 75 percent will survive; of the adults, two out of three will live. In the

1940s, just one in four cancer patients pulled through. As treatments and drugs improve, as early detection becomes an art form, doctors have been forced to recognize a new front in the so-called war on cancer: Survivorship. What happens when people recover and live 20 years or more past their diagnosis, their lives forever altered by their struggle, physically and emotionally? With the disease's reach being so pervasive, eventually all of us will have to deal with cancer.

WHAT HAPPENS WHEN YOU LIVE?

There are more than 10 million cancer survivors in the United States today, up from a mere 3 million in 1971. If the cancer survivors joined hands, they would crisscross the country four times. With improved chemotherapy, the advent of targeted treatments, and better screening and detection methods, for many, cancer is now less a death threat than it is a chronic condition. But even after leaving the world of wigs and gamma rays and bad biopsies, those who fought so hard don't just live happily ever after.

Oddly, many survivors say they felt safe as long as they were getting hooked up to the IVs full of Kool-Aid–colored chemicals, but the day treatment ended, they felt as if they were being tossed to the sharks. "Now what?" they wonder. "What am I supposed to do now?"

Until recently, experts were still shrugging their shoulders. As the ranks of survivors swelled, the information that could improve their lives lagged behind. For decades, the medical world (understandably) focused its heavy artillery on killing cancer cells and saving lives. Only recently has a new front emerged—survivorship, the rigorous study of what happens when cancer patients live.

There are dozens of unknowns: Which chemotherapy treatments cause secondary cancers 20 years later? Which patients are at greatest risk of developing heart problems as a result of treatment? Does going mano a mano with death make a person a Buddhist sage or a neurotic lifelong hypochondriac? How many cancer survivors reach their career goals? How do people disfigured by surgery handle dating in a world obsessed with beauty and physical perfection? Until recently, the posttreatment life of a survivor was like the blank part of a medieval map labeled "Here be dragons." That is about to change.

"One thing we're learning is that cancer affects every domain of life," says Julia H. Rowland, PhD, director of the Office of Cancer Survivorship, which was established in 1996 by the National Cancer Institute in response to growing advocacy by survivors. Problems run the gamut from persistent medical complaints—chronic pain and fatigue, arm swelling, infertility, the fuzzy mind state known as chemobrain—to insurance and employment problems, drastically altered love lives, social stigmatization, and depression.

Of 1,020 cancer survivors polled by the Lance Armstrong Foundation in October 2004, 57 percent said that although cancer may leave their bodies, it will always be a part of their lives. Seventy percent have struggled with depression; 54 percent, with chronic pain; and 53 percent, with secondary health problems. The majority said the practical and emotional consequences of the disease were more painful than the medical issues. Being denied life or health insurance, losing a job or a promotion, and going into debt are not uncommon sequels to a cancer diagnosis. Forty-nine percent of survivors said their nonmedical needs were not being met by the health care system. And, lest we forget, they are the lucky ones.

"We're not blaming oncologists," says Doug Ulman, director of survivorship at the foundation. "Doctors truly want to offer more to their patients, but they need to know what to do. The oncologist may hand you a brochure about your problem, but if you're too depressed or overwhelmed, you might not be able to make the call."

Often the patients want to break off contact. "In the first years after my diagnosis, my highest aspiration was to leave behind the survival statistics—10 years disease free—and melt back into normal life," says Judith Hooper, cancer survivor. "I didn't want medical statisticians tracking me, wondering about relatives with cancer or how many drinks I had last week. My goal was all too attainable, I've since learned, as about 95 percent of adults with cancer simply don't participate in clinical trials." (Parents tend to have better follow-through: 75 percent of children with cancer do join trials.)

"Yet I was hungry for information," Hooper continues. "There was a time, 2 or 3 years postdiagnosis, when all I read were books about mountain climbing—about mountain climbing disasters, to be precise." (To meet her standards, someone had to fall into a crevasse or nearly perish from hypothermia.) "After accumulating an impressive armchair knowledge of the use of carabiners and crampons on icy precipices, I moved on to memoirs by people who had been shipwrecked, lost en route to either pole, marooned on an island, or stranded by airplane crashes. Several years passed before it hit me that there was a connection between these survival stories and my own near brush with death: I wanted to find out what happened to people who had peered into the abyss, what they saw, and how they managed afterward."

David H. Johnson, MD, a lymphoma survivor and outgoing president of the American Society for Clinical Oncology (ASCO), notes, "We all live with this sword of Damocles hanging over us, and we want to know what to do to stay well." After completing his treatment for lymphoma in 1989, Dr. Johnson recalls, "I asked my colleagues, 'What do you do when you finish treatment?' and they said, 'Well, uh . . .' There are rehabilitative programs for heart patients. I thought,

'Where's the cancer rehab program?' I had to create my own."

Dr. Johnson appointed a task force that is developing guidelines to address the physical, emotional, and practical needs of survivors. The group will also revise the organization's oncology training curriculum and support research to improve the care of long-term survivors.

Dr. Johnson, the deputy director of the Vanderbilt-Ingram Cancer Center in Nashville, was the first cancer survivor to head ASCO. His successor, Sandra J. Horning, MD, is the second—surely, a sign of the times. A few hours after getting her breast cancer diagnosis 9 years ago, Dr. Horning, a professor of medicine at Stanford University Medical Center, had to present a federal grant proposal. "Having cancer made me understand the grief of losing your concept of being a healthy person," she says. Wracked with insomnia for the first time in her life, she empathized with her sleep-challenged patients, and she is still struggling with the occasional subtle cognitive lapses of chemobrain.

"It's not that I can't balance my checkbook," she says, "but I sometimes have trouble finding a word or recalling a name. Oddly, I often know the letter it starts with." The very existence of chemobrain is being questioned by new studies.

"The long-term consequences of these drugs weren't studied in the past because they were only used in women with metastatic disease who did not last long enough to find out," says surgeon/ author/activist Susan Love, MD. "Now survivors are dealing with questions about premature menopause, osteoporosis, and chemobrain, as well as the fears of recurrence or second cancers."

Common medical aftereffects in men also include sexual dysfunction, among other genitourinary problems following treatment for prostate, bladder, or colorectal cancer. In premenopausal women, treatment for cancers of the pelvic region or breast can result in low libido, vaginal dryness, or sexual difficulties. Cancer treatments, including chemotherapy, hormone therapy, radiation, and surgery, can all bring on cardiovascular and kidney trouble, lymphedema (an often persistent swelling in the arm or leg following surgery or radiation to sites containing lymph nodes), chronic pain, chronic fatigue, and infertility. Whew. And those are only the physical effects.

"When I got cancer, I half expected the universe to balance the books,"

Hooper says. "I should win the state lottery or at least get a lucrative book contract, and certainly the people with whom I did business should be extra nice to me. Instead, all the hassles that punctuate normal life tend to worsen. Money flies out the window; your kids act out; you argue with your spouse and haggle with your insurer; and your brilliant career may hit the skids. So could your partner's. For a time, you and your entire family are in a lifeboat, bailing like crazy. You need lots of emotional support."

"Whether it's a support group or something else, you need a team to get through cancer," says UCLA's Patricia A. Ganz, MD, an oncologist who has been on the forefront of survivorship research for 2 decades. "Many patients are asymptomatic when diagnosed, and it's a shock to switch from the world of the well to the world of the sick."

Cancer is another country—especially if you're young. Ulman, then a 19-year-old college student in Rhode Island, was recovering from a rare cartilage cancer that required the removal of part of his rib cage while his college dormmates were attending keg parties and dealing with midterms. "I felt about 80 years old. I had this premature maturity."

And if you're dating? Should you mention biopsies on the third date—or the fifth? Withhold information about your partial mastectomy when you describe yourself on Match.com?

"Because I've written about having cancer, it's right there on Google," says Denise, a breast cancer survivor. "That became an issue when I started cyberdating. Once, a reporter for a major newspaper wrote me online, and for 2 weeks, we had a good time talking on the phone every night. When we made a date, I told him my full name. 'Good! I can look you up,' he teased.

"He sure did. When I got to the restaurant, there was one tall, thin, annoyed-looking guy standing outside." All flirtation was gone. Throughout dinner, her date was brusque, "acting as if he were being ripped off." He frowned while glancing repeatedly at her breasts, signed the check before they could order dessert, and fled as if from a plague-infested city. (The upside: Cancer weeds out the jerks. Like many survivors, this woman has gone on to a full, happy romantic life. As one survivor put it, "We have more to offer. Our hearts are bigger.")

A 2002 quality-of-life survey by Dr. Ganz and colleagues found that the majority of the 763 breast cancer survivors polled were doing remarkably well 5 to 10 years after diagnosis. Their brush with cancer inspired better health habits (diet, exercise, supplements) and renewed religious belief in many; the impact, both positive and negative, was strongest in younger women. The worst fallout was in the arena of "love life."

Sigmund Freud observed that love and work are the two poles of existence, and both suffer after cancer. Younger breast cancer survivors, according to Dr. Ganz's survey, took significant hits in the "job or career" department—and no wonder. The current health care system traps many survivors or their spouses in a form of de facto indentured servitude, like a woman in Minneapolis who continues in a sales job she loathes, 6 years after a stem cell transplant: "I can't quit," she says, "I'm uninsurable."

"We find this all the time," says Ulman, "especially with survivors between 20 and 40. The average college graduate changes jobs five or six times in his or her career; it's part of moving ahead. But cancer survivors and their partners may feel they can't take the risk." Many turn down promotions because they may need to take time off or because it is too disruptive to move away from their medical network.

Hoping for some sort of relief for survivors begins to feel Pollyannaish. How can an already overburdened health care system manage to sort out survivors' bank accounts, love lives, and depression, in addition to their persistent medical complaints? Nevertheless, some experts are optimistic. "The future will be better," says Dr. Love.

"Some very smart people," Dr. Johnson says, "are studying the issues we're talking about, and things will start to change in as little as 2 to 5 years, possibly sooner."

For starters, predicts Dr. Rowland: "You'll leave your active treatment phase with a standardized summary stating your illness, all the medications you got, the radiation you received and at which sites, and a prescription for follow-up care and surveillance."

Passport for Care, being developed at the Texas Children's Cancer Center of Baylor College of Medicine, is one prototype. This secure, online, interactive resource will provide long-term pediatric cancer survivors with immediate access to abstracts of their medical histories and physician recommendations for maintaining health. The database will be up and running in 2 to 3 years; ultimately, it will be adapted for adult survivors.

As more survivor data is gathered, treatment can become more personalized, and subsequent problems—such as cardiac defects, chemobrain, or infertility due to certain drugs—anticipated or even prevented.

"We are beginning to study the genetic factors that determine how people will respond to a certain chemotherapy drug, whether it will be effective and whether it will cause side effects," says Dr. Horning. "For example, I felt I might have a genetic sensitivity to a chemo drug, 5-FU. My mother had also taken it, and it caused physical problems for both of us." (When top clinicians are left guessing about links between a treatment and its subsequent effects, it is obvious there is an urgent need for more rigorous tracking.)

As for the survivor psyche (chemobrain or not), life after cancer will never be a cakewalk. But it is easier to feel like a person instead of a walking arrangement of possibly deranged cells, now that formerly chilly cancer centers are sprouting warm and fuzzy sides— including new "survivors' centers" with social scientists and therapists onboard. Today, medical journals show a growing interest in such matters of the psyche as "intrusive cancer-related thoughts" among survivors, while the NCI's Office of Cancer Survivorship is channeling research dollars into acupuncture for menopausal hot flashes, the psychosocial impact of cancer-related infertility, and other whole-person subjects.

No longer marginalized and isolated, survivors can visit Web sites sponsored by the American Cancer Society, the NCI, the Lance Armstrong Foundation, and ASCO for help, including updated information, live chats with experts, peer-to-peer support, and links to resources for depression, post-traumatic stress, and other problems. On the practical side, the National Coalition for Cancer Survivorship offers a Web site (www.canceradvocacy.org) with a Cancer Survival Toolbox and expert legal advice on insurance and employment rights.

The best news may be that there are simple things survivors themselves can do to improve their fate, and diet and exercise—wouldn't you know it?—top the list. In a study by Rowan T. Chlebowski, MD, of the Los Angeles Biomedical Research Institute, breast cancer survivors had a lower risk of recurrence if they were eating a low-fat diet. The greatest benefit was for women with estrogen receptor–negative tumors, considered a marker of poor prognosis.

Also 2005, Harvard's Michelle D. Holmes, MD, discovered that modest exercise could make a big difference: Women who'd had breast cancer could cut their risk of dying in half by walking 3 to 5 hours per week. Exercise is thought to exert its effects in part by reducing circulating estrogens. (If it appears that breast cancer survivors, with their large numbers and unflagging advocacy, get the lion's share of attention, it's because it's true.)

However, that is not to say there is a surefire formula. It makes people more comfortable if they think they know why you got cancer and why you survived it (or didn't), and even slight acquaintances are quick to offer advice: "The most important thing is to have a positive attitude"; "You just need to accept your anger."

"Of the eight members of my original cancer support group, four of us are still standing," Hooper says. "People want to know why. Did we get in touch with our emotions? Use more or better imagery? Take the right supplements? Have stronger chemo or better radiation? Get more support from loved ones? Work off our bad Karma? I don't know. Maybe the nonsurvivors were the best of us, and they graduated while the rest of us are still trying to fill out our credits."

As every survivor knows, the first thing that cancer does is rip off the blinders. You are mortal. You know it. You can't un-know it. "When I graduated from college," recalls Ulman, "I got an offer of life insurance saying I would qualify for a great rate. Then I read the small print, which said I wasn't eligible. There are always these daily reminders."

A headache can never be just a headache; it could be brain metastases, says Hooper. "Five-year or 10-year plans make us nervous, and when we hear someone say, 'Next summer we'll . . .' we secretly mutter something like the Arabic phrase *inshallah* (God willing)."

Cancer survivors all have their little post-traumatic triggers. "There is a certain street corner I am unable to drive past without a momentary flash of nausea," Hooper says. "That was the turnoff to my oncologist's office. Because I was holding a phone to my ear when I got various pieces of bad news (the ominous calcifications, the lymph node biopsy), my subconscious still believes bad things enter via the phone. I'm apt to jump when it rings."

That is why cancer survivors are the twice-born, to borrow a word from William James. Maybe it takes a serious illness—or 6 weeks on an open raft—to see the true paradise that exists beneath the surface.

"I hear all the time from my patients that they look on each day as a gift," Dr. Johnson says. "Shortly after I recovered, I was talking to an oncologist friend and I said, 'I just feel renewed.' And he said, 'You'll get over that.'

"But I haven't. After 15 years I still have that sense of renewal."

14 Survivors Reveal the Biggest Myths

We've all seen a movie of the week about a woman with cancer who survives against all odds and gets the cute guy in the end. These stories have taught us that cancer bestows valuable lessons; that doctors always know what's best; that everyone comes together to support the heroine. Well, you'll be shocked to discover that Hollywood doesn't always get it right. So we asked the people who really know: cancer survivors from all walks of life—celebrities, authors, athletes, doctors.

Myth: Doctors know best

"The surgeon I went to initially said, 'You have so many questions. Why don't you read a book by a doctor named Susan Love? Then you won't have to annoy me.' That's a direct quote. I told him I would not only get her book—I'd ask her to do my surgery. And she did."

—Linda Ellerbee, broadcast journalist, author, breast cancer survivor

"The worst piece of advice I ever got was, 'Just listen to your doctor and do what she tells you.' I needed to do my own research and talk to people who'd been through it."

—Fran Visco, president of the National Breast Cancer Coalition, breast cancer survivor

"I was told I had 6 months to live, but after 2 years of treatment, my cancer went away, and it has never returned. It's been 15 years."

—Kevin Sharp, country singer, bone cancer survivor

Myth: You'll gain a healthy perspective on life

"I thought cancer would automatically make me centered; that it would turn me into a saint; that immediately, I would get my priorities straight and stop sweating the small stuff. But pretty quickly, I realized that I was still stressing about work, fighting with my boyfriend, yelling at my sister."

—Erin Zammett, author of *My (So-Called) Normal Life*, leukemia survivor

"I kept hearing that your attitude is the most important thing. When I had complications and my cancer returned, I kept thinking, Why can't I do this better? Is this my fault?"

—Wendy Harpham, MD, author of *Happiness in a Storm: Facing Illness and Embracing Life as a Healthy Survivor*, non-Hodgkin's lymphoma survivor

Myth: Cancer brings people closer together

"A friend of mine said, 'You know, your friends don't want to hear about your disease. You need to go to a support group with other people who have cancer.'"

—Sean Patrick, founder of HERA "Climb for Life" annual climb, ovarian cancer survivor

"You find out who your friends are. People either rally to support you or fall by the wayside."

—Corina Morariu, professional tennis player, leukemia survivor

"A lot of well-meaning people told me how many people they knew who had died of breast cancer. That's not helpful."

—Geralyn Lucas, author of *Why I Wore Lipstick to My Mastectomy*, breast cancer survivor

Myth: You will be damaged goods

"Chemo was like an inside-out exfoliation. My skin is better; I don't break out anymore; my hair is thicker than it used to be. I actually feel better and healthier now."

—Melissa Etheridge, musician, breast cancer survivor

"Cancer made me more in touch with my sexuality. Before, I never felt beautiful or that I was one of those people who deserved to wear lipstick. Finding out that I can have one boob, be balding and shedding, made me rethink what beauty is and what it means to be a woman."

—Geralyn Lucas

"After chemo, my hair came back in straight rather than curly, and I was ecstatic over that. My whole life I'd wanted straight hair!"

—Sharon Osbourne, reality TV star, founder of the Sharon Osbourne Colon Cancer Foundation, colon cancer survivor

Myth: You'll never be afraid again

"If you've had cancer, don't sleep alone! Get a pet if you don't have a mate. Sometimes you wake up in the middle of the night and your mind plays tricks on you. That's when you need something alive that you can hold on to."

—Fran Drescher, actress, author, uterine cancer survivor

"Even after my treatment was finished, there was never a feeling that it was over. I kept waiting for the other shoe to drop."

—Sandra Steingraber, PhD, author of *Living Downstream*, biologist, bladder cancer survivor

Myth: Treatment will be terrible

"I quickly learned that chemo ruled my Fridays, but it didn't have to rule my life."

—JoAnna Lund, coauthor of *When Life Hands You Lemons, Make Lemon Meringue Pie*, breast cancer survivor

"I thought chemotherapy was going to ravage my body, but I never felt very sick. At its worst, I had a really unpleasant taste in my mouth and was queasy the first day and a half after treatment."

—Randi Rosenberg, president of the Young Survival Coalition, breast cancer survivor

Not a myth: Life will never be the same

"The difficult part of having cancer isn't the actual disease; it's figuring out what to do once you've survived. You have to go about living your life after it's been turned upside down."

—Corina Morariu

"The day before my diagnosis, I thought I was healthy, and the day after, I knew that I wasn't. There's a sense of loss for the rest of your life, knowing that your health is flawed."

—David H. Johnson, MD, deputy director of Vanderbilt-Ingram Cancer Center, non-Hodgkin's lymphoma survivor

MEDICAL BREAKTHROUGHS

Besides heart disease and cancer, diabetes can welcome other unwanted complications into your life. Here's the latest research on them.

PEER INTO THIS CRYSTAL BALL

Wondering about your future health? Skip the fortune-teller and click on Diabetes PHD—a sophisticated health risk calculator that predicts your odds for developing devastating complications of diabetes such as heart attack, stroke, blindness, or kidney failure.

"Thinking about health risks is really abstract, but when you plug your own health information—such as your age, weight, blood sugar, blood pressure, cholesterol levels, and medications—into this program, you see exactly what you're in for," says Robert Rizza, MD, professor of medicine at Mayo Clinic in Rochester, Minnesota, and president of the American Diabetes Association, which sponsors this online health tool. Even better, you can see how your risk changes if you make lifestyle changes.

Powering this virtual crystal ball is software used by medical centers and health care corporations to predict the success of new treatment plans. Best of all, it's free. Click on www.diabetes.org/diabetesphd to get started.

PROTECT YOURSELF AGAINST "TYPE 3" DIABETES

Intriguing new research from Brown University suggests that Alzheimer's disease (AD) may actually be a third type of diabetes—after insulin- and noninsulin-dependent types. What if you could reduce your chances of developing Alzheimer's the same way you can cut your risk of type 2 diabetes: by maintaining a healthy weight and staying active?

By looking at postmortem brain tissue from 28 people who'd had AD and 26 who hadn't, they found that insulin levels were five to six times lower in brains affected by AD, a sign of insulin resistance. If brain cells develop insulin resistance, that could explain AD's tangled fibers and plaques, the scientists say.

One way to reduce your risk might be some cutting-edge calorie counting: Learn to eat in response to true hunger and fullness cues from your body by eating mindfully—chewing slowly and eating only when you're sitting down.

TAKE THIS TEST

How many animals can you name in a minute? This is a fun keep-the-kids-occupied-in-the-car game, but when UK scientists asked 136 volunteers to play, they found a way to detect early-stage dementia. People with early Alzheimer's named an average of 10 to 15 animals or fruits within the time allowed. Healthy adults, however, listed 20 to 25. While the Alzheimer's group thought of every-day words such as cat and apple, they left out others that aren't used as often, such as zebra and kiwi.

The pattern was so consistent that researchers correctly identified ill patients based solely on word lists. The potential payoff: Early detection may someday give scientists a better shot at slowing disease progression.

ASK FOR THIS TEST BY NAME

Kidney disease is sneaking up on Americans: One in nine of us already has it, and anyone with high blood pressure, diabetes, or a family history of kidney disorders is at increased risk of getting it. At least now you can get an accurate diagnosis. A new test is far more likely than older tests to detect the disorder before it leads to kidney failure.

Accumin, a urine test, catches 98 percent of cases, diagnosing them an average of 4 years earlier than older tests (which also miss more than a third of cases). With no obvious symptoms in the early stages, the disease can lead to kidney failure. Then, a patient's only options are dialysis or a transplant.

The National Kidney Foundation advises adults to get tested for the disease yearly, so ask your doctor for Accumin. It's covered by most insurers.

SEE THIS SIGHT SOLUTION

Diabetes steals the eyesight of 24,000 Americans each year. The fix? Control high blood pressure, say British scientists.

When they compared 758 people with diabetes who kept their blood pressure (BP) under strict control (around 144/82) with 390 whose levels stayed higher (157/88), the lower BP group had a 47 percent lower risk of dimmed eyesight. High blood pressure can damage blood vessels in the eyes, explains study author David Matthews, FRCP, chairman of the Oxford Centre for Diabetes, Endocrinology, and Metabolism. Control BP with exercise; weight loss; eating plenty of fruits, veggies, whole grains, and low-fat dairy; and, if needed, drugs.

SKIP OPEN-TOED SHOES

If you have diabetes, watch what you slip on your feet. People with diabetes who wear thong sandals have twice the leg-amputation risk, according to a Diabetes Care study. Researchers blame the greater likelihood of stubbed toes and stepped-on feet. Choose shoes and sandals that cover your toes.

LISTEN UP!

In an ongoing Department of Veterans Affairs report of nearly 700 former members of the armed forces, researchers recently found that those with type 2 diabetes experienced age-related declines in hearing earlier than people without diabetes did. High blood sugar may prompt tiny blood vessels in the inner ear to narrow, disrupting the normal reception of sound, says lead author

Nancy Vaughan, PhD, of the Department of Veterans Affairs' National Center for Rehabilitative Auditory Research in Portland, Oregon. If you have type 2 diabetes, wear hearing protection in noisy situations, such as at rock concerts or while using power tools.

SHOW A LITTLE LEG

Every September, doctors and health centers across the nation offer free screenings for peripheral arterial disease (PAD)—a condition in which plaque accumulates inside leg arteries, leading to pain, difficulty walking, and ultimately even amputation. One out of every three people with diabetes over age 50 has PAD.

"If undetected, peripheral arterial disease can increase a person's risk of having a heart attack and stroke. The progression of PAD results in death for about one-third of patients," says Harvey Wiener, DO, chief of interventional radiology at Phoenix Baptist Hospital in Arizona and head of the 2005 Legs for Life program, the national screening program sponsored by the Society of Interventional Radiology. "Diabetics and their physicians need to get in the habit of an annual ankle brachial index (ABI) test to look for PAD. We want diabetics to know their ABI number the way they know their blood sugar number—both can save their life."

An ABI test compares blood pressure in the legs and arms to assess bloodflow. The treatment for PAD? Stop smoking and start exercising; you may need medications to reduce pain and also surgery to remove plaque. Visit www.legsforlife.org to find a screening location near you.

Q&A

"I have diabetes and seem to get urinary tract infections (UTIs) all the time. Can I do anything to help prevent them?"

Although you are more likely to get UTIs than a person who doesn't have diabetes, the preventive steps are the same: Always urinate after sexual intercourse, avoid diaphragms and spermicidal foam, drink plenty of fluids throughout the day, don't wait to urinate, don't rush when you do go, and wipe from front to back to prevent bacteria around the anus from entering the vagina or urethra.

These precautions are especially important for you because diabetes impairs the immune system, making you more vulnerable to infection, explains Christopher A. Czaja, MD, fellow in infectious diseases at the University of Washington. Plus, high levels of sugar in your urine make it easier for UTI-causing bacteria to grow. Diabetes may also damage nerves in the bladder, so you don't completely empty it when you urinate, creating a breeding ground for bacteria. If you notice signs of an infection, such as a burning sensation when you pee or frequent urination, call your doctor promptly: You are three times more likely than a person without diabetes to develop a potentially life-threatening blood infection (bacteremia) from a UTI.

PART VII

DIABETES COOKBOOK

CHAPTER 29

EFFORTLESS MEAL PLANNING

Whip up healthy, delicious meals and snacks

You already know that eating well is an essential part of managing diabetes. The right foods can help to keep your blood sugar and fats at steady levels, and that's key to both taking control of diabetes and avoiding diabetes-related problems. Studies show that people with type 2 diabetes who ate a diet high in fiber and complex carbohydrates improved their blood sugar control by an average of 95 percent! And those with type 1 diabetes experienced a considerable 30 percent improvement.

The Diabetes Food Exchange System—organized by the American Dietetic Association and the American Diabetes Association—makes it easy to ensure you're getting the right amounts of fiber-rich, low-fat foods and other wholesome, healing nutrients.

To use the exchange system, determine your target calorie level based on whether you need to maintain your weight or lose weight. (See "How Many Calories Do You Need?" on page 277.) We recommend losing 1 to 2 pounds a week for optimal weight loss. Then see "Find Your Exchange Allowance" on page 279 to see how many servings of the various food groups you should eat each day. All the recipes in this book include dietary exchanges to simplify meal planning.

HOW MUCH IS AN EXCHANGE SERVING?

Knowing serving sizes is crucial to making any meal plan work. Unfortunately, because we eat in restaurants (where the portions are huge), we've gotten accustomed to eating more than we should. When in doubt about what makes a serving, minimize—don't supersize. Here are the specifics of exchange servings. (Some of these vary from food pyramid serving sizes. See "Pyramids Compared" on page 278 for a comparison.)

Bread: The bread group, also called starches, encompasses all carbohydrate-rich foods, such as cereals, grains, pastas, breads, crackers, and snacks. Starchy vegetables such as corn, green peas, plantains, potatoes, winter squash, and yams are also included here. In general, one serving (cooked, where applicable) is . . .

- $^1/_2$ cup cereal or starchy vegetable
- $^1/_3$ cup rice or pasta
- 1 slice bread

Fruit: These can be fresh, frozen, canned, or dried fruit or fruit juice. One fruit serving equals . . .

- 1 small to medium piece of fresh fruit
- $^1/_2$ cup canned fruit (with a small amount of juice), cut fruit, or fruit juice
- $^1/_4$ cup dried fruit

Milk: Fat-free milk and yogurt are included here. (To count cheeses, see the meat group. Cream and other dairy fats are counted in the fat group.) One serving of milk equals . . .

- 1 cup ($^1/_2$ pint or 8 fluid ounces) fat-free milk
- 1 cup fat-free or low-fat yogurt

Vegetable: This includes all vegetables except the starchy ones mentioned previously. Go for the richest colors you can find. Dark green and dark yellow vegetables are the most nutritious. These include spinach, broccoli, romaine lettuce, carrots, bell peppers, and chile peppers. In general, one vegetable serving is . . .

- $^1/_2$ cup cooked vegetables or vegetable juice
- 1 cup raw vegetables

How Many Calories Do You Need?

Here's a way to quickly estimate how many calories you should be eating. Just find your activity level in the chart below, then multiply that number by your weight in pounds. Use the resulting "daily calorie needs" number to look up your exchange allowance on page 279.

1. Find your activity level.

IF YOU ARE A . . .	YOUR ACTIVITY LEVEL IS . . .
Sedentary woman	12
Sedentary man	13
Lightly active woman	14
Lightly active man	15
Active woman	16
Active man	17
Very active woman	18
Very active man	20

2. Determine your calorie needs.

Note: If you're trying to lose weight, use your goal weight instead of your actual weight.

Activity level × weight in pounds = calorie needs

Meat: When buying meats, choose those labeled "lean" or "very lean." "Select" and "choice" grades are leaner than "prime." Look for ground beef rather than meat labeled "hamburger," because the latter may contain more fat.

In addition to meats, this group includes other protein-based foods such as cheese, eggs, and beans. (Bacon is counted in the fat group.)

Note that the serving size for meat and cheese is 1 ounce. But don't worry, you can still eat plenty of meat. We recommend that you get somewhere between 5 and 10 servings (5 to 10 ounces) from the meat group each day. (You'll find your recommended number of servings in "Find Your Exchange Allowance" on page 279.) Just remember that there may be several ounces (or several servings) of meat in any one meal you eat. Generally, 1 serving of meat equals . . .

• 1 ounce cooked lean beef, pork, lamb, skinless poultry, fish, or shellfish
• 1 ounce cheese

• ¹/₂ cup cooked dried beans, peas, or lentils
• 1 egg

Fat: Most fats have the same number of calories per serving. But some fats are better for you than others. The good monounsaturated and polyunsaturated fats are generally found in plant foods such as olive oil and nuts and in some seafood. Generally, one serving of fat equals . . .

• 1 teaspoon butter, regular margarine, or vegetable oil

Pyramids Compared

The American Diabetes Association's diabetes food pyramid is a variation of the USDA Food Guide Pyramid that you're probably already familiar with. If you choose to use the diabetes food pyramid as a guide, take note that a few of its servings are different in size than a diabetes exchange serving. The differences are listed below.

FOOD	DIABETES EXCHANGE SERVING	DIABETES PYRAMID SERVING
Lean meat	1 oz	2–3 oz poultry or fish
Cheese	1 oz (a meat exchange)	1¹/₂ oz
Dry cereal	¹/₂ c (a bread exchange)	1 oz
Fruit juice	¹/₂ c	³/₄ c
Peanut butter	2 tsp (a fat exchange)	2 Tbsp (a meat group serving)

Find Your Exchange Allowance

In the chart below, pick the "daily calorie needs" level closest to the one you have chosen to maintain your current weight or to reach your goal weight. (If possible, ask a dietitian to help you choose.) Then scan the food groups to see how many servings of each food to eat in a day. These numbers are meant only as a guide. Some days, you may end up eating more or less in any given food category.

FOOD GROUP	DAILY CALORIE NEEDS				
	1,200	1,500	1,800	2,000	2,500
Bread	5	6	8	9	10
Fruit	3	3	5	5	6
Milk	1½	2	2	2	4
Vegetable	2	5	5	5	5
Meat	5	6	6	8	10
Fat	3	4	5	5	6

- 1 tablespoon regular salad dressing
- ⅛ of a medium avocado
- 8 to 10 olives
- 6 to 10 nuts
- 2 teaspoons peanut butter
- 2 teaspoons tahini paste
- 1 tablespoon sesame seeds
- 1 slice bacon
- 2 tablespoons half-and-half
- 2 tablespoons coconut
- 3 tablespoons reduced-fat sour cream

COUNT CARBOHYDRATES, TOO

Carbohydrates include both starches and sugars. But the total amount of carbs you consume is more important than the type; both starches and sugars affect your blood sugar in the same way. Carbohydrates that are refined or processed include sweets such as candy and soft drinks. Naturally occurring carbs come from milk, fruit, pasta,

Avoid the Trans Fats

A recent study showed that high intakes of trans fatty acids may increase your risk of developing type 2 diabetes. Trans fatty acids are found in margarine and foods cooked in hydrogenated vegetable oil, such as crackers, potato chips, cookies, and cakes. Reduce your risk by cutting back on stick margarine, using canola or olive oil for cooking, and limiting the aforementioned foods.

bread, rice, dried beans and peas, and starchy vegetables such as potatoes, corn, and green peas.

Carbohydrates from sugary foods have little nutritional value, so it's best to limit these. Instead, choose carbs in the form of grains, fruits, and milk, which contain vitamins, minerals, and fiber. If you do eat sugary foods, they have to be substituted for other carbs and not simply added to your meal plan.

One serving of grain, fruit, or milk provides about 15 grams of carbohydrate and is considered one carbohydrate exchange. For most people, a reasonable guideline is 45 to 75 grams of carbohydrate per meal and no more than 15 to 30 grams per snack. (You can get carbohydrate counts from recipes and food labels.) But it's best to have a registered dietitian develop a meal plan that meets your individual requirements.

CHAPTER 30

THE RECIPES

100 Delicious, Nutritious, Diabetes-Fighting Meals and Snacks

You can protect your health and eat great at the same time with these simple recipes. They're good for you, and the entire family will love them. Enjoy!

BREAKFASTS

Vegetable Omelet

(photo on page 311)

3 eggs, well beaten

3 Tbsp chopped red bell pepper

2 Tbsp chopped green bell pepper

2 Tbsp seeded and chopped tomato

2 Tbsp chopped mushrooms

2 Tbsp chopped zucchini

1. Heat large skillet coated with olive oil cooking spray over medium heat. Add eggs, allowing them to cover bottom of pan. Cook 3 minutes or until bottom begins to set.

2. When nearly cooked, top one half of omelet with peppers, tomato, mushrooms, zucchini, and salt and black pepper to taste. Carefully fold remaining half over filling and cook 2 minutes or until cooked through.

Makes 1 serving

Per serving: 257 cal, 21 g pro, 9 g carb, 15 g fat, 4.5 g sat fat, 637 mg chol, 2 g fiber, 194 mg sodium

Diet Exchanges: 0 milk, 1$^1/_2$ vegetable, 0 fruit, 0 starch/bread, 3 meat, 2 fat

Spinach Omelet

2 lg eggs

6 egg whites

1 Tbsp 1% milk

1 tsp trans-free margarine or butter

1$^1/_2$ c loosely packed baby spinach

$^1/_4$ c (about 1 oz) shredded part-skim mozzarella or reduced-fat Cheddar cheese

1. In medium bowl, beat eggs, egg whites, and milk.

2. In large skillet over medium heat, melt margarine. Add the beaten egg mixture and cook until it begins to set. Sprinkle spinach and cheese on top, cook 1 or 2 minutes longer, then gently fold into an omelet. Cook until spinach appears wilted and eggs are completely set.

3. Season to taste with salt and black pepper and serve immediately.

Makes 2 servings

Per serving: 190 cal, 22 g pro, 4 g carb, 10 g fat, 4 g sat fat, 220 mg chol, 0 g fiber, 500 mg sodium

Diet Exchanges: 0 milk, $^1/_2$ vegetable, 0 fruit, 0 starch/bread, 3 meat, 1 fat

Austrian Anytime Scramble

2 med eggs

4 egg whites

2 Tbsp finely chopped fresh parsley

$^1/_4$ c (about 1 oz) shredded Asiago cheese

Tomato slices (optional)

1. Coat medium skillet with cooking spray.

2. In medium bowl, beat eggs and egg whites, then add parsley and cheese. Season to taste with salt and black pepper.

3. Set skillet over medium-high heat and add the egg mixture. Scramble until set and serve with fresh tomato slices, if desired.

Makes 2 servings

Per serving: 160 cal, 18 g pro, 2 g carb, 9 g fat, 4 g sat fat, 225 mg chol, 0 g fiber, 370 mg sodium

Diet Exchanges: 0 milk, 0 vegetable, 0 fruit, 0 starch/bread, $2^1/_2$ meat, 1 fat

Breakfast in a Cup

4 oz reduced-fat loose breakfast sausage

$^1/_4$ c chopped green bell pepper

$^1/_4$ c chopped onion

1 c liquid egg substitute or 4 egg whites

1 lg egg

1 can (4 oz) sliced mushrooms, drained

$^1/_2$ cup (2 oz) shredded reduced-fat Cheddar cheese

1. Coat 6-cup muffin pan with cooking spray. Preheat oven to 350°F.

2. In medium nonstick skillet over medium-high heat, cook sausage, pepper, and onion 5 minutes, or until the sausage is browned. Spoon the mixture into a bowl and cool slightly. Stir in egg substitute, egg, and mushrooms. Spoon the mixture evenly into the prepared muffin pan. Sprinkle with cheese.

3. Bake 20 minutes or until the egg is set.

Makes 6 servings

Per serving: 91 cal, 11 g pro, 3 g carb, 4 g fat, 2 g sat fat, 42 mg chol, 1 g fiber, 344 mg sodium

Diet Exchanges: 0 milk, 0 vegetable, 0 fruit, 0 starch/bread, $1^1/_2$ meat, $^1/_2$ fat

Egg-chiladas with Ranchero Sauce

Sauce

1 med onion, chopped

1 jalapeño chile pepper, seeded and chopped

1 lg clove garlic, chopped

1 tsp olive or peanut oil

1 c vegetable (V8) or tomato juice

2 tsp chopped fresh oregano or $1/2$ tsp dried

$1/4$ tsp chili powder

$1/4$ tsp ground black pepper

$1/4$ tsp salt

Egg-chiladas

16 oz liquid egg substitute or 16 egg whites

1 c finely shredded reduced-fat Cheddar/ Monterey Jack cheese mixture

4 stone-ground corn tortillas, warmed

2 c shredded romaine lettuce

1. *To prepare sauce:* In large saucepan, sauté onion, jalapeño pepper, and garlic in oil 5 minutes over medium-high heat. Add vegetable juice, oregano, chili powder, black pepper, and salt. Reduce heat to medium-low and simmer 10 minutes. Cool slightly. Ladle sauce into blender or food processor and puree. Use immediately or keep warm in the saucepan over low heat.

2. *To prepare egg-chiladas:* In nonstick skillet, scramble egg substitute and season to taste. Divide the warm eggs and $1/2$ cup of the cheese among the tortillas. Fold. Lay the filled wraps on beds of lettuce. Top with warm Ranchero Sauce and sprinkle with remaining $1/2$ cup cheese.

Makes 4 wraps with $1/4$ cup sauce per wrap

Per serving: 242 cal, 21 g pro, 23 g carb, 8 g fat, 3 g sat fat, 18 mg chol, 3 g fiber, 701 mg sodium

Diet Exchanges: 0 milk, 1 vegetable, 0 fruit, 1 starch/bread, 3 meat, 1 fat

Fried Eggs with Vinegar

2 Tbsp butter

8 lg eggs

1 tsp salt

$1/4$ tsp ground black pepper

$1/8$ tsp dried marjoram or basil

4 tsp red wine vinegar

1 tsp chopped parsley (optional)

1. Melt 1 tablespoon of the butter in large nonstick skillet over medium-low heat. Add eggs and sprinkle with salt, pepper, and marjoram (work in batches

if necessary). Cover and cook until the whites are set and the yolks are almost set, 3 to 5 minutes. (For steam-basted eggs, add 1 teaspoon of water to the pan and cover with a lid.)

2. Remove to plates. Place skillet over low heat and add remaining 1 tablespoon butter. Cook until the butter turns light brown, 1 to 2 minutes. Add vinegar. Pour the vinegar mixture over the eggs. Sprinkle with parsley (if using). Serve hot.

Makes 4 servings

Per serving: 206 cal, 13 g pro, 1 g carb, 16 g fat, 7 g sat fat, 440 mg chol, 0 g fiber, 764 mg sodium

Diet Exchanges: 0 milk, 0 vegetable, 0 fruit, 0 starch/bread, 2 meat, 2½ fat

Cornmeal Flapjacks

(photo on page 312)

    1 c cornmeal

    ³/₄ c whole grain pastry flour

    1 tsp baking soda

    ¹/₂ tsp salt

    1¹/₄ c low-fat buttermilk

    1 egg

    2 Tbsp maple syrup

    1 Tbsp vegetable oil

1. Preheat oven to 200°F. Coat baking sheet with cooking spray.

2. In large bowl, combine cornmeal, flour, baking soda, and salt.

3. In medium bowl, combine buttermilk, egg, maple syrup, and oil. Beat with a fork or whisk until blended. Add to the flour mixture. Stir until a smooth batter forms.

4. Coat large nonstick skillet with cooking spray. Warm over medium heat. Pour batter by ¹/₄ cupfuls into skillet. Cook 2 minutes, or until tiny bubbles appear on the surface and the edges begin to look dry. Flip the pancakes. Cook 1 to 2 minutes or until golden on the bottom. Transfer pancakes to the prepared baking sheet. Place in the oven to keep warm.

5. Coat the skillet with cooking spray. Repeat with the remaining batter to make a total of 15 pancakes.

Makes 5 servings

Per serving: 235 cal, 8 g pro, 41 g carb, 6 g fat, 1 g sat fat, 45 mg chol, 6 g fiber, 472 mg sodium

Diet Exchanges: ¹/₂ milk, 0 vegetable, 0 fruit, 2¹/₂ starch/bread, ¹/₂ meat, 1 fat

Fast French Toast

2 egg whites, beaten

$1/2$ c 1% milk

$1/4$ tsp vanilla extract

$1/8$ tsp ground cinnamon

4 slices bread

1. In shallow bowl, combine egg whites, milk, vanilla extract, and cinnamon. Beat until frothy. Dip bread into the egg white mixture, turning to coat both sides.

2. Heat large skillet coated with cooking spray over medium heat. Working in batches if necessary, place bread in pan and cook 3 minutes. Turn bread. Cook 3 minutes longer or until golden brown on both sides.

Makes 2 servings

Per serving: 174 cal, 11 g pro, 28 g carb, 3 g fat, 1 g sat fat, 2 mg chol, 3 g fiber, 339 mg sodium

Diet Exchanges: $1/2$ milk, 0 vegetable, 0 fruit, $1 1/2$ starch/bread, $1/2$ meat, 0 fat

Stuffed French Toast

Filling

4 oz whipped light cream cheese

2 Tbsp strawberry or raspberry all-fruit preserves

French Toast

1 loaf French bread, about 16" long (16 oz)

3 egg whites

3 eggs

1 c fat-free evaporated milk

1 tsp vanilla extract

$1/2$ tsp ground allspice

1. *To prepare filling:* In small bowl, using electric mixer, beat cream cheese. Mix in preserves.

2. *To prepare French toast:* Trim $1/2$" off each end of bread loaf and discard. Cut the loaf into ten $1 1/2$"-thick slices. Cut a pocket in the top of each slice without cutting all the way through. Fill each pocket with about $1 1/2$ tablespoons of the filling.

3. Coat nonstick griddle or large skillet with cooking spray and warm over medium heat.

4. In shallow bowl, beat together egg whites, eggs, milk, vanilla extract, and

allspice. Using tongs, dip the bread in the egg mixture to coat completely (take care not to squeeze out the filling).

5. Cook the bread in batches over medium heat 2 minutes on each side or until golden brown. (Using tongs, hold the crusts against the griddle for a few seconds to cook all sides.)

Makes 10 slices

Per slice: 212 cal, 11 g pro, 29 g carb, 6 g fat, 2 g sat fat, 73 mg chol, 1 g fiber, 363 mg sodium

Diet Exchanges: $\frac{1}{2}$ milk, 0 vegetable, 0 fruit, 2 starch/bread, 1 meat, 1 fat

Breakfast Cookies

$1\frac{1}{2}$ c whole wheat flour or whole grain pastry flour

1 tsp baking soda

1 tsp salt

$\frac{3}{4}$ c olive oil

$\frac{1}{2}$ c sugar

$\frac{1}{2}$ c honey

2 med eggs, lightly beaten

2 Tbsp fat-free milk

$1\frac{1}{2}$ Tbsp vanilla extract

$2\frac{1}{4}$ c quick-cooking oats

1 c golden raisins

$\frac{1}{4}$ c semisweet mini-chocolate chips (or a dark chocolate bar broken into bits)

1. Preheat oven to 350°F.

2. In large bowl, combine flour, baking soda, and salt.

3. In another large bowl, whisk oil, sugar, and honey until creamy. Add eggs and stir until thoroughly combined. Add milk and vanilla extract and stir again. Add the flour mixture and stir until just combined, then fold in oats, raisins, and chocolate chips. Drop dough by tablespoonfuls onto ungreased baking sheet.

4. Bake 9 to 13 minutes or until slightly brown but still very soft. Cool on the baking sheet several minutes, then carefully transfer to a rack.

5. When completely cool, store in airtight container.

Makes 36

Per cookie: 126 cal, 2 g pro, 18 g carb, 6 g fat, 1 g sat fat, 10 mg chol, 1 g fiber, 106 mg sodium

Diet Exchanges: 0 milk, 0 vegetable, 0 fruit, 1 starch/bread, 0 meat, 1 fat

Lemon Scones

1 c whole grain pastry flour

1 c all-purpose flour

1 Tbsp baking powder

1 tsp ground cardamom or coriander

$\frac{1}{2}$ tsp salt

3 Tbsp sugar

1 Tbsp canola oil

3 egg whites

$\frac{1}{2}$ c (4 oz) low-fat plain or lemon yogurt

1 Tbsp grated lemon peel

1. Preheat oven to 400°F. Coat baking sheet with cooking spray.

2. In large bowl, combine flours, baking powder, cardamom, salt, and 2 tablespoons of the sugar. Drizzle with oil and mix with a fork until evenly distributed.

3. Reserve 1 tablespoon of the egg whites.

4. Stir yogurt, lemon peel, and remaining egg whites into the flour mixture. Stir gently with a fork until the mixture holds together. Turn onto a lightly floured surface. Knead about 8 strokes to mix the dough thoroughly. Pat out the dough to form an 8" circle. With a sharp knife, cut evenly into 8 wedges. Arrange the wedges, about 1" apart, on the prepared baking sheet. Brush with

the reserved egg white. Sprinkle with remaining 1 tablespoon sugar.

5. Bake 15 minutes or until golden brown.

Makes 8

Per scone: 153 cal, 6 g pro, 28 g carb, 2 g fat, 1 g sat fat, 1 mg chol, 2 g fiber, 288 mg sodium

Diet Exchanges: 0 milk, 0 vegetable, 0 fruit, 2 starch/bread, 0 meat, $\frac{1}{2}$ fat

Blueberry Tea Scones

$\frac{1}{2}$ c dried blueberries

1 c boiling water

1 egg

$\frac{1}{2}$ c soy milk

$\frac{1}{4}$ c fat-free milk

2 c all-purpose flour

$\frac{1}{4}$ c sugar

$1\frac{1}{2}$ tsp baking powder

6 Tbsp trans-free margarine (such as Smart Balance)

$\frac{1}{4}$ c English toffee chips

2 Tbsp ground flaxseed

1 Tbsp wheat germ

1. Preheat oven to 400°F. Coat 2 large baking sheets with cooking spray.

2. Place blueberries in bowl and cover with boiling water. Set aside.

3. Beat egg in 8-ounce measuring cup

and add soy milk to $^1/_4$-cup line. Fill to 1-cup line with fat-free milk. Set aside.

4. In large bowl, sift together flour, sugar, and baking powder. Add margarine using pastry blender or fork until the mixture resembles coarse meal.

5. Drain blueberries. Add to the flour mixture along with toffee chips, flaxseed, and wheat germ. Stir to distribute evenly. Stir the egg-and-milk mixture and add to the dough. Stir until dough just clings together. Do not overmix. Drop by $^1/_4$ cupfuls onto the prepared baking sheets.

6. Bake 12 minutes or until golden brown. Serve warm.

Makes 12

Per scone: 200 cal, 4 g pro, 28 g carb, 8 g fat, 2 g sat fat, 19 mg chol, 2 g fiber, 127 mg sodium

Diet Exchanges 0 milk, 0 vegetable, $^1/_2$ fruit, $1^1/_2$ starch/bread, 0 meat, $1^1/_2$ fat

Whole Wheat Cranberry-Orange Muffins

1 Tbsp trans-free margarine or butter, melted

$^1/_2$ c packed brown sugar

$^1/_2$ tsp ground cinnamon

2 c whole wheat flour or whole grain pastry flour

$^1/_2$ c granulated sugar

2 tsp baking powder

1 tsp salt

$^1/_4$ tsp baking soda

3 Tbsp grated orange zest

1 c orange juice

$^1/_2$ c unsweetened applesauce

2 med eggs, lightly beaten

1 c fresh cranberries, chopped

1. Preheat oven to 350°F. Generously coat 12-cup muffin pan with cooking spray.

2. In small bowl, combine margarine, brown sugar, and cinnamon.

3. In large bowl, combine flour, granulated sugar, baking powder, salt, baking soda, and orange zest. In another large bowl, mix orange juice, applesauce, eggs, and cranberries. Add to the flour mixture and stir until just combined. Do not overmix.

4. Evenly divide batter among the prepared muffin cups. Sprinkle each muffin with the sugar-cinnamon mixture. Bake 20 to 25 minutes or until a wooden pick inserted in the center of a muffin comes out clean. Cool on rack 10 minutes before serving.

Makes 12

Per muffin: 210 cal, 4 g pro, 45 g carb, 2 g fat, 0.5 g sat fat, 36 mg chol, 3 g fiber, 315 mg sodium

Diet Exchanges: 0 milk, 0 vegetable, $^1/_2$ fruit, 2 starch/bread, 0 meat, $^1/_2$ fat

Raspberry Muffins

1 c whole grain pastry flour

$^1/_2$ c all-purpose flour

2 tsp baking powder

1 tsp baking soda

$^1/_4$ tsp salt

$^3/_4$ c low-fat buttermilk

3 Tbsp vegetable oil

1 egg

$^1/_3$ c sugar

1 tsp grated lemon peel

1 c raspberries

1. Preheat oven to 400°F. Spray a 12-cup muffin pan with cooking spray.

2. In medium bowl, combine flours, baking powder, baking soda, and salt.

3. In large bowl, stir together buttermilk, oil, egg, sugar, and lemon peel until well blended. Stir in the flour mixture until just combined. Do not overmix. Gently fold in raspberries.

4. Divide the batter evenly among the prepared muffin cups, filling them about two-thirds full. Bake 12 to 15 minutes or until a wooden pick inserted in the center of a muffin comes out clean. Cool on rack 5 minutes. Remove to rack and cool completely.

Makes 12

Per muffin: 120 cal, 3 g pro, 18 g carb, 4 g fat, 1 g sat fat, 18 mg chol, 2 g fiber, 190 mg sodium

Diet Exchanges: $^1/_2$ milk, 0 vegetable, $^1/_2$ fruit, $1^1/_2$ starch/bread, $^1/_2$ meat, 1 fat

Pecan Muffins

$1^1/_2$ c whole grain pastry flour

$^1/_4$ c soy flour

$2^1/_2$ tsp baking powder

$^1/_2$ tsp salt

$^1/_2$ tsp ground nutmeg

$^1/_2$ c toasted pecans, chopped

$^1/_2$ c vegetable oil

$^1/_2$ c apricot or peach fruit spread

2 lg eggs, lightly beaten

$1^1/_2$ tsp vanilla extract

$^1/_8$ tsp liquid stevia

1. Place a rack in the middle position in the oven and preheat oven to 375°F. Coat 12-cup muffin pan with cooking spray or line with paper cups.

2. In large bowl, combine flours, baking powder, salt, nutmeg, and pecans.

3. In small bowl, combine oil, fruit spread, eggs, vanilla extract, and stevia.

Add to the flour mixture and stir just until the dry ingredients are moistened.

4. Spoon into the prepared muffin cups, filling them three-quarters full. Bake 12 to 14 minutes or until a wooden pick inserted in the center of a muffin comes out clean. Serve warm.

Makes 12

Per muffin: 218 cal, 4 g pro, 20 g carb, 12 g fat, 1 g sat fat, 35 mg chol, 3 g fiber, 193 mg sodium

Diet Exchanges: 0 milk, 0 vegetable, 0 fruit, 1 starch/bread, $^1/_2$ meat, $2^1/_2$ fat

Cherry Cream of Rye Cereal

$1^1/_4$ c water

$1^1/_4$ c apple cider

$^1/_4$ tsp salt

1 c cream of rye cereal

$1^1/_4$ Tbsp cherry fruit spread

$^1/_8$ tsp ground nutmeg

$^1/_8$ tsp ground cardamom

$1^1/_2$ Tbsp chopped hazelnuts (optional)

1. Combine water, cider, and salt in a saucepan and bring to a boil over medium heat. Stir in cereal and reduce heat to low. Cook, uncovered, until thick, stirring occasionally, 3 to 5 minutes. Remove from heat and stir in fruit spread.

2. Spoon into bowls and sprinkle with nutmeg, cardamom, and hazelnuts (if using). Serve hot.

Makes 4 servings (3 cups)

Per serving: 208 cal, 4 g pro, 45 g carb, 1 g fat, 0 g sat fat, 0 mg chol, 6 g fiber, 168 mg sodium

Diet Exchanges: 0 milk, 0 vegetable, 1 fruit, 2 starch/bread, 0 meat, 0 fat

Baked Apple Oatmeal

1 med cooking apple, cored and chopped

1/2 c old-fashioned rolled oats

2 Tbsp raisins

1/2 tsp ground cinnamon

Pinch of salt

1 c water

1. Preheat oven to 350°F.

2. In small baking dish, combine apple, oats, raisins, cinnamon, salt, and water and stir well.

3. Bake, uncovered, stirring once or twice, 15 to 20 minutes or until mixture becomes thick and apple pieces are fork-tender.

Makes 1 serving

Per serving 350 cal, 8 g pro, 74 g carb, 4 g fat, 0.5 g sat fat, 0 mg chol, 11 g fiber, 310 mg sodium

Diet Exchanges: 0 milk, 0 vegetable, 2 $^1/_2$ fruit, 2 $^1/_2$ bread, 0 meat, $^1/_2$ fat

Berry Morning Mix

(photo on page 313)

1 c fat-free blueberry yogurt

$1/2$ c 1% cottage cheese

$1/2$ c blueberries and/or sliced strawberries

1–2 Tbsp low-fat granola

1 tsp crushed walnuts or almonds

2 tsp grated dark chocolate

1. In individual cups or large bowl, combine yogurt, cottage cheese, berries, granola, and nuts.

2. Sprinkle chocolate on top.

Makes 2 servings

Per serving: 159 cal, 12 g pro, 22 g carb, 3 g fat, 1.5 g sat fat, 5 mg chol, 2 g fiber, 290 mg sodium

Diet Exchanges: 1 milk, 0 vegetable, $1/2$ fruit, 0 starch/bread, 1 meat, $1/2$ fat

Citrus Fruit Bowl

4 med navel oranges

3 lg pink grapefruits

$1/3$ c dried sweetened cranberries

Fresh mint leaves (optional)

1. Cut off the peel and pith from oranges and grapefruits. Working over a large bowl, cut out the sections of fruit from between the membranes, letting the sections fall into the bowl. Squeeze the juice from the membranes over the fruit. Discard the membranes.

2. Add cranberries and stir to combine. Garnish with mint, if desired.

Makes 6 servings

Per serving: 100 cal, 2 g pro, 25 g carb, 0 g fat, 0 g sat fat, 0 mg chol, 4 g fiber, 0 mg sodium

Diet Exchanges: 0 milk, 0 vegetable, 2 fruit, 0 starch/bread, 0 meat, 0 fat

LUNCH
Veggie Bagel

- 1 med bagel, split
- 1 Tbsp fat-free cream cheese
- $1/3$ cucumber, thinly sliced
- $1/3$ tomato, finely chopped
- 1 portobello mushroom, thinly sliced
- 2 slices reduced-fat or fat-free Swiss cheese

1. Preheat broiler.

2. Lightly toast bagel in toaster oven. Spread cream cheese on each half of bagel. Top each half with cucumber, tomato, mushroom, and 1 slice cheese.

3. Place on broiler-pan rack and broil 4 minutes or until cheese is melted.

Makes 2 servings

Per serving: 170 cal, 13 g pro, 22 g carb, 4.5 g fat, 2 g sat fat, 10 mg chol, 2 g fiber, 230 mg sodium

Diet Exchanges: 0 milk, 1 vegetable, 0 fruit, 1 starch/bread, 1 meat, 0 fat

Mediterranean Tuna Sandwiches

- 1 can (6 oz) water-packed tuna, drained
- 1 Tbsp olive oil
- 1 Tbsp red wine vinegar
- 1 clove garlic, minced
- 3 Tbsp chopped red onion
- $1/2$ tsp chopped parsley
- 2 leaves lettuce
- $1/2$ tomato, sliced
- 2 hard rolls, split

1. In medium bowl, combine tuna, oil, vinegar, garlic, onion, and parsley until thoroughly mixed. Cover and refrigerate 2 hours to allow flavors to blend.

2. Place lettuce, tomato, and tuna mixture on bottom halves of rolls. Close sandwiches with top halves of rolls and serve.

Makes 2 servings

Per serving: 340 cal, 28 g pro, 35 g carb, 10 g fat, 1.5 g sat fat, 35 mg chol, 1 g fiber, 600 mg sodium

Diet Exchanges: 0 milk, $1/2$ vegetable, 0 fruit, 2 starch/bread, 3 meat, $1^1/2$ fat

Meatball Souvlaki

(photo on page 314)

Meatballs

1 med egg

¹/₄ c dried bread crumbs

1 tsp Dijon mustard

¹/₂ tsp dried oregano

¹/₄ tsp salt

¹/₄ tsp black pepper

1 lb lean ground beef

Sandwiches

1 c low-fat plain yogurt

¹/₂ c grated English cucumber

1 clove garlic, minced

2 Tbsp dried mint

6 whole wheat pitas

2 c shredded lettuce

2 sm tomatoes, chopped

6 thin slices red onion

1. Preheat oven to 400°F. Line baking sheet with foil.

2. *To prepare meatballs:* In large bowl, whisk egg, bread crumbs, mustard, oregano, salt, and pepper. Mix in beef. Shape mixture into 24 meatballs and place on baking sheet. Bake 15 minutes or until meatballs are no longer pink inside.

3. *To prepare sandwiches:* In small bowl, combine yogurt, cucumber, garlic, mint, and black pepper to taste. Lay pitas on clean work surface and spread ¹/₄ cup yogurt mixture over each. Sprinkle equal portions of lettuce, tomatoes, and onion over each pita. Top with 4 meatballs each. Fold pitas in half and serve.

Makes 6 servings

Per serving: 370 cal, 26 g pro, 46 g carb, 10 g fat, 3.5 g sat fat, 65 mg chol, 6 g fiber, 600 mg sodium

Diet Exchanges: 0 milk, ¹/₂ vegetable, 0 fruit, 2¹/₂ starch/bread, 2¹/₂ meat, ¹/₂ fat

Club Sandwiches

Lemon-Caper Mayonnaise

¹/₂ c low-fat mayonnaise

1 tsp lemon juice

2 tsp drained capers, coarsely chopped

Sandwiches

12 thin slices multigrain bread, toasted

¹/₂ lb cooked skinless chicken breast, sliced

2 oz alfalfa sprouts

¹/₃ English cucumber, thinly sliced

1 lg tomato, cut into 8 slices

8 slices turkey bacon, cooked

4 leaves lettuce

1. *To prepare lemon-caper mayonnaise:* In small bowl, combine mayonnaise, lemon juice, and capers.

2. *To prepare sandwiches:* Place 4 of the bread slices on a work surface. Spread 2 teaspoons of lemon-caper mayonnaise on each slice. Top with layers of chicken, sprouts, and cucumber.

3. Spread 4 of the remaining bread slices each with 2 teaspoons of lemon-caper mayonnaise. Place the slices, mayonnaise side up, on the 4 sandwiches. Top with layers of tomato, bacon, and lettuce.

4. Spread remaining 4 bread slices with remaining lemon-caper mayonnaise. Place, mayonnaise side down, on top of the sandwiches. Cut in half diagonally. Secure with wooden picks.

Makes 4 servings

Per serving: 303 cal, 21 g pro, 39 g carb, 10 g fat, 1 g sat fat, 40 mg chol, 10 g fiber, 664 mg sodium

Diet Exchanges: 0 milk, $^1/_2$ vegetable, 0 fruit, 2 starch/bread, 2 meat, 0 fat

Open-Faced Chicken Quesadillas

4 flour tortillas (10" diameter)

$^1/_2$ c mayonnaise

1 Tbsp roasted garlic and red pepper spice blend

2 c shredded cooked chicken

1 c (4 oz) shredded Monterey Jack cheese

2 med tomatoes, seeded and chopped

2 c shredded romaine lettuce

1. Preheat oven to 350°F. Place tortillas on baking sheets and toast 5 minutes.

2. In small bowl, combine mayonnaise and spice blend. Spread 2 tablespoons of the mixture over each tortilla. Evenly top the center of each tortilla with chicken, then sprinkle with cheese. Arrange tomatoes around the chicken.

3. Bake 10 minutes or until heated through. Sprinkle lettuce around the tomato.

Makes 4 servings

Per serving: 380 cal, 31 g pro, 31 g carb, 14 g fat, 4 g sat fat, 63 mg chol, 1 g fiber, 586 mg sodium

Diet Exchanges: 0 milk, $^1/_2$ vegetable, 0 fruit, 2 starch/bread, 4 meat, $1^1/_2$ fat

Peanut Butter, Ham, and Pickle Sandwich

2 Tbsp creamy or crunchy peanut butter

2 slices whole grain bread

2 Tbsp pickle relish

1 slice ($^1/_2$ oz) low-fat deli ham

Spread peanut butter on 1 slice of the bread. Spread pickle relish on top of the peanut butter, add ham, and top with remaining slice of bread.

Makes 1 serving

Per serving: 376 cal, 16 g pro, 41 g carb, 19 g fat, 4 g sat fat, 4 mg chol, 6 g fiber, 817 mg sodium

Diet Exchanges: 0 milk, 0 vegetable, 0 fruit, $2^1/_2$ starch/bread, $^1/_2$ meat, $^1/_2$ fat

Strawberry and Bacon Salad

2 slices turkey bacon

2 lg leaves green leaf lettuce

1 tomato, chopped

3–4 slices avocado, halved

$^1/_2$ c sliced strawberries

1 Tbsp balsamic vinegar or rice vinegar

1. Prepare turkey bacon according to package directions. Slice into bite-size pieces.

2. Line 2 plates with lettuce leaves. Top with tomato, avocado, strawberries, and bacon. Drizzle with vinegar.

Makes 2 servings

Per serving: 92 cal, 3 g pro, 9 g carb, 6 g fat, 1.5 g sat fat, 12 mg chol, 3 g fiber, 195 mg sodium

Diet Exchanges: 0 milk, $^1/_2$ vegetable, $^1/_2$ fruit, 0 starch/bread, $^1/_2$ meat, 1 fat

Chicken-Pasta Salad

$1^1/_2$ c rotini pasta

1 pkg (6 oz) cooked chicken breast, cut into bite-size pieces

2 c broccoli florets

$^1/_2$ green bell pepper, chopped

$^1/_2$ red bell pepper, chopped

$^1/_2$ red onion, finely chopped

$^3/_4$ c light salad dressing, such as Italian or ranch

1. Prepare pasta according to package directions. Drain and place in serving bowl.

2. Add chicken, broccoli, peppers, onion, and salad dressing. Toss to combine.

3. Refrigerate 30 minutes or until chilled.

Makes 6 servings

Per serving: 203 cal, 13 g pro, 25 g carb, 6 g fat, 1 g sat fat, 26 mg chol, 2 g fiber, 264 mg sodium

Diet Exchanges: 0 milk, $^1/_2$ vegetable, 0 fruit, $1^1/_2$ starch/bread, $1^1/_2$ meat, 1 fat

Tortellini and Broccoli Salad

1 pkg (16 oz) cheese- or meat-filled tortellini

3 c broccoli florets

1/4 c olive oil

2 Tbsp red wine vinegar

1 Tbsp coarse grain mustard

2 cloves garlic, minced

2 tsp honey

2 tsp dried basil

1/2 tsp salt

1 sm red onion, chopped

4 scallions, sliced 1/2" thick

1/2 pt cherry tomatoes, halved

3/4 c (3 oz) shredded Romano cheese

1. Prepare tortellini according to package directions. Add broccoli during the last 3 minutes of cooking. Rinse under cold water and drain.

2. In large bowl, whisk together oil, vinegar, mustard, garlic, honey, basil, and salt. Add tortellini, broccoli, onion, scallions, tomatoes, and cheese. Toss to coat well.

3. Serve immediately or refrigerate up to 24 hours.

Makes 6 servings

Per serving: 294 cal, 15 g pro, 41 g carb, 8 g fat, 4 g sat fat, 33 mg chol, 3 g fiber, 630 mg sodium

Diet Exchanges: 0 milk, 1 vegetable, 0 fruit, 2 1/2 starch/bread, 1 meat, 1/2 fat

Southwestern Salad

1 c brown rice

1 can (14 1/2 oz) low-sodium black beans, rinsed and drained

2 c frozen corn kernels, thawed

1 med red bell pepper, chopped

1 sm onion, chopped

1/3 c white wine vinegar

1/4 c chopped cilantro

1 jalapeño chile pepper, finely chopped (wear plastic gloves when handling)

1 tsp chili powder

1. Cook rice according to package directions.

2. Transfer the rice to large bowl and add beans, corn, bell pepper, onion, vinegar, cilantro, jalapeño pepper, and chili powder. Toss gently and let stand, refrigerated or at room temperature, 1 hour before serving.

Makes 4 servings

Per serving: 320 cal, 10 g pro, 72 g carb, 2 g fat, 0 g sat fat, 0 mg chol, 9 g fiber, 180 mg sodium

Diet Exchanges: 0 milk, 1 vegetable, 0 fruit, 4 starch/bread, 0 meat, 0 fat

Steak Salad

1 Tbsp light soy sauce

1 clove garlic, minced

6 oz beef tenderloin, thinly sliced

2 tsp toasted sesame oil

$1/4$ c reduced-fat beef broth

1 med red bell pepper, sliced

$1/2$ med onion, sliced into rings

$1/2$ lb mushrooms of your choice, sliced

$1/2$ head leaf lettuce, washed and torn into
    bite-size pieces

1. In shallow glass dish, mix soy sauce and garlic. Lay beef slices in sauce and turn several times to coat. Cover and refrigerate at least 30 minutes or overnight.

2. Warm oil in large skillet or wok over medium-high heat. When hot, add beef and its marinade and cook, stirring constantly, 5 minutes or until no longer pink. Transfer beef to large bowl and set aside. Add broth to skillet and cook with pepper, onion, and mushrooms about 1 minute or until vegetables are bright and crisp-tender.

3. In large bowl, toss vegetables and beef with lettuce and serve.

Makes 2 servings

Per serving: 240 cal, 24 g pro, 14 g carb, 11 g fat, 3 g sat fat, 55 mg chol, 3 g fiber, 440 mg sodium

Diet Exchanges: 0 milk, $2^{1}/_{2}$ vegetable, 0 fruit, 0 starch/bread, 3 meat, 2 fat

Roasted Beet and Orange Salad

4 med beets (about 1 lb), stems trimmed to 1"

2 Tbsp apricot all-fruit spread

1 Tbsp white balsamic vinegar

$1^{1}/_{2}$ tsp olive oil

$1^{1}/_{2}$ tsp flaxseed oil

2 Tbsp snipped fresh chives or thinly sliced
    scallion greens

$1/2$ tsp salt

$1/4$ tsp freshly ground black pepper

2 med navel oranges

4 c mixed bitter salad greens, such as
    arugula, watercress, endive, and
    escarole

1. Preheat oven to 400°F. Coat 9" baking pan with cooking spray.

2. Place beets in the prepared baking pan and cover tightly with foil. Roast 1 hour or until very tender. Uncover and let the beets stand until cool enough to handle.

3. Meanwhile, in large bowl, whisk fruit spread, vinegar, olive oil, flaxseed oil, chives, salt, and pepper.

4. Slip the skins off the beets and discard the skins. Chop the beets. Cut off the peel and white pith from the oranges. Section the oranges into the bowl with the dressing. Add the beets and toss to coat well. Let stand for at least 15 minutes to allow the flavors to blend.

5. Just before serving, arrange the greens on a serving plate. Top with the beet mixture.

Makes 4 servings

Per serving: 140 cal, 4 g pro, 28 g carb, 3 g fat, 0 g sat fat, 0 mg chol, 5 g fiber, 396 mg sodium

Diet Exchanges: 0 milk, $1/2$ vegetable, 1 fruit, 1 starch/bread, 0 meat, $1/2$ fat

Fruited Turkey Salad

(photo on page 315)

- $1/2$ c (4 oz) fat-free sour cream
- $1/4$ c low-fat mayonnaise
- 2 tsp chopped fresh thyme or 1 tsp dried, crushed
- 2 tsp lemon juice
- $1/2$ tsp grated lemon peel
- 1 lb cooked skinless turkey breasts, cut into $1/2$" cubes
- 2 ribs celery, chopped
- 1 apple, cut into $1/2$" cubes
- $1/3$ c dried apricots, sliced
- 2 Tbsp toasted coarsely chopped walnuts

In large bowl, combine sour cream, mayonnaise, thyme, lemon juice, and lemon peel. Add turkey, celery, apple, and apricots. Toss gently to coat. Sprinkle with walnuts.

Makes 4 servings

Per serving: 320 cal, 29 g pro, 26 g carb, 11 g fat, 2 g sat fat, 76 mg chol, 3 g fiber, 258 mg sodium

Diet Exchanges: $1/2$ milk, $1/2$ vegetable, 1 fruit, $1/2$ starch/bread, $3^1/2$ meat, 2 fat

Minestrone Soup

(photo on page 316)

2 cans (10³/₄ oz each) low-sodium chicken
    or vegetable broth

1 can (14–19 oz) red kidney beans, rinsed
    and drained

1 can (14–19 oz) white kidney beans, rinsed
    and drained

2 cans (14¹/₂ oz each) diced tomatoes

6 carrots, sliced

1 bunch scallions, sliced

³/₄ tsp Italian seasoning

¹/₄ tsp salt

¹/₄ tsp black pepper

12 oz rotini pasta

1 pkg (10 oz) frozen spinach, thawed and
    squeezed dry

Fat-free Parmesan cheese (optional garnish)

1. In large pot, combine broth, beans,
tomatoes (with juice), carrots, scallions,
Italian seasoning, salt, and pepper.
Cover and cook on low heat 6 to 8
hours.

2. Prepare pasta according to package
directions. Drain and stir into soup
along with spinach until heated
through. Serve sprinkled with cheese,
if using.

Makes 10 (1¹/₂-cup) servings

Per serving: 250 cal, 13 g pro, 50 g carb, 1 g fat,
0 g sat fat, 1 mg chol, 11 g fiber, 350 mg sodium

Diet Exchanges: 0 milk, 2 vegetable, 0 fruit,
3 starch/bread, 0 meat, 0 fat

Turkey Chili

2 Tbsp vegetable oil

1 lg onion, chopped

1 med green bell pepper, chopped

1 med red bell pepper, chopped

3 cloves garlic, minced

1–3 tsp chili powder

1 Tbsp ground cumin

1 lb lean ground turkey breast

2 cans (14¹/₂ oz each) pinto beans, rinsed
    and drained

1 can (28 oz) diced tomatoes

1 sm bunch cilantro, stemmed and chopped

Juice of ¹/₂ lime

1. Warm oil in large pot over medium
heat. When hot, add onion and peppers
and cook 5 to 10 minutes or until soft.
Add garlic, chili powder, and cumin
and cook, stirring, 2 to 3 minutes. Add
turkey and cook, stirring, until no
longer pink. Add beans and tomatoes
(with juice) and bring to a boil.

2. Reduce heat and simmer, uncovered, about 20 minutes. Stir in cilantro and lime juice and season with salt and black pepper to taste.

Makes 6 (1½-cup) servings

Per serving: 270 cal, 26 g pro, 28 g carb, 6 g fat, 1 g sat fat, 45 mg chol, 9 g fiber, 570 mg sodium

Diet Exchanges: 0 milk, 2 vegetable, 0 fruit, 1 starch/bread, 2½ meat, 1 fat

Thai Squash Soup

5–6 shallots, unpeeled

1 can (13½ oz) light coconut milk

2 c reduced-sodium chicken broth

1½ lb butternut squash, peeled and cut into ½" cubes

½ c packed cilantro + 1 Tbsp chopped, for garnish

¼ tsp salt

2 Tbsp fish sauce

¼ c minced scallions, green part only

1. Preheat broiler. Coat sheet of heavy foil with cooking spray and place shallots on top. Broil shallots, turning occasionally, about 5 to 7 minutes or until softened and blackened. Remove from the broiler, let cool, then peel and halve lengthwise.

2. In large pot over medium-high heat, combine shallots, coconut milk, broth, squash, and ½ cup of the cilantro. Cook just until the mixture begins to boil. Reduce heat, add salt, and simmer about 10 minutes or until the squash is tender. Stir in fish sauce and cook 2 to 3 minutes.

3. Garnish each serving with sprinkling of scallions and the remaining chopped cilantro. Season with black pepper to taste.

Makes 6 (1-cup) servings

Per serving: 130 cal, 5 g pro, 19 g carb, 5 g fat, 3.5 g sat fat, 0 mg chol, 2 g fiber, 600 mg sodium

Diet Exchanges: 0 milk, 2½ vegetable, 0 fruit, 0 starch/bread, ½ meat, 0 fat

Caramelized Onion and Sweet Potato Soup

2 Tbsp trans-free margarine or butter

5 lg sweet onions, thinly sliced

1¹⁄₂ Tbsp sugar

4 med sweet potatoes, peeled and cubed

2 qt chicken broth

¹⁄₂ tsp ground allspice

¹⁄₂ tsp dried thyme

¹⁄₂ tsp ground nutmeg

¹⁄₂ tsp salt

¹⁄₂ tsp black pepper

In large pot over medium-high heat, melt margarine. Add onions and cook, stirring constantly, 5 to 7 minutes or until browned. Add sugar and cook, stirring, 3 minutes. Add sweet potatoes, broth, allspice, thyme, nutmeg, salt, and pepper and bring to a boil. Quickly reduce heat to low and continue to simmer, uncovered, 15 to 20 minutes or until sweet potatoes are fork-tender. Adjust seasonings and serve.

Makes 14 (1-cup) servings

Per serving: 80 cal, 2 g pro, 16 g carb, 1.5 g fat, 0 g sat fat, 0 mg chol, 2 g fiber, 330 mg sodium

Diet Exchanges: 0 milk, 1 vegetable, 0 fruit, ¹⁄₂ starch/bread, 0 meat, 0 fat

Spicy Chicken Tortilla Soup

1 can (15 oz) diced tomatoes

1¹⁄₂ tsp chili powder

1¹⁄₂ tsp ground cumin

¹⁄₄ tsp black pepper

2 tsp Worcestershire sauce

¹⁄₂ tsp hot-pepper sauce

2 tsp olive oil

1 lb boneless, skinless chicken breasts, cut into 1" pieces

1 med onion, chopped

1–2 jalapeño chile peppers, chopped (wear plastic gloves when handling)

2 cloves garlic, minced

2 cans (14¹⁄₂ oz each) reduced-sodium chicken broth

¹⁄₄ c all-purpose flour

¹⁄₂ c water

¹⁄₃ c fat-free sour cream

¹⁄₃ c chopped cilantro

4 oz reduced-fat tortilla chips, crushed

1. In food processor or blender, combine tomatoes (with juice), chili powder, cumin, black pepper, Worcestershire sauce, and hot-pepper sauce. Process to smooth, thick consistency and set aside.

2. Warm oil in large pot over medium-high heat. When hot, cook chicken, onion, jalapeño pepper, and garlic, stirring frequently, 5 minutes or until chicken is no longer pink and onion is softened. Reduce heat to low, add the tomato mixture and broth and simmer uncovered, 15 minutes.

3. Meanwhile, in small bowl, whisk flour and water until smooth paste forms. Add to soup and raise tempera-ture if necessary to keep soup just barely boiling. Simmer 5 minutes.

4. Remove from heat, add sour cream, and stir until well blended. Stir in cilantro, garnish with tortilla chips, and serve.

Makes 8 (1-cup) servings

Per serving: 190 cal, 19 g pro, 22 g carb, 3.5 g fat, 0.5 g sat fat, 34 mg chol, 2 g fiber, 230 mg sodium

Diet Exchanges: 0 milk, 1 vegetable, 0 fruit, 1 starch/bread, 2 meat, $1/2$ fat

BEVERAGES AND SNACKS

Peanut Butter Shake

1 c fat-free milk

1 sm ripe banana

2 Tbsp toasted wheat germ

2 Tbsp creamy peanut butter

In blender, combine milk, banana, wheat germ, and peanut butter. Process until smooth.

Makes 1 serving

Per serving: 433 cal, 22 g pro, 52 g carb, 18 g fat, 4 g sat fat, 4 mg chol, 6 g fiber, 281 mg sodium

Diet Exchanges: 1 milk, 0 vegetable, 2 fruit, $1/2$ starch/bread, $1^1/2$ meat, 3 fat

Citrus Crush

1 c unsweetened pineapple juice

1 c orange juice

3 Tbsp lemon juice

2 Tbsp lime juice

2 c crushed ice

In blender, combine pineapple juice, orange juice, lemon juice, lime juice, and ice. Puree until smooth and frothy.

Makes 2 servings

Per serving: 135 cal, 2 g pro, 34 g carb, 0 g fat, 0 g sat fat, 0 mg chol, 1 g fiber, 10 mg sodium

Diet Exchanges: 0 milk, 0 vegetable, $2^1/2$ fruit, 0 starch/bread, 0 meat, 0 fat

Hot Chocolate

1 c fat-free milk

1 Tbsp sugar

1 Tbsp unsweetened, nonalkalinized cocoa powder

Dash of salt

$1/8$ tsp vanilla extract

1. Combine milk, sugar, cocoa, and salt in small saucepan.

2. Cook, stirring occasionally, over medium heat until the milk begins to steam—about 2 minutes. Do not boil.

3. Remove from heat, stir in vanilla extract, and serve.

Makes 1 serving

Per serving: 150 cal, 9 g pro, 27 g carb, 1 g fat, 0 g sat fat, 5 mg chol, 2 g fiber, 270 mg sodium

Diet Exchanges: 1 milk, 0 vegetable, 0 fruit, 1 starch/bread, 0 meat, 0 fat

Italian Salsa and Chips

(photo on page 317)

Chips

 1 pkg (10 oz) pitas (6" diameter)

 ¹/₄ c (1 oz) grated Parmesan cheese

 1¹/₂ tsp Italian seasoning

Salsa

 5 plum tomatoes, chopped

 1 sm onion, chopped

 ³/₄ c chopped fresh basil

 3 Tbsp balsamic or wine vinegar

 2 Tbsp chopped kalamata olives

 1 Tbsp olive oil

 2 cloves garlic, chopped

 ¹/₄ tsp salt

 ¹/₄ tsp ground black pepper

1. *To prepare chips:* Preheat oven to 375°F. Cover baking sheet with foil.

2. Cut pitas into quarters. Separate each wedge into 2 pieces. Place on the baking sheet. Lightly coat the pitas with cooking spray.

3. In small bowl, combine Parmesan and Italian seasoning. Sprinkle over the pitas. Bake 8 to 10 minutes or until golden and crisp. Transfer to platter or serving basket.

4. *To prepare salsa:* Meanwhile, in medium bowl, combine tomatoes, onion, basil, vinegar, olives, oil, garlic, salt, and pepper. Serve with the chips.

Makes 6 servings

Per serving: 204 cal, 7 g pro, 33 g carb, 5 g fat, 1 g sat fat, 3 mg chol, 2 g fiber, 471 mg sodium

Diet Exchanges: 0 milk, 1 vegetable, 0 fruit, 2 starch/bread, ¹/₂ meat, 1 fat

Quick 'n' Cool Chicken Bites

Sauce

1/2 c plum preserves

2 Tbsp lime juice

1 Tbsp soy sauce

1 Tbsp Dijon mustard

3 tsp prepared chopped ginger

Chicken

1/4 c sesame seeds

6 c toasted rice cereal

3 Tbsp vegetable oil

3/4 tsp salt

1/2 tsp garlic powder

1/2 c buttermilk

2 lg eggs

2 lb boneless, skinless chicken breast
   halves, cut into 1" pieces

1. *To prepare sauce:* In medium bowl, combine preserves, lime juice, soy sauce, mustard, and ginger. Set aside until ready to serve.

2. *To prepare chicken:* Place rack in upper third of oven and preheat to 450°F. Spread sesame seeds on baking sheet and toast 2 to 4 minutes or until golden. Transfer to plate to cool slightly. Coat the same baking sheet and another with cooking spray and set aside.

3. In food processor, combine cereal, oil, salt, and garlic powder. Add cooled sesame seeds and process to fine crumbs. Transfer to large bowl.

4. In another medium bowl, whisk buttermilk and eggs until well combined. With one hand, dip each piece of chicken in the buttermilk mixture, then drop into the crumb mixture. With other hand, roll the chicken firmly in the crumbs and place on baking sheets.

5. Bake 8 to 10 minutes or until golden. Serve with plum dipping sauce.

Makes 36 pieces

Per piece: 80 cal, 7 g pro, 8 g carb, 2.5 g fat, 0 g sat fat, 26 mg chol, 0 g fiber, 148 mg sodium

Diet Exchanges: 0 milk, 0 vegetable, 0 fruit, 1/2 starch/bread, 1 meat, 1/2 fat

Peanut Butter–Stuffed Celery

1/4 c creamy or crunchy peanut butter

2 Tbsp horseradish

2 ribs celery

1. In small bowl, mix peanut butter and horseradish. If necessary, add a

small amount of water to soften the mixture.

2. Spread half of the mixture in each celery rib. Wrap the stuffed celery in plastic wrap or aluminum foil. Chill.

Makes 2 servings

Per serving: 200 cal, 8 g pro, 10 g carb, 16 g fat, 3 g sat fat, 0 mg chol, 3 g fiber, 350 mg sodium

Diet Exchanges: 0 milk, $\frac{1}{2}$ vegetable, 0 fruit, 0 starch/bread, $1\frac{1}{2}$ meat, $2\frac{1}{2}$ fat

Peanut Butter S'Mores

1 honey graham cracker

2 Tbsp creamy peanut butter

2 Hershey's Kisses

Spread graham cracker with peanut butter and dot with Hershey's Kisses.

Makes 1 serving

Per serving: 268 cal, 9 g pro, 17 g carb, 20 g fat, 5 g sat fat, 3 mg chol, 3 g fiber, 195 mg sodium

Diet Exchanges: 0 milk, 0 vegetable, 0 fruit, 1 starch/bread, $1\frac{1}{2}$ meat, $3\frac{1}{2}$ fat

Whoopie Pies

1 c all-purpose flour

$\frac{1}{4}$ c unsweetened cocoa powder

1 tsp baking soda

$\frac{1}{4}$ tsp salt

$\frac{1}{2}$ c sugar

$\frac{1}{4}$ c butter

1 egg white

$\frac{1}{2}$ c 1% milk

$\frac{3}{4}$ c marshmallow crème

1. Preheat oven to 425°F.

2. In medium bowl, combine flour, cocoa, baking soda, and salt.

3. In large bowl, combine sugar, butter, and egg white. With electric mixer on medium speed, beat 2 minutes or until fluffy. Stir in the flour mixture, then milk, until just blended.

4. Drop dough by rounded tablespoons onto large, ungreased baking sheets to make 32 cookies. Bake 5 minutes or until tops spring back when lightly touched.

5. Place the baking sheets on racks to cool completely. Spoon about 2 teaspoons of marshmallow crème on bottoms of 16 cookies. Top with remaining 16 cookies.

Makes 16

Per pie: 97 cal, 2 g pro, 16 g carb, 3 g fat, 2 g sat fat, 10 mg chol, 1 g fiber, 160 mg sodium

Diet Exchanges: 0 milk, 0 vegetable, 0 fruit, 1 starch/bread, 0 meat, $\frac{1}{2}$ fat

Orange-Walnut Biscotti

$^2/_3$ c walnuts

$^1/_4$ c sugar

$1^1/_4$ c whole grain pastry flour

$^1/_4$ c cornmeal

1 tsp baking powder

$^1/_4$ tsp salt

$^1/_4$ c butter, softened

$^1/_4$ c Splenda

2 eggs

2 tsp grated orange peel

$^1/_2$ tsp orange extract

1. In food processor, combine walnuts and 2 tablespoons of the sugar. Process until the walnuts are coarsely ground but not made into a paste. Transfer to large bowl and add flour, cornmeal, baking powder, and salt. Stir until combined.

2. In large bowl, using an electric mixer, beat the butter, Splenda, and remaining 2 tablespoons sugar until light and fluffy. Beat in eggs, orange peel, and orange extract. Gradually beat in the flour mixture until smooth and thick. Divide the dough into two equal-size pieces. Refrigerate 30 minutes or until firm.

3. Preheat oven to 350°F. Coat baking sheet with cooking spray.

4. Shape each piece of dough into a 12"-long log and place both on the prepared baking sheet. Bake 25 to 30 minutes or until golden. Remove the logs to racks to cool.

5. Cut each log on a slight diagonal into $^1/_2$"-thick slices. Place the slices, cut side down, on the baking sheet and bake 5 minutes. Turn the slices over and bake 5 minutes longer or until dry. Remove to racks to cool.

Makes 24

Per biscotti: 76 cal, 2 g pro, 8 g carb, 5 g fat, 2 g sat fat, 23 mg chol, 1 g fiber, 68 mg sodium

Diet Exchanges: 0 milk, 0 vegetable, 0 fruit, $^1/_2$ starch/bread, 0 meat, 1 fat

Vanilla Crisps

2 med eggs, separated

$^1/_2$ tsp baking powder

$^1/_8$ tsp salt

$^1/_4$ c granulated sugar

2 tsp vanilla extract

$^1/_4$ tsp grated lemon zest

$^1/_3$ c all-purpose flour

Confectioners' sugar

1. Preheat oven to 375°F. Line baking sheets with parchment.

2. In large bowl, with electric mixer on medium speed, beat egg whites until foamy. Slowly add baking powder, salt, and sugar and continue beating on medium speed until stiff peaks form.

3. In another large bowl, combine egg yolks, vanilla extract, and lemon zest and beat with a fork until thoroughly mixed. Fold into beaten egg whites just until combined. Sift flour over egg mixture and fold in until the batter is smooth and light. Drop 2 teaspoons of batter per cookie about 2" apart onto the baking sheets.

4. Bake 12 to 15 minutes or until golden. Cool on the sheets 5 minutes, then remove to racks to cool completely. Cookies will crisp upon cooling. Dust with confectioners' sugar before serving. For best results, store covered.

Makes 24

Per cookie: 21 cal, 1 g pro, 4 g carb, 0 g fat, 0 g sat fat, 20 mg chol, 0 g fiber, 30 mg sodium

Diet Exchanges: 0 milk, 0 vegetable, 0 fruit, 0 starch/bread, 0 meat, 0 fat

Chocolate-Covered Strawberries

3$\frac{1}{2}$ oz high-quality dark chocolate

1 Tbsp fat-free milk

20 med ripe strawberries with stems

1. Line baking sheet with parchment.

2. Place chocolate and milk in top of double boiler over boiling water. Lower heat to medium and allow chocolate to melt, about 3 minutes. Stir to combine milk and chocolate. Remove from heat.

3. Holding stem, dip each strawberry into chocolate three-quarters of the way up. Place on parchment, leaving 1" of space around each berry.

4. Refrigerate 30 minutes to set the chocolate.

Makes 4 servings

Per serving: 160 cal, 2 g pro, 22 g carb, 8 g fat, 5 g sat fat, 0 mg chol, 4 g fiber, 0 mg sodium

Diet Exchanges: 0 milk, 0 vegetable, $\frac{1}{2}$ fruit, 1 starch/bread, 0 meat, 1$\frac{1}{2}$ fat

Melon-Mango Sorbet

1 mango, peeled and cubed

2 c frozen unsweetened melon balls

$^1/_4$ c superfine sugar

$^1/_4$ c lime juice

1. In blender or food processor, combine mango, melon, sugar, and lime juice. Puree.

2. Spoon into 4 margarita glasses or glass custard cups. Cover with plastic wrap and freeze 30 to 40 minutes or until firm, stirring once to break up any ice crystals.

Makes 4 servings

Per serving: 117 cal, 1 g pro, 30 g carb, 1 g fat, 0 g sat fat, 0 mg chol, 2 g fiber, 9 mg sodium

Diet Exchanges: 0 milk, 0 vegetable, $^1/_2$ fruit, 1 starch/bread, 0 meat, 0 fat

Cantaloupe Sorbet

4 c frozen cantaloupe, slightly thawed

1 frozen banana, sliced

$^1/_4$ c Splenda

1 Tbsp crème de menthe liqueur (optional)

1 Tbsp lime juice

2 tsp grated lime peel

$^1/_8$–$^1/_4$ tsp ground cinnamon

1. In food processor, combine cantaloupe, banana, Splenda, liqueur (if using), lime juice, lime peel, and cinnamon. Process until smooth.

2. Scrape into a shallow metal pan. Cover and freeze 4 hours or overnight. Using a knife, break the mixture into chunks. Process briefly in a food processor before serving.

Makes 6 servings

Per serving: 61 cal, 1 g pro, 15 g carb, 0 g fat, 0 g sat fat, 0 mg chol, 2 g fiber, 11 mg sodium

Diet Exchanges: 0 milk, 0 vegetable, 1 fruit, 0 starch/bread, 0 meat, 0 fat

Vegetable Omelet
Recipe on page 282

Cornmeal Flapjacks
Recipe on page 285

Berry Morning Mix
Recipe on page 292

Meatball Souvlaki
Recipe on page 294

Fruited Turkey Salad
Recipe on page 299

Minestrone Soup
Recipe on page 300

Italian Salsa and Chips
Recipe on page 305

Bacon-Asparagus Wraps
Recipe on page 320

Chocolate Sorbet

$2^1/_3$ c water

$^1/_4$ c sugar

$^1/_2$ c Splenda

$^3/_4$ c Dutch cocoa powder

4 oz dark chocolate, chopped

$^1/_2$ tsp vanilla extract

1. Bring water, sugar, and Splenda to a boil in medium saucepan. Reduce heat to medium. Whisk in cocoa until smooth. Return to a boil. Reduce heat to low and simmer 1 minute.

2. Pour the cocoa mixture over chocolate in medium bowl and whisk until smooth. Add vanilla extract.

3. Place bowl in ice-water bath. Stir occasionally until the mixture is cool to the touch, about 15 minutes. (Or refrigerate, loosely covered, $1^1/_2$ hours, until cool to the touch.)

4. Transfer the mixture to ice cream maker and follow manufacturer's instructions.

5. When frozen, transfer to freezer container, press piece of wax paper to top and freeze until firm, at least 3 hours.

Makes 6 servings

Per serving: 180 cal, 3 g pro, 26 g carb, 18 g fat, 4 g sat fat, 0 mg chol, 3 g fiber, 0 mg sodium

Diet Exchanges: 0 milk, 0 vegetable, 0 fruit, $1^1/_2$ starch/bread, 0 meat, $1^1/_2$ fat

Yogurt Pops

8 oz fat-free plain or flavored yogurt

6 oz concentrated unsweetened fruit juice, such as mixed berry flavor

Dash of vanilla extract or honey

1. In medium bowl, combine yogurt, juice, and vanilla extract. Pour into four 3-ounce paper cups and partially freeze 1 hour.

2. Insert wooden sticks into each cup and freeze 4 hours or until solid.

Makes 4

Per pop: 70 cal, 4 g pro, 14 g carb, 0 g fat, 0 g sat fat, 0 mg chol, 0 g fiber, 45 mg sodium

Diet Exchanges: $^1/_2$ milk, 0 vegetable, $^1/_2$ fruit, 0 starch/bread, 0 meat, 0 fat

SIDES
Bacon-Asparagus Wraps

(photo on page 318)

24 spears asparagus

8 slices low-fat turkey bacon

3 Tbsp sesame seeds, lightly toasted

1 Tbsp soy sauce

1. Preheat broiler.

2. Wrap 3 spears asparagus together around the middle with 1 strip bacon. Secure with wooden pick. Repeat to use remaining asparagus and bacon.

3. Place sesame seeds in shallow dish. Spritz asparagus wraps with olive oil and roll in sesame seeds. Place on baking sheet. Drizzle with soy sauce.

4. Broil on top rack 7 minutes or until bacon is cooked and asparagus is crisp-tender and light green.

Makes 8

Per wrap: 73 cal, 4 g pro, 4 g carb, 4 g fat, 1.5 g sat fat, 12 mg chol, 1 g fiber, 348 mg sodium

Diet Exchanges: 0 milk, $^1/_2$ vegetable, 0 fruit, 0 starch/bread, $^1/_2$ meat, $^1/_2$ fat

Skinny Scalloped Potatoes

(photo on page 351)

4 russet potatoes, scrubbed and very thinly sliced

1 med sweet onion, chopped

2 cloves garlic, minced

2 Tbsp all-purpose flour

2 Tbsp trans-free margarine or butter

$1^1/_2$ c 2% milk

$^1/_2$ tsp mustard powder

$^1/_4$ c (1 oz) grated Parmesan cheese

Chives (optional)

1. Preheat oven to 350°F. Coat $1^1/_2$-quart baking dish with cooking spray.

2. Arrange potatoes, onion, and garlic in baking dish in alternating layers. Sprinkle flour on top and toss lightly. Dot with margarine.

3. In small saucepan over low heat, whisk milk and mustard powder and heat until warm. Remove from heat, stir in cheese, and pour over potatoes. Season with salt and black pepper to taste.

4. Cover and bake 30 minutes. Uncover and bake 15 minutes longer or until lightly browned and bubbling. Garnish with chives, if desired.

Makes 4 servings

Per serving: 280 cal, 10 g pro, 42 g carb, 9 g fat, 4 g sat fat, 18 mg chol, 3 g fiber, 280 mg sodium

Diet Exchanges: ¹/₂ milk, ¹/₂ vegetable, 0 fruit, 2 starch/bread, ¹/₂ meat, 1 fat

Corn and Zucchini Cakes

¹/₄ c whole grain pastry flour

¹/₄ c cornmeal

¹/₂ tsp baking powder

¹/₂ tsp salt

2 c fresh or frozen corn kernels, thawed

¹/₃ c water

1 sm zucchini, cut into ¹/₄" pieces

1 sm onion, chopped

2 Tbsp chopped fresh basil or 1 tsp dried

¹/₄ c fat-free milk

2 eggs

1. In large bowl, combine flour, cornmeal, baking powder, and salt. Stir to mix. Set aside.

2. Place corn and water in medium skillet over medium-high heat. Cook 2 to 3 minutes or until the corn is tender and the water has evaporated. Place about 1 cup in food processor or blender and set aside. Add remaining corn to reserved flour mixture.

3. Wipe out the skillet and coat it with cooking spray. Set over medium heat. Add zucchini, onion, and basil. Cook 3 to 4 minutes or until soft. Add to the reserved flour mixture.

4. Meanwhile, add milk and eggs to the reserved corn in the food processor or blender. Process to make a coarse puree. Add to the reserved flour mixture. Stir to combine.

5. Coat large skillet with cooking spray. Set over medium heat. Spoon about 2 tablespoons of the batter per cake into skillet to form 3"-wide cakes. Cook 3 minutes or until golden brown and crisp on the bottom. Flip the cakes and cook 3 minutes or until golden brown and heated through. Repeat with the remaining batter to make a total of 12 cakes.

Makes 4 servings

Per serving: 196 cal, 10 g pro, 34 g carb, 4 g fat, 1 g sat fat, 107 mg chol, 6 g fiber, 393 mg sodium

Diet Exchanges: 0 milk, 4 vegetable, 0 fruit, ¹/₂ starch/bread, ¹/₂ meat, ¹/₂ fat

Green Beans and Carrots Parmesan

(photo on page 352)

4 med carrots, cut into 3" matchsticks

1 pkg (8–10 oz) frozen whole green beans

1 Tbsp canola oil

2 Tbsp grated Parmesan cheese

1. Place steamer basket in large pot with 2" of water. Bring to a boil over high heat. Place carrots and beans in basket and steam about 10 minutes or until tender. Drain and toss with oil.

2. Place in serving dish and sprinkle with cheese.

Makes 4 servings

Per serving: 82 cal, 2 g pro, 9 g carb, 4.5 g fat, 0.5 g sat fat, 0 mg chol, 3 g fiber, 80 mg sodium

Diet Exchanges: 0 milk, 2 vegetable, 0 fruit, 0 starch/bread, 0 meat, 1 fat

Sausage, Egg, and Vegetable Casserole

1 lb sweet Italian sausage, casing removed and meat cut into 1" pieces

1 Tbsp + 1½ tsp olive oil

½ sm head (4 oz total) escarole, chopped

2 zucchini (8 oz), thinly sliced

1 red bell pepper, chopped

1 sm red onion, thinly sliced

¼ tsp salt

¼ tsp ground black pepper

7 lg eggs, at room temperature

½ c 2% milk, at room temperature

¼ c (1 oz) grated Parmesan cheese

1. Preheat oven to 350°F. Coat 8" × 8" baking dish with cooking spray.

2. Cook sausage in large skillet over medium-high heat until half-cooked, 6 to 8 minutes, stirring occasionally. Spread over the bottom of the prepared dish. Discard fat from the skillet. Pour oil into the same skillet and stir in escarole, zucchini, bell pepper, onion, salt, and ⅛ teaspoon of the black pepper.

3. Reduce heat to medium. Cook, stirring occasionally, until vegetables are tender and the liquid evaporates, 8 to 10 minutes. Let cool 10 minutes and arrange over the sausage.

4. Meanwhile, in large bowl, combine eggs, milk, cheese, and remaining ⅛ teaspoon of black pepper. Pour over the vegetables.

5. Bake until eggs are set, 40 to 45 minutes. Cut into squares to serve.

Makes 6 servings

Per serving: 352 cal, 23 g pro, 7 g carb, 26 g fat, 7 g sat fat, 308 mg chol, 2 g fiber, 657 mg sodium

Diet Exchanges: 0 milk, 1 vegetable, 0 fruit, 0 starch/bread, 3 meat, 3½ fat

DINNERS

Roasted Red Pepper Chicken

4 boneless, skinless chicken breast halves

1 bottle (8 oz) fat-free Italian dressing

4 lg red bell peppers

4 thin slices fresh mozzarella cheese

Fresh basil leaves (garnish)

1. Place chicken in 13" × 9" baking dish and pierce in several places with fork. Pour dressing over chicken and turn to coat both sides. Cover and refrigerate 1 hour.

2. Preheat broiler.

3. Cut tops off peppers and cut peppers in half. Remove stems and seeds. Place peppers, cut sides down, on baking sheet. Broil 10 minutes or until skins are charred. Place in paper bag and allow to cool. When cool enough to handle, remove and discard skins. Cut pepper halves into $1/2$" strips.

4. Change oven temperature to 350°F. Remove chicken from marinade and discard marinade.

5. Cut pocket into thick end of each breast. Stuff each piece with some sliced peppers. Place 1 slice cheese on top of each piece. Top with remaining pepper strips, covering the cheese.

6. Place chicken in clean 13" x 9" baking dish and bake uncovered 40 minutes or until thermometer inserted in thickest portion registers 160°F and juices run clear. Let stand 5 minutes before serving. Garnish with basil.

Makes 4 servings

Per serving: 270 cal, 38 g pro, 16 g carb, 6 g fat, 3 g sat fat, 88 mg chol, 4 g fiber, 950 mg sodium

Diet Exchanges: 0 milk, $1/2$ vegetable, 0 fruit, 1 starch/bread, $4^1/2$ meat, 1 fat

Lime Chicken

(photo on page 353)

$^1/_2$ c lime juice

$^1/_4$ c chopped cilantro

2 boneless, skinless chicken breasts (about 12 oz)

1 Tbsp olive oil

1. In ziplock bag, combine lime juice and cilantro, then season with salt and black pepper to taste. Rub chicken with oil and place in same bag. Refrigerate 2 hours.

2. Preheat grill to medium-high and cook the chicken about 10 minutes per side or until meat thermometer inserted in thickest portion registers 170°F and juices run clear.

Makes 4 servings

Per serving: 130 cal, 20 g pro, 3 g carb, 4.5 g fat, 0.5 g sat fat, 50 mg chol, 0 g fiber, 130 mg sodium

Diet Exchanges: 0 milk, 0 vegetable, 0 fruit, 0 starch/bread, 3 meat, 1 fat

Mandarin Chicken

1 Tbsp olive oil

4 boneless, skinless chicken breast halves (about $1^1/_4$ lb)

1 c brown basmati rice

1 clove garlic, minced

$2^1/_2$ c reduced-sodium chicken broth

1 can (6 oz) mandarin oranges, drained

2 scallions, sliced

1 Tbsp chopped cilantro

1. Warm oil in large skillet over medium to high heat. When hot, add chicken and cook about 5 minutes per side or until lightly golden. Add rice and garlic and continue cooking until grains turn golden. Add broth and heat just until boiling, then cover and reduce heat to low.

2. Simmer 25 to 30 minutes or until rice is tender and meat thermometer inserted in thickest part of chicken registers 170°F and juices run clear. Remove from heat and add oranges, tossing gently. Top with scallions and cilantro and serve.

Makes 4 servings

Per serving: 390 cal, 39 g pro, 44 g carb, 6 g fat, 1 g sat fat, 85 mg chol, 2 g fiber, 180 mg sodium

Diet Exchanges: 0 milk, 0 vegetable, $^1/_2$ fruit, 2 starch/bread, 5 meat, 1 fat

Angel Hair Pasta with Chicken and Vegetables

$^1/_2$ lb angel hair pasta

2 boneless, skinless chicken breasts, cut
    into thin strips

1 Tbsp olive oil

1 c snow peas

1 c thinly sliced white mushrooms

2–3 carrots, cut into matchsticks (about 1 c)

$^1/_2$ red bell pepper, cut into matchsticks
    (about $^1/_2$ c)

2 cloves garlic, minced

$^1/_4$ c mild oyster sauce

2 scallions, thinly sliced

1. In large pot, cook pasta according to package directions. Drain and set aside.

2. Meanwhile, coat large skillet with cooking spray and set over medium heat. Add chicken and cook, stirring constantly, 3 to 4 minutes or until chicken is no longer pink and juices run clear. Transfer to medium bowl and set aside.

3. Wipe out the skillet with a paper towel and increase heat to medium-high. Add oil and heat about 1 minute, then add snow peas, mushrooms, carrots, and pepper. Cook, stirring constantly, about 5 minutes or until vegetables brighten in color and become slightly tender.

4. Add garlic and chicken for the last minute or two of cooking and heat through. Add cooked pasta, oyster sauce, and scallions and toss until thoroughly coated. Serve immediately.

Makes 4 servings

Per serving: 360 cal, 29 g pro, 49 g carb, 5 g fat, 1 g sat fat, 50 mg chol, 4 g fiber, 190 mg sodium

Diet Exchanges: 0 milk, 1 vegetable, 0 fruit, 3 starch/bread, 3 meat, 1 fat

Stuffed Peppers

$^1/_2$ c brown rice

8 lg bell peppers (any color)

1 lb ground turkey breast

1 onion, chopped

3 cloves garlic, chopped

1 tsp parsley

$^1/_2$ tsp seasoning salt

$^1/_2$ tsp ground black pepper

$^1/_2$ tsp dried thyme

$^1/_2$ tsp dried basil

$^1/_2$ tsp dried oregano

$^1/_8$ tsp ground red pepper

1 can (8 oz) tomato sauce

1 c salsa

2 Tbsp Worcestershire sauce

1 can (11 oz) corn niblets, drained

1 c (4 oz) shredded low-fat or fat-free
    mozzarella cheese

1. Prepare rice according to package directions.

2. Meanwhile, cut tops from bell peppers and remove and discard stems and seeds. Chop tops. Reserve shells.

3. In large nonstick skillet over medium heat, cook turkey 5 minutes or until no longer pink. Add pepper tops, onion, garlic, parsley, seasoning salt, black pepper, thyme, basil, oregano, and ground red pepper. Cook 7 minutes or until vegetables are soft. Remove to large bowl.

4. In small bowl, combine tomato sauce, salsa, and Worcestershire. Reserve $1^1/_2$ cups.

5. Preheat oven to 400°F.

6. Add rice, corn, $^1/_2$ cup of cheese, and reserved sauce mixture to the turkey mixture. Stir to combine. Spoon into pepper shells. Top with remaining $^1/_2$ cup sauce mixture. Place in two 13" × 9" baking dishes.

7. Cover with foil and bake 35 minutes. Sprinkle with remaining $^1/_2$ cup cheese and bake 10 minutes longer or until cheese is melted.

Makes 8 servings

Per serving: 240 cal, 22 g pro, 30 g carb, 4.5 g fat, 2.5 g sat fat, 45 mg chol, 5 g fiber, 570 mg sodium

Diet Exchanges: 0 milk, 3 vegetable, 0 fruit, 1 starch/bread, 2 meat, $^1/_2$ fat

Chipotle-Grilled Turkey

Relish

  1 c coarsely chopped tomatillos

  Juice and grated zest from $1/2$ lime

  3 Tbsp olive oil

  1 Tbsp chopped cilantro

  2 cloves garlic, minced

  $1/4$ tsp salt

  $1/4$ tsp black pepper

  Pinch of sugar

Turkey

  $1/2$ c chipotle salsa

  $1/3$ c lime juice

  1 tsp sugar

  $1/8$ tsp ground cumin

  1 lb turkey breast cutlet, lightly pounded to
    1" thick

  1 c pickled jalapeño chile peppers, drained

  1 Tbsp cider vinegar

  2 Tbsp chopped cilantro

  Baked tortilla chips

1. *To prepare relish:* In food processor, combine tomatillos, lime juice, lime zest, oil, cilantro, garlic, salt, pepper, and sugar. Pulse until chunky. Transfer to small bowl, cover, and refrigerate until ready to serve.

2. *To prepare turkey:* In small glass bowl, combine salsa, lime juice, sugar, cumin, and black pepper to taste. Spread evenly on turkey and refrigerate in ziplock bag for no longer than 2 to 3 hours.

3. Preheat oven to 400°F. Remove turkey from marinade (reserve 3 table-spoons) and pat dry. On heatproof grill pan set over high heat, cook turkey 4 minutes per side. Transfer to plate and set aside.

4. Spread jalapeño peppers on grill pan. Pour vinegar over chiles, followed by reserved marinade. Lay turkey over the peppers. Cover loosely with foil and bake 15 to 20 minutes. Bake uncovered 5 minutes longer or until juices run clear.

5. Let turkey rest about 5 minutes, then slice against grain into $1/4$" strips. Top with tomatillo relish and cilantro and serve with tortilla chips.

Makes 4 servings

Per serving: 380 cal, 32 g pro, 4 g carb, 11 g fat, 1.5 g sat fat, 70 mg chol, 1 g fiber, 202 mg sodium

Diet Exchanges: 0 milk, $1/2$ vegetable, 0 fruit, 0 starch/bread, $3^1/2$ meat, 2 fat

Beef and Vegetables

1 Tbsp vegetable oil

1½ lb eye of round roast, trimmed

2 onions, cut into wedges

3 carrots, coarsely chopped

1 green bell pepper, coarsely chopped

1 qt beef broth

2 heads broccoli, coarsely chopped

1. Preheat oven to 350°F.

2. Heat oil in ovenproof Dutch oven over medium-high heat. Add beef and onions and cook 7 minutes or until browned. Add carrots, pepper, and broth and bring to a boil. Remove from heat and place in oven.

3. Bake uncovered 1 hour. Stir in broccoli and bake 20 minutes longer or until thermometer inserted in center of beef registers 160°F for medium doneness. Let stand 10 minutes before slicing.

Makes 6 servings

Per serving: 293 cal, 30 g pro, 19 g carb, 12 g fat, 3.5 g sat fat, 55 mg chol, 8 g fiber, 440 mg sodium

Diet Exchanges: 0 milk, 4 vegetable, 0 fruit, 0 starch/bread, 5 meat, ½ fat

Beef and Broccoli

1 can (14 ½ oz) reduced-sodium beef broth

2 Tbsp cornstarch

2 Tbsp light soy sauce

2 Tbsp oyster sauce

1 Tbsp vegetable oil

1 lb boneless sirloin steak, cut into thin strips

4 c fresh broccoli florets

1 med onion, sliced

1 clove garlic, minced

1. In small bowl, combine broth, cornstarch, soy sauce, and oyster sauce and whisk until smooth. Set aside.

2. Warm oil in large skillet or wok over medium-high heat 1 minute. Add steak and cook, stirring constantly, 5 to 7 minutes or until beef is browned. Transfer to covered bowl to keep warm.

3. Add broccoli, onion, and garlic to skillet and cook, stirring constantly, 1 to 2 minutes or until broccoli is bright green and crisp-tender. Add broth mixture and bring to a boil, stirring. Reduce heat, add beef, and simmer 5 minutes or until sauce thickens.

Makes 4 servings

Per serving 270 cal, 30 g pro, 11 g carb, 11 g fat, 3 g sat fat, 75 mg chol, 3 g fiber, 640 mg sodium

Diet Exchanges 0 milk, 1 vegetable, 0 fruit, 1/2 bread, 4 meat, 1 1/2 fat

Stir-Fry Beef

1 c brown rice

2 low-sodium beef bouillon cubes

1 3/4 c boiling water

1/4 c light soy sauce

1/4 c red wine (optional)

1/2 tsp minced garlic

2 tsp Montreal steak spice

1 sirloin steak (8 oz), trimmed of visible fat
    and sliced in 1" pieces

1 green bell pepper, sliced

1 orange or red bell pepper, sliced

1 onion, sliced

4 oz mushrooms, sliced

2 tsp cornstarch

1. Prepare rice according to package directions.

2. In large bowl, combine bouillon cubes and water. Stir to dissolve. Add soy sauce, wine (if using), garlic, and steak spice. Stir to combine. Add steak and stir to coat. Cover and refrigerate 1 hour.

3. Heat large nonstick skillet over medium-high heat. Remove steak from marinade and add to the skillet. Reserve 1 cup of marinade. Cook steak, stirring constantly, 5 minutes or until lightly browned. Add peppers, onion, and mushrooms and cook, stirring constantly, 5 minutes or until steak is no longer pink and vegetables are crisp-tender.

4. Add cornstarch to reserved marinade and stir into pan. Cook 5 minutes or until sauce is thickened. Serve over the rice.

Makes 4 servings

Per serving: 340 cal, 16 g pro, 45 g carb, 11 g fat, 4 g sat fat, 40 mg chol, 3 g fiber, 990 mg sodium

Diet Exchanges: 0 milk, 1 vegetable, 0 fruit, 2 1/2 starch/bread, 3 1/2 meat, 1 fat

Onion-Grilled London Broil

1 med sweet onion, quartered

1 clove garlic

2 Tbsp light soy sauce

1 Tbsp Dijon mustard

1 Tbsp honey

1 Tbsp olive oil

1 tsp black pepper

1 lb London broil

1. In food processor, combine onion, garlic, soy sauce, mustard, honey, oil, and pepper. Pulse until smooth, then transfer to ziplock bag. Add London broil and refrigerate at least 2 hours, or preferably overnight.

2. Let steak stand at room temperature about 30 minutes before grilling (cold meat is more likely to stick to a hot grill). Preheat grill to high.

3. Remove steak from the bag and discard the onion mixture. Grill steak about 10 minutes per side or until meat thermometer inserted in center registers 145°F for medium-rare, 160°F for medium, or 165°F for well-done.

4. Transfer to cutting board and let stand 10 minutes, then slice thinly across grain and serve.

Makes 4 servings

Per serving: 230 cal, 25 g pro, 8 g carb, 10 g fat, 3 g sat fat, 35 mg chol, 0 g fiber, 420 mg sodium

Diet Exchanges: 0 milk, 0 vegetable, 0 fruit, 0 starch/bread, $3\frac{1}{2}$ meat, $1\frac{1}{2}$ fat

Pork Chops Baked with Cabbage and Cream

1 sm head ($1\frac{1}{2}$ lb) green cabbage, cored and finely shredded

4 boneless pork chops (6 oz each), each $\frac{3}{4}$" thick

$\frac{1}{4}$ tsp ground black pepper

$\frac{1}{2}$ tsp salt

2 tsp olive oil

$\frac{1}{2}$ c half-and-half

1 tsp caraway seeds

$\frac{1}{2}$ tsp sweet Hungarian paprika

1 tsp dried marjoram or thyme

$\frac{1}{2}$ c (2 oz) shredded Swiss cheese

1. Preheat oven to 350°F.

2. Bring a large pot of salted water to a boil over high heat. Add cabbage and cook until soft, 4 to 5 minutes. Drain in colander and dry well with paper towels.

3. Season meat with pepper and $\frac{1}{4}$ teaspoon of the salt. Heat oil in an oven-proof, large, heavy skillet over high heat. Add the meat and cook just

until browned, 1 to 2 minutes. Remove to a plate.

4. Discard any fat in the skillet and heat skillet over low heat. Stir in the cabbage, half-and-half, caraway seeds, paprika, marjoram, and remaining $1/4$ teaspoon salt. Cook and stir until heated through, about 1 minute. Remove from the heat and arrange the pork over the cabbage, adding any juices accumulated on the plate. Sprinkle with cheese. Bake until a meat thermometer registers 160°F for medium-well, about 25 minutes.

Makes 4 servings

Per serving: 463 cal, 53 g pro, 12 g carb, 20 g fat, 9 g sat fat, 165 mg chol, 4 g fiber, 460 mg sodium

Diet Exchanges: 0 milk, $2^1/2$ vegetable, 0 fruit, 0 starch/bread, 7 meat, $3^1/2$ fat

Stuffed Lamb Chops

$1^1/2$ c fresh spinach

2 Tbsp Italian-style bread crumbs

2 Tbsp feta cheese, crumbled

1 Tbsp pine nuts

1 tsp cornstarch

$1/4$ tsp dried thyme

4 loin lamb chops (about 4 oz each)

1 tsp olive oil

2 Tbsp red wine

1. In small skillet over low heat, combine spinach, bread crumbs, cheese, pine nuts, and cornstarch. Cook gently until spinach is bright green and wilted. Remove from heat, add thyme, and season with salt and black pepper to taste. Let cool.

2. Cut a small pocket into the side of each chop and stuff with equal amounts of the spinach mixture.

3. Warm oil in large skillet over medium heat. When hot, add stuffed chops and cook about 4 minutes per side. Add wine and cook 2 to 3 minutes or until most of liquid has evaporated.

4. Drizzle lamb chops with any pan sauce and serve.

Makes 4 servings

Per serving: 230 cal, 17 g pro, 5 g carb, 15 g fat, 7 g sat fat, 60 mg chol, 1 g fiber, 280 mg sodium

Diet Exchanges: 0 milk, 0 vegetable, 0 fruit, $1/2$ starch/bread, $2^1/2$ meat, 2 fat

Stuffed Flounder

1 Tbsp olive oil

$^1/_2$ lb peeled and deveined shrimp, cut up

$^1/_2$ tsp minced garlic

$^1/_3$–$^1/_2$ c unseasoned dried bread crumbs

2 Tbsp grated Parmesan cheese

1 lb flounder fillets

$^1/_4$ c white wine or nonalcoholic white wine

$^1/_2$ Tbsp parsley

1. Preheat oven to 350°F.

2. Heat oil in large skillet over medium-high heat. Add shrimp and garlic and cook, stirring frequently, 5 minutes or until shrimp is opaque. Remove to large bowl. Add bread crumbs and cheese and stir to combine.

3. Place flounder on work surface. Evenly divide the shrimp mixture among fillets, spreading almost to edge. Roll fillets from short end to enclose filling. Secure with wooden picks.

4. Place rolls in 13" × 9" baking dish. Pour wine into dish. Sprinkle with parsley. Bake, uncovered, 15 minutes or until fish flakes easily.

Makes 4 servings

Per serving: 250 cal, 35 g pro, 7 g carb, 7 g fat, 1.5 g sat fat, 145 mg chol, 0 g fiber, 300 mg sodium

Diet Exchanges: 0 milk, 0 vegetable, 0 fruit, $^1/_2$ starch/bread, 5 meat, 1 fat

Baked Halibut

3 Tbsp lemon juice

1 tsp salt

$^1/_2$ tsp paprika

6 halibut steaks (5–6 oz each)

2 Tbsp trans-free margarine

$^1/_2$ c chopped onion

1 lg bell pepper, cut into strips

1. In shallow bowl, combine lemon juice, salt, and paprika. Add fish, cover, and refrigerate 1 hour, turning once.

2. Preheat oven to 450°F. Coat 13" × 9" baking dish with cooking spray.

3. Melt margarine in medium skillet over medium-high heat and cook onion 5 to 10 minutes or until brown. Place fish in baking dish and top with onion and pepper strips.

4. Bake 10 minutes or until fish is just opaque.

Makes 6 servings

Per serving: 171 cal, 24 g pro, 3 g carb, 6 g fat, 1.5 g sat fat, 40 mg chol, 1 g fiber, 492 mg sodium

Diet Exchanges: 0 milk, $^1/_2$ vegetable, 0 fruit, 0 starch/bread, 4 meat, 1 fat

Tropical Mahi Mahi

2 Tbsp reduced-sodium soy sauce

1 can (8 oz) pineapple chunks, drained,
   juice reserved

2 cloves garlic, minced

4 mahi mahi fillets (about 6 oz each)

1 Tbsp olive oil

1 med tomato, finely chopped

$1/2$ med yellow onion, finely chopped

$1/2$ med red bell pepper, finely chopped

$1/2$ med yellow bell pepper, finely chopped

1 c brown basmati rice

$2^1/_2$ c water

2 scallions, sliced

1. In large, shallow baking dish, combine soy sauce, reserved pineapple juice, and garlic. Add fish and turn to coat. Cover and refrigerate 30 minutes.

2. Meanwhile, warm oil in medium skillet over medium-high heat. When hot, add tomato, onion, and bell peppers and cook 2 to 3 minutes or until softened. Add rice and cook, stirring, about 5 minutes or until fragrant. Add water, bring to a boil, then cover and reduce heat. Simmer 45 minutes or until rice is tender.

3. Meanwhile, preheat oven to 450°F. Bake fish in baking dish 10 to 15 minutes or until it flakes easily. Serve with rice and garnish with pineapple chunks and scallions.

Makes 4 servings

Per serving: 366 cal, 36 g pro, 45 g carb, 6 g fat, 1 g sat fat, 125 mg chol, 4 g fiber, 460 mg sodium

Diet Exchanges: 0 milk, 1 vegetable, $1/2$ fruit, 2 starch/bread, $4^1/_2$ meat, 1 fat

Creole Tilapia

$1/2$ c quick-cooking brown rice

1 med onion, sliced

2 ribs celery, sliced

2 lg carrots, sliced

2 tilapia fillets (5–6 oz each)

1 c canned diced tomatoes, drained

2 Tbsp chopped cilantro, parsley, or basil

Seasoning salt

1. Cook rice according to package directions.

2. Meanwhile, coat large skillet with cooking spray. Over medium-high heat, cook onion, celery, and carrots 5 minutes or until tender. Add tilapia and cook 3 minutes. Carefully turn fish and add tomatoes and herbs. Add seasoning salt to taste. Simmer 2 minutes or until fish flakes easily. Serve over rice.

Makes 2 servings

Per serving: 280 cal, 31 g pro, 38 g carb, 2 g fat, 0.5 g sat fat, 70 mg chol, 7 g fiber, 460 mg sodium

Diet Exchanges: 0 milk, $3^1/_2$ vegetable, 0 fruit, 1 starch/bread, 2 meat, 0 fat

Scallops in Tarragon Cream

1 Tbsp butter, softened

1½ lb fresh or thawed frozen sea scallops, rinsed

1½ tsp chopped fresh tarragon or ½ tsp dried

¼ tsp ground black pepper

¼ c half-and-half

1 Tbsp Pernod or 2 Tbsp dry sherry (optional)

2 Tbsp lemon juice

1 Tbsp chopped fresh parsley

1. Melt butter in large skillet over medium-high heat. When butter foams, add scallops, tarragon, and pepper. Cook 2 to 3 minutes, stirring constantly.

2. Stir in half-and-half, Pernod (if using), and lemon juice. Reduce heat to medium-low, and cook until scallops look opaque throughout and feel slightly springy when lightly pressed, 1 to 2 minutes.

3. Stir in parsley.

Makes 4 servings

Per serving: 201 cal, 29 g pro, 5 g carb, 6 g fat, 3 g sat fat, 71 mg chol, 0 g fiber, 312 mg sodium

Diet Exchanges: 0 milk, 0 vegetable, 0 fruit, 0 starch/bread, 4 meat, 1 fat

Crab-Stuffed Tiger Shrimp

(photo on page 354)

Sauce

1 tsp olive oil

2 cloves garlic, minced

2 med shallots, finely chopped

¼ c finely chopped roasted red peppers

1 c fat-free half-and-half

1 c 2% milk

¼ c grated Parmesan cheese

Stuffing

1 can (6 oz) special or lump crabmeat

1 Tbsp light mayonnaise

1 c soft whole wheat bread crumbs

½ tsp crab-boil seasoning

¼ c finely chopped roasted red peppers

Shrimp

1 lb large shrimp

1 Tbsp olive oil

Paprika

2 Tbsp chopped fresh parsley

2 Tbsp finely chopped roasted red peppers

1. *To prepare sauce:* Warm oil in medium saucepan over medium heat. When hot, add garlic and shallots and

cook 1 minute or until fragrant. Season to taste with black pepper, then add red peppers, half-and-half, and milk. Whisking constantly, bring mixture almost to a boil, then add cheese. Continue to whisk until thickened. Cover to keep warm and set aside.

2. *To prepare stuffing:* In medium bowl, combine crabmeat, mayonnaise, bread crumbs, crab-boil seasoning, red peppers, and black pepper to taste. Mix carefully and set aside.

3. Preheat oven to 350°F. Coat baking sheet with cooking spray.

4. *To prepare shrimp:* Peel and devein shrimp, cutting along back of each shrimp to make flat surface for stuffing. Arrange shrimp on baking sheet about 2" or 3" apart. On each shrimp, place about 1 tablespoon of stuffing, then drizzle with oil and dust with paprika.

5. Bake about 20 minutes or until shrimp turn pink and opaque. Transfer to serving plate, drizzle with sauce, top with parsley and red peppers, and serve.

Makes 4 servings

Per serving: 371 cal, 39 g pro, 17 g carb, 15 g fat, 3.5 g sat fat, 238 mg chol, 1 g fiber, 604 mg sodium

Diet Exchanges: $1/2$ milk, $1/2$ vegetable, 0 fruit, $1/2$ starch/bread, 5 meat, 2 fat

Delicious Veggies

1 lg onion, sliced

1 red bell pepper, finely chopped

$1/2$ eggplant, cubed

$1/2$ head cauliflower, cut into florets

1 lg zucchini, sliced

1 c sliced mushrooms

1 c salsa

$1/4$ c balsamic vinegar

$1/4$–$1/2$ tsp dried oregano

$1/4$–$1/2$ tsp dried basil

Pinch of ground red pepper

1 head broccoli, cut into florets

1. Heat large skillet coated with cooking spray over medium heat. Add onion and bell pepper and cook 2 minutes. Add eggplant, cauliflower, zucchini, and mushrooms and cook 3 minutes.

2. Stir in salsa, vinegar, oregano, basil, and red pepper. Stir in broccoli and cover. Cook 12 minutes or until vegetables are tender. Season with additional oregano and basil, if desired.

Makes 8 servings

Per serving: 80 cal, 4 g pro, 17 g carb, 0 g fat, 0 g sat fat, 0 mg chol, 6 g fiber, 250 mg sodium

Diet Exchanges: 0 milk, $2^{1/2}$ vegetable, 0 fruit, 0 starch/bread, 0 meat, 0 fat

Penne with Vegetables

(photo on page 355)

2 Tbsp olive oil

$1^1/_2$ c mixed finely chopped bell peppers

$^1/_2$ med onion, finely chopped

1 sm clove garlic, minced

8 oz white mushrooms, sliced

4 c broccoli florets

$^1/_2$ c marsala wine

$1^1/_2$ c penne

$^1/_2$ c grated Parmesan cheese

1. Warm oil in large nonstick skillet over medium heat. Add peppers, onion, and garlic and cook, stirring, about 2 minutes or until crisp-tender. Add mushrooms and cook about 2 minutes. Add broccoli and stir. Add wine, partially cover pan, and cook about 10 minutes.

2. Meanwhile, in large pot, cook penne per package directions, drain, and place in large bowl. Add the broccoli mixture and toss gently. Sprinkle with cheese, season with salt and black pepper to taste.

Makes 4 servings

Per serving: 340 cal, 13 g pro, 43 g carb, 11 g fat, 2.5 g sat fat, 10 mg chol, 4 g fiber, 180 mg sodium

Diet Exchanges: 0 milk, 2 vegetable, 0 fruit, 2 starch/bread, 1 meat, $1^1/_2$ fat

Pesto Pasta

8 oz linguine

$2^1/_2$ c packed fresh basil

$^3/_4$ c packed fresh parsley

2 Tbsp olive oil

3 cloves garlic

2 Tbsp toasted pine nuts or walnuts

2 Tbsp freshly grated Parmesan cheese

$^1/_4$ c chicken broth

1. Prepare pasta according to package directions.

2. Meanwhile, in food processor or blender, combine basil, parsley, oil, garlic, and nuts. Pulse to finely chop. Sprinkle with cheese. With the machine running, add broth, 1 tablespoon at a time, until mixture is the consistency of prepared mustard.

3. Toss pesto with pasta and serve.

Makes 4 servings

Per serving: 326 cal, 11 g pro, 46 g carb, 11 g fat, 2 g sat fat, 2 mg chol, 4 g fiber, 70 mg sodium

Diet Exchanges: 0 milk, $^1/_2$ vegetable, 0 fruit, 3 starch/bread, $^1/_2$ meat, $1^1/_2$ fat

Creamy Black Bean Enchiladas

²/₃ c brown rice

³/₄ c (6 oz) fat-free sour cream

3 oz reduced-fat cream cheese, softened

3 scallions, finely chopped

1 jar (4 oz) chopped green chile peppers, drained

¹/₂ tsp ground cumin

1 can (15 oz) black beans, rinsed and drained

6 corn or whole wheat flour tortillas (6" diameter)

1 c (4 oz) shredded low-fat Monterey Jack or Cheddar cheese

¹/₂ c mild red taco sauce

1. Preheat oven to 375°F. Coat 13" x 9" baking dish with cooking spray.

2. Cook rice per package directions.

3. Meanwhile, in medium bowl, combine sour cream, cream cheese, scallions, peppers, and cumin. Stir until well blended. Add beans and rice. Stir gently to mix.

4. Place tortillas on a work surface. Spoon some of the bean filling down the center of each tortilla. Sprinkle with cheese. Roll into cylinders. Place, seam side down, in the prepared baking dish. Drizzle with taco sauce.

5. Bake 12 to 15 minutes or until heated through.

Makes 6 servings

Per enchilada: 318 cal, 16 g pro, 54 g carb, 9 g fat, 4 g sat fat, 21 mg chol, 6 g fiber, 643 mg sodium

Diet Exchanges: ¹/₂ milk, ¹/₂ vegetable, 0 fruit, 2 starch/bread, 1 meat, 1 fat

Grilled Portobello Burgers

$^1/_2$ c balsamic vinegar

$^1/_4$ c soy sauce

1 Tbsp dried oregano

2 cloves garlic, chopped

2 tsp olive oil

4 lg portobello mushroom caps

4 slices ($^1/_4$" thick) sweet onion

4 slices (2 oz) fontina cheese

4 kaiser rolls, halved

4 leaves lettuce

2 roasted red peppers, halved

1. In a 13" x 9" baking dish, combine vinegar, soy sauce, oregano, garlic, and oil. Add mushroom caps, turning to coat. Set aside, turning occasionally, 30 minutes.

2. Coat grill rack or broiler pan with cooking spray. Preheat grill or broiler. Remove mushroom caps and reserve the marinade. Grill or broil mushroom caps and onion 6" from the heat for 3 minutes per side or until golden. Top mushrooms with cheese. Cook 1 to 2 minutes or until the cheese melts.

3. Meanwhile, toast the cut side of the rolls on the grill or under the broiler for 1 minute or until golden. Remove and place lettuce on the bottoms of the rolls. Top each with a pepper half, onion slice, and mushroom cap. Drizzle with a bit of the reserved marinade. Cover with the tops of the rolls. Cut in half.

Makes 4 servings

Per serving: 336 cal, 15 g pro, 47 g carb, 10 g fat, 5 g sat fat, 16 mg chol, 6 g fiber, 996 mg sodium

Diet Exchanges: 0 milk, 2 vegetable, 0 fruit, $2^1/_2$ starch/bread, $^1/_2$ meat, $1^1/_2$ fat

DESSERTS

Simple Chocolate Cake

1 c all-purpose flour

$^1/_2$ c sugar

3 Tbsp unsweetened cocoa powder

1 tsp ground cinnamon

1 tsp baking soda

$^1/_4$ tsp salt

8 oz fat-free vanilla yogurt

2 Tbsp vegetable oil

1 tsp vanilla extract

2 eggs, separated

1. Preheat oven to 350°F. Grease 8" or 9" round cake pan.

2. In medium bowl, combine flour, sugar, cocoa, cinnamon, baking soda, and salt.

3. In large bowl, combine yogurt, oil, vanilla extract, and egg yolks.

4. In medium bowl, with electric mixer on high speed, beat egg whites until stiff peaks form.

5. Stir the flour mixture into the yogurt mixture until just blended. Fold the egg whites into the flour mixture. Pour into the prepared pan.

6. Bake 35 minutes or until a wooden pick inserted in the center comes out clean. Cool on rack 5 minutes. Remove to rack and cool completely.

Makes 12 servings

Per serving: 119 cal, 3 g pro, 19 g carb, 3 g fat, 1 g sat fat, 36 mg chol, 1 g fiber, 135 mg sodium

Diet exchanges: $^1/_2$ milk, 0 vegetable, 0 fruit, $1^1/_2$ starch/bread, $^1/_2$ meat, 1 fat

Almond-Cocoa Angel Food Cake

Cocoa Cake

$^{1}/_{2}$ c all-purpose flour, sifted

2 Tbsp unsweetened cocoa powder, sifted

$^{1}/_{8}$ tsp salt

6 Tbsp + $^{1}/_{2}$ c sugar

6 egg whites, at room temperature

1 tsp cream of tartar

1 tsp almond extract

Fruit Sauce

$^{1}/_{4}$ c orange juice

1 Tbsp cornstarch

1 Tbsp sugar

2 peaches, sliced

$^{1}/_{2}$ pt raspberries

1. Preheat oven to 350°F.

2. *To prepare cocoa cake:* In medium bowl, combine flour, cocoa, salt, and 6 tablespoons of the sugar.

3. In large bowl, with electric mixer on medium speed, beat egg whites until foamy. Add cream of tartar and almond extract. Increase mixer speed to high. Gradually add remaining $^{1}/_{2}$ cup sugar and beat until stiff, glossy peaks form and the sugar dissolves.

4. Fold the flour mixture, one-third at a time, into the beaten whites. Place in ungreased 9" x 5" loaf pan and bake 25 minutes or until a wooden pick inserted in the center comes out clean. Turn upside down on a rack and cool for 30 minutes.

5. *To prepare fruit sauce:* In small saucepan, whisk together orange juice, cornstarch, and sugar. Bring to a boil over medium heat. Boil for 2 minutes or until thickened. Remove from heat and stir in peaches and raspberries. Let cool.

6. When the cake has cooled, using a knife, release the sides of the cake. Remove to a serving plate. Cut into 16 slices.

7. To serve, place 2 slices of cake on each of 8 dessert plates. Top slices with the fruit sauce.

Makes 8 servings

Per serving: 154 cal, 4 g pro, 35 g carb, 0 g fat, 0 g sat fat, 0 mg chol, 2 g fiber, 63 mg sodium

Diet Exchanges: 0 milk, 0 vegetable, $^{1}/_{2}$ fruit, 2 starch/bread, $^{1}/_{2}$ meat, 0 fat

Apple Soufflé Cake

1¼ c all-purpose flour

¼ tsp baking powder

3 med Granny Smith apples, peeled, cored, and thinly sliced

2 tsp ground cinnamon

½ c sugar

⅓ c trans-free margarine or butter, softened

½ c Splenda

1 med egg

½ c 1% milk

1. Preheat oven to 350°F. Lightly coat 9" springform pan with cooking spray.

2. In small bowl, combine flour and baking powder.

3. In medium bowl, toss apples with cinnamon and ¼ cup of the sugar. Spread evenly in springform pan.

4. In large bowl, with electric mixer on medium speed, blend margarine with Splenda and remaining ¼ cup sugar for 2 minutes or until fluffy. Add egg and mix until thoroughly combined. Add the flour mixture, alternating with milk. Pour batter over apples.

5. Bake 45 to 50 minutes or until golden brown. Cool in pan 10 minutes, then release ring and carefully invert onto serving plate. Serve warm or chilled.

Makes 8 servings

Per serving: 222 cal, 4 g pro, 37 g carb, 7 g fat, 2 g sat fat, 25 mg chol, 2 g fiber, 95 mg sodium

Diet Exchanges: 0 milk, 0 vegetable, ½ fruit, 2½ starch/bread, 0 meat, ½ fat

Carrot Cake with Cream Cheese Frosting

(photo on page 356)

Cake

- 2 c whole grain pastry flour
- 2 tsp baking powder
- 2 tsp baking soda
- 1 tsp ground cinnamon
- $1/4$ tsp salt
- 1 c granulated sugar
- 2 eggs
- 2 egg whites
- $1/3$ c canola oil
- 2 tsp vanilla extract
- 1 c low-fat buttermilk or fat-free plain yogurt
- 2 c finely shredded carrots
- $1/2$ c golden raisins
- $1/2$ c well-drained crushed pineapple

Frosting

- 2 oz reduced-fat cream cheese, at room temperature
- 2 Tbsp unsalted butter, at room temperature
- $1^1/4$ c confectioners' sugar
- $1/2$ tsp vanilla extract
- 3 Tbsp chopped walnuts or pecans

1. *To prepare cake:* Preheat oven to 350°F. Coat two 8" round cake pans with cooking spray.

2. In medium bowl, combine flour, baking powder, baking soda, cinnamon, and salt.

3. In large bowl, using a wire whisk, beat granulated sugar, eggs, egg whites, oil, and vanilla extract until well blended and frothy. Whisk in buttermilk. Stir in carrots, raisins, and pineapple. Add the flour mixture and stir just until blended.

4. Evenly divide batter between prepared cake pans. Bake 25 minutes or until a wooden pick inserted in the center comes out clean.

5. Cool cakes in the pans on racks 30 minutes. Loosen edges and turn cakes out onto racks to cool completely.

6. *To prepare frosting:* In medium bowl, with electric mixer on medium-high speed, beat cream cheese and butter just until blended. Beat in confectioners' sugar and vanilla extract until light and fluffy.

7. Place one cake layer on a plate. Spread the top of the layer, but not the sides, with frosting. Place the other cake layer on top. Spread the top of the layer with the remaining frosting. Sprinkle with walnuts.

Makes 10 servings

Per serving: 382 cal, 7 g pro, 61 g carb, 14 g fat, 4 g sat fat, 54 mg chol, 4 g fiber, 367 mg sodium

Diet Exchanges: $1/2$ milk, $1/2$ vegetable, $1/2$ fruit, $3^1/_2$ starch/bread, $1/2$ meat, 3 fat

Triple Chocolate Cheesecake

Crust

$1/_2$ c vanilla wafer crumbs (about 15 wafers)

3 Tbsp confectioners' sugar

1 Tbsp Dutch-process cocoa powder

1 Tbsp butter or margarine, melted

Filling

$1^1/_2$ c dark chocolate chips (9 oz), such as Hershey's Special Dark chips

Layers

2 pkg (8 oz each) cream cheese, softened

8 oz 1% cottage cheese

$1/_3$ c granulated sugar

$1/_3$ c Splenda

4 lg eggs

$1/_4$ c half-and-half

1 Tbsp vanilla extract

$1/_4$ tsp salt

1. *To prepare crust:* Toss crumbs, sugar, cocoa, and butter in medium bowl until moistened. Press mixture onto bottom and $1^1/_2$" up side of 9" springform pan. Preheat oven to 350°F.

2. *To prepare filling:* Place chips in large microwaveable bowl and microwave on high $1^1/_2$ minutes. Stir until chocolate is melted. Set aside.

3. *To prepare layers:* Beat cream cheese, cottage cheese, granulated sugar, and Splenda in large bowl with electric mixer on medium-high speed until smooth. Beat in eggs, then half-and-half, vanilla extract, and salt.

4. With rubber spatula, fold $1^1/_2$ cups of cheesecake batter into melted chocolate. Spread 2 cups of chocolate mixture onto crust. Blend 2 cups of cheesecake batter into remaining chocolate mixture. Spread 2 cups of mixture over first layer. Stir remaining cheesecake batter into remaining chocolate mixture and spread over second layer.

5. Bake 50 to 55 minutes or until center is almost set. Transfer cheesecake to rack. With knife, immediately loosen cake from side of pan. Cool to room temperature. Cover and refrigerate several hours, until thoroughly chilled. Remove from pan to serve.

Makes 16 servings

Per serving: 240 cal, 8 g pro, 25 g carb, 13 g fat, 7 g sat fat, 75 mg chol, 0 g fiber, 220 mg sodium

Diet Exchanges: 0 milk, 0 vegetable, 0 fruit, 1 starch/bread, 1 meat, 2 fat

Strawberry Cheesecake

1 pkg (8 oz) light cream cheese

1 pkg (8 oz) light firm silken tofu

$1/2$ c Splenda Sugar Blend for Baking

2 egg whites

1 reduced-fat prepared graham cracker crust

1 c sliced strawberries (garnish)

1. Preheat oven to 350°F.

2. In large bowl or food processor, blend cream cheese, tofu, Splenda, and egg whites about 1 minute or until smooth. Pour mixture into graham cracker crust.

3. Bake 30 minutes or until set. Let cheesecake cool. Garnish with strawberries.

Makes 8 servings

Per serving: 210 cal, 7 g pro, 27 g carb, 8 g fat, 3.5 g sat fat, 15 mg chol, 1 g fiber, 260 mg sodium

Diet Exchanges: 0 milk, 0 vegetable, 0 fruit, $1/2$ starch/bread, 1 meat, 1 fat

Lemon Cheesecake

$1^1/4$ c graham cracker crumbs

$2^1/4$ c sugar

3 Tbsp butter, melted

3 egg whites, divided

2 pkg (8 oz each) fat-free cream cheese

1 pkg (8 oz) reduced-fat cream cheese

$1/4$ c all-purpose flour

$1/2$ c lemon juice

2 eggs

2 c (16 oz) fat-free sour cream

1. Preheat oven to 350°F. Coat 9" springform pan with cooking spray.

2. In large bowl, combine cracker crumbs, $1/4$ cup of the sugar, and butter. Lightly beat 1 of the egg whites in a cup. Add half of the egg white to the bowl. (Reserve the remainder for another use or discard.) Mix well. Press mixture into the bottom and 1" up the side of the prepared pan. Bake 10 minutes or until lightly browned. Cool on a rack.

3. Meanwhile, place cream cheeses in a food processor. Process 1 minute or until smooth. Add flour and $1^1/2$ cups of the remaining sugar. Process 3 minutes or until light and fluffy. Stop and scrape sides of bowl as necessary. Add lemon juice and process briefly. Add eggs and remaining 2 egg whites, one at a time. Process until just incorporated.

4. Place mixture in prepared crust. Bake 1 hour. Remove from oven. Do not turn off oven.

5. In small bowl, combine sour cream and remaining $1/2$ cup sugar. Spread over the hot cheesecake. Bake 10 minutes. Place on a rack and let cool to room

temperature. Cover and refrigerate at least 8 hours.

Makes 16 servings

Per serving: 264 cal, 10 g pro, 42 g carb, 6 g fat, 4 g sat fat, 42 mg chol, 1 g fiber, 363 mg sodium

Diet Exchanges: $\frac{1}{2}$ milk, 0 vegetable, $\frac{1}{2}$ fruit, 3 starch/bread, $1\frac{1}{2}$ meat, 1 fat

Lemon Angel Food Cake Squares

$1\frac{1}{4}$ c granulated sugar

$\frac{1}{4}$ c cornstarch

$\frac{2}{3}$ c fresh lemon juice (from about 3 lg lemons)

1 lg egg yolk

1 c water

1 Tbsp trans-free margarine or butter

1 box angel food cake mix

1 tsp grated lemon zest

$\frac{1}{4}$ tsp lemon extract

Confectioners' sugar

1. In 2-quart saucepan, whisk granulated sugar and cornstarch until combined. Add lemon juice, egg yolk, and water and whisk until well blended. Whisking constantly, cook lemon mixture over medium heat for about 2 to 3 minutes or until just boiling. Reduce heat to low and simmer, whisking constantly, 1 to 2 minutes longer or until thick enough to coat back of a spoon.

2. Remove from heat and stir in margarine. Pour into medium bowl and cover with plastic wrap. Refrigerate this lemon curd about $1\frac{1}{2}$ hours or until cool.

3. Preheat oven to 350°F. Coat $15\frac{1}{2}$" × $10\frac{1}{2}$" jelly-roll pan with cooking spray and line bottom with parchment.

4. Prepare cake according to package directions. Add lemon zest and lemon extract while beating. Spread batter evenly into the prepared pan.

5. Bake 20 minutes or until cake is golden and top springs back when touched. Cool in pan on rack 10 minutes, then invert onto rack. Carefully remove parchment and allow cake to cool completely, then cut horizontally into thirds. Cut each third through the middle and spread one-third of cooled lemon curd over 3 halves. Top each with remaining halves and cut each piece into 5 equal portions. Sprinkle with confectioners' sugar and serve.

Makes 15 servings

Per serving: 188 cal, 3 g pro, 43 g carb, 1 g fat, 0 g sat fat, 15 mg chol, 0 g fiber, 211 mg sodium

Diet Exchanges: 0 milk, 0 vegetable, 0 fruit, $2\frac{1}{2}$ starch/bread, 0 meat, 0 fat

Fresh Berry Shortcakes

2 c whole grain pastry flour

3 Tbsp + $1/3$ c sugar

2 tsp baking powder

$1/4$ tsp baking soda

$1/4$ c butter, cut into small pieces

$2/3$ c + 2 Tbsp low-fat buttermilk

$1^1/2$ pt assorted berries

2 Tbsp orange juice

2 c (16 oz) fat-free vanilla yogurt

1. Preheat oven to 400°F. Coat baking sheet with cooking spray.

2. In large bowl, combine flour, 2 tablespoons of the sugar, baking powder, and baking soda. Cut in butter until the mixture resembles cornmeal. Add $2/3$ cup of the buttermilk, stirring with a fork until dough comes together.

3. Turn dough out onto a lightly floured surface. Pat to $1/2$" thickness. Using a 3" round cutter, cut 8 shortcakes. (Pat dough scraps together and use completely.) Place on the prepared baking sheet. Brush with the remaining 2 tablespoons buttermilk. Sprinkle with 1 tablespoon of the remaining sugar.

Bake 12 minutes or until golden brown. Remove to rack to cool.

4. Meanwhile, in large bowl, combine berries, orange juice, and remaining $1/3$ cup sugar. Let stand 10 minutes.

5. Split the shortcakes crosswise in half. Place the bottom piece on each of 8 dessert plates. Top with the berry filling and a scoop of frozen yogurt. Cover with the top piece.

Makes 8 servings

Per serving: 273 cal, 7 g pro, 50 g carb, 7 g fat, 4 g sat fat, 19 mg chol, 5 g fiber, 229 mg sodium

Diet Exchanges: $1/2$ milk, 0 vegetable, $1/2$ fruit, 3 starch/bread, 0 meat, $1^1/2$ fat

Brownie Pie

1 c all-purpose flour

1 tsp baking soda

$\frac{1}{3}$ c cocoa powder

$\frac{1}{4}$ c butter

$\frac{1}{3}$ c dark corn syrup

3 lg egg whites

1 tsp vanilla extract

6 walnut halves

Confectioners' sugar

1. Preheat oven to 350°F. Grease a 9" round tart pan with a removable bottom.

2. In medium bowl, combine flour and baking soda.

3. Place cocoa powder and butter in a microwaveable bowl. Microwave on high 1 to 2 minutes or until butter is melted.

4. Remove from microwave, stirring constantly to fully melt the chocolate. Stir in corn syrup. Add egg whites, one at a time, stirring after each addition, until well blended. Stir in vanilla extract and the flour mixture.

5. Spread into the prepared pan. Bake 25 minutes or until a wooden pick inserted in the center comes out clean. Cool in pan on rack 10 minutes. Remove from pan. Arrange walnut halves on top. Dust with confectioners' sugar.

Makes 12 servings

Per brownie: 117 cal, 3 g pro, 17 g carb, 5 g fat, 3 g sat. fat, 10 mg chol, 1 g fiber, 172 mg sodium

Diet Exchanges: 0 milk, 0 vegetable, 0 fruit, $1\frac{1}{2}$ starch/bread, $\frac{1}{2}$ meat, 1 fat

Peanut Butter Pie

(photo on page 357)

- 8 chocolate wafer cookies, crushed
- $^1/_3$ c creamy peanut butter
- 3 oz light cream cheese
- 5 oz fat-free cream cheese
- $^3/_4$ c confectioners' sugar
- 8 oz frozen fat-free whipped topping, thawed
- 2 tsp chocolate syrup

1. Lightly coat 9" pie plate with cooking spray. Scatter cookie crumbs evenly over the bottom. Set aside.

2. In large bowl, using electric mixer set on medium speed, beat together peanut butter and cream cheeses until smooth. Gradually beat in sugar. Fold in whipped topping. Spoon into pie plate, spreading evenly over the crumbs. Drizzle with chocolate syrup. Using the tip of a knife, decoratively swirl the syrup. Cover with plastic wrap and chill at least 4 hours or until set.

Makes 8 servings

Per serving: 228 cal, 7 g pro, 30 g carb, 7 g fat, 3 g sat fat, 7 mg chol, 1 g fiber, 261 mg sodium

Diet Exchanges: 0 milk, 0 vegetable, 0 fruit, 2 starch/bread, 1 meat, 1$^1/_2$ fat

Peaches and Cream Pie

- $^3/_4$ c all-purpose flour
- 1 pkg (3.4 oz) instant vanilla pudding mix
- $^1/_2$ c + 3 Tbsp 1% milk
- 1 med egg
- 1 tsp baking powder
- $^1/_2$ tsp salt
- 1 can (20 oz) sliced peaches, drained
- 1 pkg (8 oz) fat-free cream cheese, softened
- $^1/_2$ c + 2 tsp sugar
- $^1/_2$ tsp ground cinnamon

1. Preheat oven to 350°F. Coat 9" glass pie plate with cooking spray.

2. In medium bowl, combine flour, pudding mix, $^1/_2$ cup of the milk, egg, baking powder, and salt and stir until blended. Pour into pie plate and arrange peaches on top.

3. In small bowl, combine cream cheese, $^1/_2$ cup of the sugar, and remaining 3 tablespoons milk and stir until thoroughly combined. Pour over peaches and sprinkle with cinnamon and remaining 2 teaspoons sugar.

4. Bake 35 minutes or until set. Serve warm or cold.

Makes 8 servings

Per serving: 203 cal, 7 g pro, 41 g carb, 1.5 g fat, 0.5 g sat fat, 29 mg chol, 2 g fiber, 740 mg sodium

Diet Exchanges: 0 milk, 0 vegetable, $1/2$ fruit, 2 starch/bread, $1/2$ meat, 0 fat

Banana Cream Pie

Crust

$1^1/_4$ c reduced-fat graham cracker crumbs

3 Tbsp trans-free margarine or butter, melted

2 Tbsp sugar

$1/4$ c semisweet mini–chocolate chips

Filling

1 c fat-free sour cream

$1/2$ c fat-free milk

1 pkg (3.4 oz) instant French vanilla pudding mix

12 oz frozen light whipped topping, thawed

3 lg bananas, sliced

2 tsp lemon juice

2 Tbsp semisweet mini–chocolate chips

1. Preheat oven to 350°F. Lightly coat 9" springform pan with cooking spray.

2. *To prepare crust:* In medium bowl, combine crumbs, margarine, and sugar, then press into the prepared springform pan.

3. Bake 10 minutes. Remove from the oven and sprinkle with chocolate chips.

4. *To prepare filling:* While crust cools, in large bowl, whisk sour cream and milk until blended. Add pudding mix and whisk until dissolved, then add whipped topping and blend. Spread half of the filling over the prepared crust. Place bananas in small bowl and drizzle with lemon juice, then layer bananas over filling. Spread remaining filling over bananas and sprinkle chocolate chips on top. Cover and refrigerate overnight.

Makes 10 servings

Per serving: 282 cal, 3 g pro, 45 g carb, 9 g fat, 6 g sat fat, 0 mg chol, 2 g fiber, 250 mg sodium

Diet Exchanges: $1/2$ milk, 0 vegetable, $1/2$ fruit, 2 starch/bread, 0 meat, 1 fat

Walnut-Pumpkin Pie

Filling

1 can (16 oz) pumpkin

1 can (12 oz) evaporated milk

2 med eggs

$1/2$ c packed brown sugar

$1/4$ c Splenda

$1^1/2$ tsp ground cinnamon

$1/2$ tsp ground cloves

$1/2$ tsp ground ginger

$1/2$ tsp ground nutmeg

$1/4$ tsp salt

Crust

1 reduced-fat graham cracker crust (9"
diameter)

Walnut Topping

1 Tbsp trans-free margarine or butter

$1/4$ c finely chopped walnuts

$1/4$ c packed brown sugar

Fat-free whipped topping (optional)

1. Preheat oven to 375°F.

2. *To prepare filling:* In large bowl, combine pumpkin, milk, eggs, sugar, Splenda, cinnamon, cloves, ginger, nutmeg, and salt. With electric mixer on medium speed, beat 2 to 3 minutes or until smooth. Fill pie crust, leaving $1/2$" border at top.

3. Bake 35 to 40 minutes or until top is set and beginning to brown.

4. *To prepare topping:* While pie is baking, in small saucepan, combine margarine, walnuts, and sugar. Cook over medium heat, stirring constantly, 2 to 3 minutes or until butter and sugar are melted. Remove pie from oven and spread walnut topping evenly over top. Return to oven and bake 10 minutes longer. Before serving, top with whipped topping, if desired.

Makes 8 servings

Per serving: 305 cal, 6 g pro, 43 g carb, 9 g fat, 3.5 g sat fat, 70 mg chol, 2 g fiber, 234 mg sodium

Diet Exchanges: $1/2$ milk, 0 vegetable, 0 fruit, 2 starch/bread, $1/2$ meat, 1 fat

Skinny Scalloped Potatoes
Recipe on page 320

Green Beans and Carrots Parmesan
Recipe on page 322

Lime Chicken
Recipe on page 324

Crab-Stuffed Tiger Shrimp
Recipe on page 334

Penne with Vegetables
Recipe on page 336

356 Carrot Cake with Cream Cheese Frosting
Recipe on page 342

Peanut Butter Pie
Recipe on page 348

Plum-Blueberry Cobbler
Recipe on page 362

Fresh Fruit Tart

1$^1/_2$ c all-purpose flour

1 Tbsp + $^1/_2$ c sugar

$^1/_2$ tsp + $^1/_8$ tsp salt

5 Tbsp light (or regular) olive oil

$^1/_2$ tsp white vinegar

2 Tbsp water

1$^1/_2$ c 1% milk

1 egg

$^1/_4$ c cornstarch

$^1/_2$ c fat-free half-and-half

1 tsp vanilla extract

4 sm apricots (or 2 sm peaches), sliced into
thin wedges

2 kiwifruit, peeled and sliced into thin half-
rounds

$^1/_2$ c fresh raspberries

Mint leaves (garnish, optional)

1. Preheat oven to 400°F. Coat 10$^1/_2$"
tart pan with cooking spray.

2. In medium bowl, combine flour,
1 tablespoon of the sugar, and
$^1/_2$ teaspoon of the salt. Stir in oil
and vinegar with a fork until well
combined. Add water, stirring until
dough holds together.

3. Shape dough into a disk and roll
between 2 sheets of plastic wrap into a
12$^1/_2$"-diameter circle. Freeze on a
baking sheet for 15 minutes. Remove
the top sheet of plastic, invert the pastry
into the prepared pan, and mold to fit.
Remove the other plastic sheet and
trim the edges of the dough. Prick with
a fork. Bake 16 to 18 minutes or until
golden brown.

4. In medium saucepan, whisk together
milk, egg, cornstarch, remaining
$^1/_2$ cup sugar, and remaining $^1/_8$ teaspoon salt. Bring to a boil over medium
heat, then lower heat, whisking constantly as the mixture begins to
thicken. Cook 30 seconds or until
smooth. Gradually whisk in half-and-
half and cook 1 minute longer. Remove
from heat and stir in vanilla extract.
Pour the filling into the warm shell,
cover it with the plastic touching the
surface, and chill 2 hours or overnight.

5. Just before serving, arrange the fruit
in a decorative pattern on top. Garnish
with mint leaves, if desired, and serve.

Makes 8 servings

Per serving: 287 cal, 5 g pro, 44 g carb, 10 g fat,
2 g sat fat, 28 mg chol, 2 g fiber, 185 mg sodium

Diet Exchanges: $^1/_2$ milk, 0 vegetable, $^1/_2$ fruit,
2$^1/_2$ starch/bread, $^1/_2$ meat, 2 fat

Strawberry Tart with Oat-Cinnamon Crust

Crust

2/3 c rolled oats

1/2 c whole grain pastry flour

1 Tbsp sugar

1 tsp ground cinnamon

1/4 tsp baking soda

2 Tbsp canola oil

2–3 Tbsp fat-free plain yogurt

Filling

1/4 c strawberry all-fruit spread

1/2 tsp vanilla extract

1 1/2 pt strawberries, hulled

1. *To prepare crust:* Preheat oven to 375°F. Coat baking sheet with cooking spray.

2. In medium bowl, combine oats, flour, sugar, cinnamon, and baking soda. Stir in oil and 2 tablespoons of the yogurt to make a soft, slightly sticky dough. If the dough is too stiff, add another 1 tablespoon yogurt.

3. Place dough on the prepared baking sheet and pat evenly into a 10" circle. If the dough sticks to your hands, coat them lightly with cooking spray.

4. Place a 9" cake pan on the dough and trace around it with a sharp knife. With your fingers, push up and pinch the dough around the outside of the circle to make a 9" circle with a rim 1/4" high. Bake 15 minutes or until firm and golden. Remove from the oven and set aside to cool.

5. *To prepare filling:* Meanwhile, in a small microwaveable bowl, combine the fruit spread and vanilla extract. Microwave on high 10 to 15 seconds or until melted. Brush a generous tablespoon evenly over the cooled crust.

6. Arrange strawberries evenly over the crust. Brush the remaining spread evenly over the strawberries, making sure to get some of the spread between the strawberries to secure them.

7. Refrigerate at least 30 minutes or until the spread has jelled.

Makes 6 servings

Per serving: 172 cal, 4 g pro, 28 g carb, 6 g fat, 0 g sat fat, 0 mg chol, 4 g fiber, 59 mg sodium

Diet Exchanges: 0 milk, 0 vegetable, 1/2 fruit, 1 1/2 starch/bread, 0 meat, 1 fat

Peach Tart

1¹/₂ c + 2 Tbsp whole grain pastry flour

2 Tbsp + ¹/₃ c granulated sugar

¹/₂ tsp salt

¹/₄ c cold butter or margarine, cut into sm
   pieces

2 Tbsp reduced-fat cream cheese

3–4 Tbsp ice water

7 ripe peaches, sliced

1 c coarsely crushed fat-free almond-
   flavored biscotti

2 Tbsp chopped almonds

2 Tbsp packed brown sugar

1 Tbsp butter or margarine, softened

1. In bowl of food processor, combine 1¹/₂ cups of the flour, 2 tablespoons of the granulated sugar, and salt. Process until blended. Add cold butter and cream cheese. Pulse until mixture resembles cornmeal. Drizzle 3 tablespoons of the water over mixture. Pulse until a crumbly dough forms that will hold together when pressed. If needed, add up to 1 tablespoon more water.

2. Turn the dough out onto a work surface. Shape into a disk and wrap in plastic wrap. Refrigerate 30 minutes.

3. Preheat oven to 375°F. Coat 10" tart pan or pie pan with cooking spray.

4. On a lightly floured surface, roll the dough into a 13" circle. Drape it over the prepared pan. Gently press the dough against the side of the pan, trimming any overhang. Prick the bottom and sides of the crust with a fork. Line with foil. Fill with pie weights or dried beans.

5. Bake 15 minutes. Remove the weights and foil. Bake 10 minutes longer or until lightly golden. Remove to a rack to cool. Do not turn off the oven.

6. Meanwhile, in large bowl, combine peaches, remaining ¹/₃ cup granulated sugar, and remaining 2 tablespoons flour. Set aside.

7. In small bowl, combine biscotti, almonds, brown sugar, and softened butter. Using your hands, combine to form coarse crumbs. Spoon the peach mixture into the tart shell. Sprinkle with the crumb topping.

8. Bake 35 to 40 minutes or until the topping is golden and bubbly. Remove to rack to cool. Serve warm or at room temperature.

Makes 10 servings

Per serving: 238 cal, 4 g pro, 42 g carb, 8 g fat, 4 g sat fat, 17 mg chol, 3 g fiber, 179 mg sodium

Diet Exchanges: 0 milk, 0 vegetable, ¹/₂ fruit, 2¹/₂ starch/bread, 0 meat, 1¹/₂ fat

Plum-Blueberry Cobbler

(photo on page 358)

8 plums, quartered

1 pt fresh or frozen blueberries

$^1/_2$ c + 4 tsp sugar

2 Tbsp + 1 c whole grain pastry flour

$^3/_4$ tsp baking powder

$^1/_8$ tsp salt

$^1/_2$ c buttermilk

1 egg white, lightly beaten

$1^1/_2$ Tbsp vegetable oil

1. Preheat oven to 375°F. Coat 8" × 8" baking dish with nonstick spray.

2. In large bowl, combine plums, blueberries, $^1/_2$ cup of the sugar, and 2 tablespoons of the flour. Pour into the prepared baking dish.

3. In medium bowl, combine baking powder, salt, 3 teaspoons of the remaining sugar, and remaining 1 cup flour.

4. In small bowl, combine buttermilk, egg white, and oil. Pour into the medium bowl with the flour mixture. Stir until a thick batter forms. Drop batter in tablespoonfuls on top of the fruit. Sprinkle with the remaining 1 teaspoon sugar.

5. Bake 35 to 40 minutes or until golden and bubbly. Remove to rack to cool. Serve warm or at room temperature.

Makes 8 servings

Per serving: 181 cal, 3 g pro, 38 g carb, 3 g fat, 0 g sat fat, 1 mg chol, 4 g fiber, 60 mg sodium

Diet Exchanges: $^1/_2$ milk, 0 vegetable, 1 fruit, 2 starch/bread, $^1/_2$ meat, $^1/_2$ fat

Raspberry Crème Brûlée

1 Tbsp butter, melted

2 c whole milk

$^1/_2$ c + $^1/_4$ c sugar

3 eggs

1 Tbsp almond-flavored liqueur

1 pt fresh raspberries

1. Preheat oven to 300°F. Grease six $^1/_2$-cup ramekins or custard cups with butter. Place in baking pan and set aside.

2. In medium saucepan over medium heat, combine milk and $^1/_2$ cup of the sugar and cook, stirring occasionally, until sugar is dissolved and mixture just comes to a boil. Remove from heat.

3. In medium bowl, whisk eggs until smooth. While whisking constantly, gradually add the milk mixture until

well blended. Stir in liqueur and raspberries. Evenly pour the custard into the prepared ramekins. Add warm water to the baking pan until it reaches halfway up the sides of the ramekins. Bake 40 minutes or until custard is set in the center. Remove from the oven and water bath and cool to room temperature. Chill at least 2 hours or overnight.

4. Preheat the broiler. Evenly divide the remaining $1/4$ cup sugar over each ramekin. Place on baking sheet and broil, rotating the baking sheet for even browning, until the sugar is melted and begins to brown, about 2 minutes. Refrigerate 30 minutes or until the custard is chilled and topping has hardened.

Makes 6 servings

Per serving: 222 cal, 6 g pro, 34 g carb, 7 g fat, 4 g sat fat, 123 mg chol, 2 g fiber, 91 mg sodium

Diet Exchanges: $1/2$ milk, 0 vegetable, $1/2$ fruit, 2 starch/bread, $1/2$ meat, $1 1/2$ fat

Strawberry Crêpes

8 prepared crêpes

2 oz reduced-fat cream cheese, softened

$1/2$ c (4 oz) reduced-fat sour cream

3 Tbsp packed brown sugar

$1/2$ tsp grated lemon peel

$1/4$ tsp vanilla extract

3 c fresh strawberries, sliced

1. Wrap crêpes in plastic wrap and microwave on high 1 minute.

2. In medium bowl, with electric mixer on medium speed, beat cream cheese, sour cream, 2 tablespoons of the sugar, lemon peel, and vanilla extract until well blended.

3. Evenly divide the cream cheese mixture among the crêpes. Evenly divide 2 cups of the strawberries over the cheese mixture. Fold each crêpe in half, then in half again. Arrange on serving plate.

4. In food processor or blender, puree $3/4$ cup of the remaining strawberries with remaining 1 tablespoon sugar. Fold in remaining $1/4$ cup strawberries. Drizzle the strawberry sauce over the crêpes.

Makes 8

Per crêpe: 124 cal, 4 g pro, 22 g carb, 3 g fat, 1 g sat fat, 57 mg chol, 2 g fiber, 60 mg sodium

Diet Exchanges: 0 milk, 0 vegetable, $1/2$ fruit, 1 starch/bread, $1/2$ meat, $1/2$ fat

Index

Boldface page references indicate illustrations and photographs. <u>Underscored</u> references indicate boxed text, charts, and tables.